MESSIANIC
WINTER HOLIDAY HELPER

MESSIANIC HELPER series

Moedim: The Appointed Times for Messianic Believers
Messianic Sabbath Helper
Shabbat: Sabbath for Messianic Believers
Messianic Kosher Helper
Kashrut: Kosher for Messianic Believers
Messianic Fall Holiday Helper
Messianic Winter Holiday Helper
Messianic Spring Holiday Helper
Messianic Torah Helper

MESSIANIC
WINTER HOLIDAY HELPER

edited by Margaret McKee Huey

MESSIANIC APOLOGETICS
messianicapologetics.net

Messianic Winter Holiday Helper

© 2003, 2009, 2017, 2021 Messianic Apologetics
edited by Margaret McKee Huey
All rights reserved. With the exception of quotations for academic purposes, no part of this publication may be reproduced without prior permission of the publisher.

Cover imagery: Kameleon007/Istockphoto

ISBN 978-1467952026 (paperback)
ISBN 979-8740329338 (hardcover)
ASIN B00679V1E2 (eBook)

Published by Messianic Apologetics, a division of Outreach Israel Ministries
P.O. Box 516
McKinney, Texas 75070
(407) 933-2002

www.outreachisrael.net
www.messianicapologetics.net

Unless otherwise noted, Scripture quotations are from the *New American Standard, Updated Edition* (NASU), © 1995, The Lockman Foundation.

Unless otherwise noted, quotations from the Apocrypha are from the *Revised Standard Version* (RSV), © 1952, Division of Education of the National Council of the Churches of Christ in the United States of America.

"The Message of. . ." chapters employ primary Scripture quotations from the *New International Version* (NIV), © 1984, published by International Bible Society.

"The Message of 1, 2 Maccabees" chapters employ primary Apocrypha quotations from the Revised *English Bible* (REB), © 1992, Oxford University Press.

Fair Use Notice: This publication contains copyrighted material the use of which has not always been specifically authorized by the copyright owner. We make use of this material as a matter of teaching, scholarship, research, and commentary. We believe in good faith that this constitutes a "fair use" of any such copyrighted material as provided for in section 107 of the US Copyright Law, and is in accordance with Title 17 U.S.C. Section 107. For more information go to: https://www.law.cornell.edu/uscode/text/17/107

Outreach Israel Ministries is a non-profit 501(c)3. All prices listed on the publications of Outreach Israel Ministries and Messianic Apologetics are suggested donations.

Table of Contents

Introduction ix

1   The Holidays 1
by Jane McKee

2   The Christmas Challenge 3
by J.K. McKee

3   "Christmas is Pagan"!?
     How to Offend Family and Alienate Friends 13
by J.K. McKee

4   The Importance of Chanukah 19
by J.K. McKee

5   A Summarization of Chanukah Traditions 29
by Margaret McKee Huey and J.K. McKee

6   Why We Should Celebrate Chanukah 37
by J.K. McKee

7   The Message of Daniel 43
by J.K. McKee

8   The Message of 1 Maccabees 61
by J.K. McKee

9   The Message of 2 Maccabees 87
by J.K. McKee

10   The Impact of the Maccabees on First Century Judaism 121
by J.K. McKee

11   The Forgotten Past 149
by J.K. McKee

12   A Restoration of Israel—Without the Jews? 157
by J.K. McKee

13   Handling the Holidays 167
by Mark Huey

14   Being Messianic in a Post-Christian World 173
by Mark Huey

| 15 | Chanukah and Encountering Worldly Philosophies | 181 |

by J.K. McKee

| 16 | Celebrating Chanukah Today | 187 |

by Margaret McKee Huey

FAQs on the Winter Holiday Season 193

Kosher Your Plate for Chanukah 209

LITURGICAL RESOURCES 221

    The Role of Liturgy 223

    Kindling the Chanukah Lights 225
    Blessing After Meals for Chanukah 227
    Hallel for Chanukah 230

The Dreidel Game 234

About the Editor 235

Bibliography 239

Abbreviation Chart and Special Terms

The following is a chart of abbreviations for reference works and special terms that are used in publications by Outreach Israel Ministries and Messianic Apologetics. Please familiarize yourself with them as the text may reference a Bible version, i.e., RSV for the Revised Standard Version, or a source such as *TWOT* for the *Theological Wordbook of the Old Testament*, solely by its abbreviation. Detailed listings of these sources are provided in the Bibliography.

Special terms that may be used have been provided in this chart:

ABD: *Anchor Bible Dictionary*
AMG: *Complete Word Study Dictionary: Old Testament, New Testament*
ANE: Ancient Near East(ern)
Apostolic Scriptures/Writings: the New Testament
Ara: Aramaic
ATS: ArtScroll Tanach (1996)
b. Babylonian Talmud (*Talmud Bavli*)
B.C.E.: Before Common Era or B.C.
BDAG: *A Greek-English Lexicon of the New Testament and Other Early Christian Literature* (Bauer, Danker, Arndt, Gingrich)
BDB: *Brown-Driver-Briggs Hebrew and English Lexicon*
BECNT: *Baker Exegetical Commentary on the New Testament*
BKCNT: *Bible Knowledge Commentary: New Testament*
C.E.: Common Era or A.D.
CEV: Contemporary English Version (1995)
CGEDNT: *Concise Greek-English Dictionary of New Testament Words* (Barclay M. Newman)
CHALOT: *Concise Hebrew and Aramaic Lexicon of the Old Testament*
CJB: Complete Jewish Bible (1998)
DRA: Douay-Rheims American Edition
DSS: Dead Sea Scrolls
ECB: *Eerdmans Commentary on the Bible*
EDB: *Eerdmans Dictionary of the Bible*
eisegesis: "reading meaning into," or interjecting a preconceived or foreign meaning into a Biblical text
EJ: *Encylopaedia Judaica*
ESV: English Standard Version (2001)
exegesis: "drawing meaning out of," or the process of trying to understand what a Biblical text means on its own
EXP: *Expositor's Bible Commentary*

Ger: German
GNT: Greek New Testament
Grk: Greek
halachah: lit. "the way to walk," how the Torah is lived out in an individual's life or faith community
HALOT: *Hebrew & Aramaic Lexicon of the Old Testament* (Koehler and Baumgartner)
HCSB: Holman Christian Standard Bible (2004)
Heb: Hebrew
HNV: Hebrew Names Version of the World English Bible
ICC: *International Critical Commentary*
IDB: *Interpreter's Dictionary of the Bible*
IDBSup: *Interpreter's Dictionary of the Bible Supplement*
ISBE: *International Standard Bible Encyclopedia*
IVPBBC: *IVP Bible Background Commentary (Old & New Testament)*
Jastrow: *Dictionary of the Targumim, Talmud Bavli, Talmud Yerushalmi, and Midrashic Literature* (Marcus Jastrow)
JBK: New Jerusalem Bible-Koren (2000)
JETS: *Journal of the Evangelical Theological Society*
KJV: King James Version
Lattimore: The New Testament by Richmond Lattimore (1996)
LITV: *Literal Translation of the Holy Bible* by Jay P. Green (1986)
LS: *A Greek-English Lexicon* (Liddell & Scott)
LXE: *Septuagint with Apocrypha* by Sir L.C.L. Brenton (1851)
LXX: Septuagint
m. Mishnah
MT: Masoretic Text

NASB: New American Standard Bible (1977)
NASU: New American Standard Update (1995)
NBCR: *New Bible Commentary: Revised*
NEB: New English Bible (1970)
Nelson: *Nelson's Expository Dictionary of Old Testament Words*
NETS: New English Translation of the Septuagint (2007)
NIB: *New Interpreter's Bible*
NIGTC: *New International Greek Testament Commentary*
NICNT: *New International Commentary on the New Testament*
NIDB: *New International Dictionary of the Bible*
NIV: New International Version (1984)
NJB: New Jerusalem Bible-Catholic (1985)
NJPS: Tanakh, A New Translation of the Holy Scriptures (1999)
NKJV: New King James Version (1982)
NRSV: New Revised Standard Version (1989)
NLT: New Living Translation (1996)
NT: New Testament
orthopraxy: lit. "the right action," how the Bible or one's theology is lived out in the world
OT: Old Testament
PreachC: *The Preacher's Commentary*

REB: Revised English Bible (1989)
RSV: Revised Standard Version (1952)
t. Tosefta
Tanach (Tanakh): the Old Testament
Thayer: *Thayer's Greek-English Lexicon of the New Testament*
TDNT: *Theological Dictionary of the New Testament*
TEV: Today's English Version (1976)
TNIV: Today's New International Version (2005)
TNTC: *Tyndale New Testament Commentaries*
TWOT: *Theological Wordbook of the Old Testament*
UBSHNT: United Bible Societies' 1991 Hebrew New Testament revised edition
v(s). verse(s)
Vine: *Vine's Complete Expository Dictionary of Old and New Testament Words*
Vul: Latin Vulgate
WBC: *Word Biblical Commentary*
Yid: Yiddish
YLT: Young's Literal Translation (1862/1898)

Introduction

During the Winter holiday season, many of us in the Messianic community are faced with the annual dilemma of how we are to handle the holidays with our Christian family and friends. How do we tell people, who celebrate Christmas, that we do not celebrate it anymore? How do we share with our friends that we now look to Yeshua as our example in **all things?** How do we share that we are now enjoying the Feast of Dedication, known in Hebrew as *Chanukah*, something that is written about in John 10:22?

I do not know about you, but our family has been dealing with the Winter holiday dilemma since 1996. It is just one more of the changes that we have experienced as we have become thoroughly Messianic. We often find that our extended family and friends can be confused or perplexed about our changing Christmas celebration to *Chanukah* observance, just as they are about our having changed Sunday Church to *Shabbat* rest! They simply do not understand why we have changed. But rather than mercilessly beat them over the head with some kind of "Christmas is pagan" stick, as has been too frequently encouraged by some, we instead believe it is best for us **to present a positive testimony of change to them**. We would encourage families of Messianic Believers to invite others into their homes during the Winter holiday season, and partake of the wonderful things that our Heavenly Father is restoring to His people.

To help you and your family, this *Messianic Winter Holiday Helper* has included a variety of articles that discuss how to deal with the Winter holiday season. We have included articles that have come from our Virtual Winter holiday series, which relate to the history of *Chanukah*, the non-Biblical practice of Christmas, insights on how to handle the holidays with our family and friends, and a practical guide to observing *Chanukah* with your family and/or Messianic fellowship. We have also included teachings on the ancient Maccabees, who were stirred by the Lord to oppose the pagan Seleucid Greeks, and whose influence greatly affected the Jewish community into the time of Yeshua. This broad array of material should not only assist you in interacting with others during this time of year, but will also be quite informative in learning about the critical lessons that the account of the Maccabees teaches us.[i]

---

[i] In order to follow much of the material in this publication, you will need to have a Bible with the Apocrypha included, where the historical Books of 1-4 Maccabees are found. Modern translations that will often include an edition of the Apocrypha are the Revised Standard Version,

Messianic Winter Holiday Helper

Our family believes that the Winter season is a very special time of year! It is a time when most people of Christian faith generally and genuinely want to reach out to others in the love of the Messiah. *As Messianics, how can we act like such behavior is wrong or evil?* We cannot! We, who are to walk as Messiah Yeshua walked, must likewise reach out to others in His love at this time of year **more than ever.** Yeshua told us that people would know that we are His disciples by the love that we have for one another (John 13:35).

I strongly encourage you to love your family and friends in such a special way, that during the Winter holidays the Holy Spirit will be able to draw them to what you have to share. Dear friends, it is only through our unconditional love, that one day your Christian family and friends will want to know what we know about walking like the Messiah. Then they will honestly want to know why we have put aside the celebration of Christmas and are remembering *Chanukah*, and how we are actually walking more like Jesus and not less. One day—should we demonstrate the right example to them—they will want to know why we have become thoroughly Messianic, and what we can teach them about their Hebraic and Jewish heritage from the Scriptures. So, let us reach out in love and show them a better way.

Similarly, only by demonstrating Yeshua's love, will anyone of us be able to demonstrate who the Messiah is to a Jewish person, celebrating *Chanukah* without the knowledge of the Light of the world who delivers us from darkness. When you go to purchase any of your *Chanukah* celebration resources: your *menorah*, candles, traditional foods for the season, etc., a non-believing Jewish person might see you in the store. You will have the opportunity to wish him or her a Happy Chanukah! If you yourself are non-Jewish, you will certainly have the ability to fulfill the Apostle Paul's mandate of the nations provoking his brethren to salvation (Romans 11:11). While Jewish people are often perplexed at why a non-Jew would want to celebrate *Chanukah*, seeds that can later germinate in them coming to salvation in the Jewish Messiah can certainly be planted!

May you enjoy your Winter holiday time within your own family, rejoicing in the history and drama of *Chanukah*!

Chag Sameach!
Margaret McKee Huey

New English Bible, New Revised Standard Version, Revised English Bible, and most recently the English Standard Version. Sir L.C.L. Brenton's *Septuagint With Apocrypha* (Peabody, MA: Hendrickson, 1999), includes both his English translation and parallel Greek text.

-1-

The Holidays

Jane McKee

The Winter holiday season is supposed to be one of love, joy, peace, and "good will toward men" (Luke 2:14, KJV). However, many of my Messianic friends have shared that the Winter holiday season is hard for them. Many of them have stopped celebrating Christmas, are now celebrating *Chanukah*, and are trying to feel comfortable with all of the changes. Many of these people have asked me for my personal view on Christmas versus *Chanukah*, and how we should approach what happens in December.

This can be a wonderful, yet difficult time of year for many of us. I believe that we must keep a balanced view of the holiday season, and not be unkind toward anyone who does not (yet) see things the way that we now do. I was raised as an evangelical Christian, and I used to celebrate Christmas. But in my family, Christmas was not about presents, Santa Claus, or a tree—it was about the miraculous virgin birth of the Messiah (i.e., Isaiah 9:2-7).

In the mid-1990s, our family stopped celebrating the traditions around Christmas. When our family sends us Christmas gifts, we send them holiday gifts. When our friends send us Christmas cards, we send them holiday cards. In stopping the traditions of Christmas, we have been careful as we steadily replaced them with the various traditions of *Chanukah*.

The story of the Maccabees and the miracle of the rededication of the Temple are wonderful to hear. The Festival of Lights can hold much delight for us. There is much fun in celebrating this event in Jewish history. Yet, we cannot forget who the Light of the World is. **We cannot forget Yeshua.**

When we say to family and friends that we do not celebrate Christmas, we must be careful to let them understand that we are primarily talking about Santa Claus and the Christmas tree. With our non-Messianic family, we have had to make it clear that we still very much believe in the virgin birth of Jesus, Bethlehem, and the baby who was born to save us from our sins.

Messianic Winter Holiday Helper

However, our holiday time now centers on *the Temple*—Yeshua, the Light of the World—the Temple who needs no cleansing and the Temple who can never be destroyed!

The same principles hold true with Easter and Passover. When you tell others that you do not believe in Easter, be very careful that you let them know that you are talking about the name Easter, the bunnies, eggs, and candy—not the Lord's resurrection. My family never did the bunny thing! In the early 1980s, my late father Kimball McKee introduced the Passover *seder* to our local church, even though we did not fully understand then that the Passover celebration was not an option for us, but a commandment for all generations of God's people to remember (Exodus 12:14).

Today, we no longer have our Easter ham and yeast rolls to commemorate the day, but in the celebration of Passover, we are very careful *not* to leave out the essential element of who the Messiah is. We must remember who conducted the Last Seder and what the Cup of Redemption means.[1]

Yeshua is the Passover Lamb. The Passover is not just a remembrance of the Ancient Israelites being set free from Egypt; it is an illustration of Yeshua setting us free from the bondage of sin. He died for us and was raised from the dead!

As we go forth as Messianic Believers, we must never forget in our celebrations of *Chanukah*, Passover, and others, about Yeshua. For it is He who makes us set-apart, and it is He who makes us Messianic.

---

[1] For a further discussion, consult the *Messianic Spring Holiday Helper*.

-2-

The Christmas Challenge

J.K. McKee

No matter who you are or what religious ideology you hold to, the Winter holiday season involving Christmas will be a challenge.[1] It is first a challenge to non-Believers as they are continually presented with the message of the birth of Yeshua the Messiah (Jesus Christ) into a world that is lost in sin. Secondly, the Christmas holiday is a challenging time for many Christians who seek to remember the birth of our Savior, but at the same time all too often indulge themselves in overly frivolous gift-giving. And thirdly, the Christmas season is a challenge to Messianic Believers, as we choose not to celebrate this holiday.

The Reformation certainly did a great deal of work eliminating many non-Biblical Roman Catholic traditions and theologies from the faith. Today, Protestants believe in salvation by grace through faith and in the priesthood of all Believers, rejecting the claim that the pope is the "vicar of Christ" on Earth. Many evangelical Believers recognize that if something is primarily Catholic, it should be tested against the inspired Word of God to see if it is truly Biblical. The Bible does not tell us to pray to saints or confess sin to a priest to be forgiven. Scripture does not teach transubstantiation. Furthermore, Scripture does not tell us that Mary, the mother of our Lord Yeshua, is the so-called "Mother of God," for our Creator has always been and ever will be (cf. Micah 5:2-3).

Many Protestants pride themselves on being *Sola Scriptura*—Scripture Only. However, it is an unfortunate reality that many Protestants today still adhere, unknowingly, to some non-Biblical Catholic tradition. There are various practices and traditions among Christians today that can neither be

---

[1] This article was originally written for J.K. McKee, *Torah In the Balance, Volume I* (Kissimmee, FL: TNN Press, 2003).

found in Scripture, nor find their origins in Scripture, but rather on customs established long since the death of the Apostles and early Believers.[2]

All too often, it has been our unfortunate observation that many in the Messianic community strongly and vehemently criticize our evangelical brothers and sisters during the Winter holidays. Statements along the lines of "Christmas is a pagan holiday!" are all too commonplace. This turns many away from hearing the origins about a holiday that cannot be specifically found in the Bible, but is seemingly good. Many Christians believe that when you denounce Christmas, you are denying the Biblical reality of the virgin birth of our Lord and Savior. Certainly, Luke ch. 2 is a part of our Holy Scriptures, and the miracle of the birth of Yeshua is a sacred Biblical event. In an effort to stress balance, grace, and understanding during the Winter season among both Christians and Messianic Believers, we offer our analysis of "the Christmas challenge."

A Brief History of Christmas

Why is it asserted among many contemporary Christians that if there are those who do not celebrate Christmas, then obviously such people cannot be true Believers? Are we dangerous cultists who do not believe in the virgin birth of the Messiah?

Obviously, Luke ch. 2, which fully details the miraculous birth of Yeshua the Messiah, the Savior of the world, is something that none of us should ever deny or consider unimportant. If Yeshua had not been born, He would not have grown up to become the perfect sacrifice for our sin. We would be unable to have His blood covering us and have no hope for permanent forgiveness of sin.

But what of the holiday we now call "Christmas"? Where did it come from? If its celebration is not specified in Holy Scripture itself, then how did we get it?

Author Susan E. Richardson makes some interesting observations in her popular book *Holidays & Holy Days*:

> "During the Roman Empire, people usually celebrated the birthdays of rulers and other outstanding people, though not necessarily on the exact date of their birth. The early Christians' desire to honor Christ's birth may come from the fact that they gave him the title and other honors that pagans gave to the 'divine' emperors. These Christians lived in a culture

---

[2] J. Theodore Mueller, "Christmas," in Everett F. Harrison, ed., *Baker's Dictionary of Theology* (Grand Rapids: Baker Book House, 1960), 117; Ronald V. Huggins, "Christmas," in David Noel Freedman, ed., *Eerdmans Dictionary of the Bible* (Grand Rapids: Eerdmans, 2000), 240; Brett Scott Provance, *Pocket Dictionary of Liturgy & Worship* (Downers Grove, IL: InterVarsity, 2009), pp 37-38.

where the birth of a ruler was a major celebration. What could be more natural than celebrating the birth of the King of Kings?

"Despite the logic of this, Christmas has long been surrounded by controversy. In A.D. 245, Origen wrote that even to consider observing it was a sin. Early Christians in Armenia and Syrians accused Roman Christians of sun worship for celebrating Christmas on December twenty-fifth."[3]

It is witnessed from ancient Christian history, that commemorating the birth of the King of Kings, is something controversial. Still, the birth of the Messiah is a recorded event in the Gospels. Typological connections are undoubtedly intended to be made between the birth of Yeshua, and the birth of Moses seen in Torah reading *Shemot* (Exodus 1:1-6:1). However, we should find serious problems remembering Yeshua's birth at a time which has historically been associated with the honoring of pagan deities, as Richardson later comments that "pagan celebrations held on December 25 included Mesopotamian celebrations for Marduk, Greek ones for Zeus, and Roman *Saturnalia* in honor of Saturn."[4] In their textbook *History of the World Christian Movement*, which I had to use for Church History I at seminary (Summer 2005), Dale T. Irvin and Scott W. Sunquist summarize,

> "Prior to the year 300 there had been no consensus among Christians concerning the date on which to celebrate the birth of Jesus Christ. Some argued for a spring date, but others suggested December 25. That latter date was the day celebrated in honor of the Invincible Sun, who had grown in imperial favor through the third century. Through the course of the fourth century most Christians came to accept December 25 as the celebration of the birth of Jesus, integrating elements of this solar monotheism with Christianity."[5]

The celebration of the Messiah's birth on December 25 came as a result of generations of Christian people, long after the death of the Apostles, employing syncretism to evangelize pagans. The original intent was to reinterpret local religious holidays with Biblical meanings, in an effort to share the gospel. Without any doubt, the motives of some were sincere, as they wanted to "adapt their faith" for the pagans around them, and use Biblical overtones of their holidays to spread the good news. However, such adaptations came at a time after the destruction of Jerusalem when anti-Semitism was at a serious high in the Roman Empire, and the Believers in

---

[3] Susan E. Richardson, *Holidays & Holy Days* (Ann Arbor, MI: Vine Books, 2001), 119.
[4] Ibid., 123.
[5] Dale T. Irvin and Scott W. Sunquist, *History of the World Christian Movement*, Vol. 1 (Maryknoll, NY: Orbis Books, 2001), 164.

Yeshua were ejected from the Synagogue. Anything perceived as "Jewish," namely the appointed times or *moedim* of Leviticus 23, would be looked down upon and not be observed. Substitute and replacement holidays had to be created instead and Christmas is a reality to this very day.

How Christmas has been celebrated over the centuries has been determinant on a variety of cultures and Christian denominations. The name Christmas comes from "Christ's mass," or a service that is held in Roman Catholic churches. Many evangelical Protestants realize many of the non-Biblical elements of the Roman Catholic service certainly derive from ancient paganism, the foremost of which might be transubstantiation,[6] so the name Christmas has already to an extent been tainted. What is perhaps more disturbing is that other such "masses" exist on the Roman Catholic service calendar, such as Michaelmass, a service to be held for the Archangel Michael, which I must admit is very strange (cf. Colossians 2:18).

What about the Christmas tree?

For many Protestants throughout the centuries, Christmas was not like we consider it today. For those living in Great Britain and colonial America, Christmas Day was a very serious occasion when a family would attend church services, sing hymns about the birth of the Lord, and return home and sometimes exchange small gifts in remembrance of the three Magi who later gave gifts to Yeshua. There would have been no Christmas tree. Up until the mid-Nineteenth Century, Christmas trees were unheard of in either Britain or the United States. Decorating a tree at Christmas time, was mainly a German or Nordic custom, which German immigrants to America brought with them in the early Nineteenth Century. Prince Albert brought the tradition to Great Britain when he married Queen Victoria.[7]

The most common modern-day association with Christmas is obviously the Christmas tree. Its usage for "honoring the Lord," of course, is not detailed anywhere in the Bible, and it is certainly not rooted in any of the events surrounding Yeshua's birth—especially given the topography of Bethlehem. Unfortunately for those Christmas tree lovers, Holy Scripture strongly prohibits God's people from introducing decorated trees into their homes for spiritual adoration. The following words from the Prophet Jeremiah

---

[6] Transubstantiation is the belief that during communion, the bread and wine actually become the *literal* body and blood of Christ. During the Protestant Reformation, Martin Luther advocated a position known as consubstantiation, where the bread and wine *did not change*, but the presence of Christ was active during communion. Today, most Protestant traditions see the practice of communion as only being a memorial of the Last Supper.

For a further discussion, consult the Messianic Apologetics FAQ, "Communion."

[7] Richardson, 132.

detail how the Christmas tree had its forbearers in Ancient Near Eastern religion:

"Thus says the LORD, 'Do not learn the way of the nations, and do not be terrified by the signs of the heavens although the nations are terrified by them; for the customs of the peoples are delusion; because it is wood cut from the forest, the work of the hands of a craftsman with a cutting tool. They decorate *it* with silver and with gold; they fasten it with nails and with hammers so that it will not totter. Like a scarecrow in a cucumber field are they, and they cannot speak; they must be carried, because they cannot walk! Do not fear them, for they can do no harm, nor can they do any good" (Jeremiah 10:2-5, NASU).

Many Christians have astutely observed that these Bible verses speak of pagan idolatry. While not wanting to directly accuse contemporary Christian people, who sincerely know Yeshua as their Savior, of participating in idol worship—it is also true that God's Torah does state, "You shall not plant for yourself an Asherah of any kind of tree beside the altar of the LORD your God, which you shall make for yourself" (Deuteronomy 16:21, NASU).

We cannot accuse all Believers of volitionally participating in idolatrous worship of trees. However, these quotations from Jeremiah and Deuteronomy, respectively, are the most explicit examples of what we can compare today to the Christmas tree in Scripture. For even if Believers, who in ignorance, have Christmas trees in their homes and do not worship them—as I have many fond personal Christmas memories—what of non-Believers who have Christmas trees? What of the non-Believers who have rejected the salvation of Yeshua (Jesus), and who celebrate Christmas by indulging themselves? What is the god that they worship during the Christmas season? Richardson observes,

> "Using trees as part of religious celebrations goes back well beyond the first recorded Christmas tree. Egyptians decorated green date palms indoors for winter solstice rites. Romans hung trinkets on pine trees during *Saturnalia* and used evergreens for *Natalis Sol Invicti*. In Britain, Druids placed candles, cakes, and gilded apples in tree branches as offerings."[8]

Some Christians when confronted with the verses forbidding Christmas trees, have stated things along the lines of, "In many cultures, trees

---

[8] Ibid., 130.
Please note that these comments specifically speak of trees involving religious ceremonies; they do not speak of having potted trees or plants for decoration, as you would find in many public buildings throughout the year, *not* including Christmas trees.

symbolized life,"[9] justifying their usage of something that has its roots in idolatry. In addition to just the Christmas tree, an evergreen is commonly employed in various decorations throughout the Christmas season. Unfortunately for them, this is not what Holy Scripture says: "For the life of the flesh is in the blood, and I have given it to you on the altar to make atonement for your souls; for it is the blood by reason of the life that makes atonement" (Leviticus 17:11, NASU). Our eternal life is neither found nor represented in evergreen trees, but rather in the shed blood of Messiah Yeshua, in which "we have confidence to enter the holy place" (Hebrews 10:19, NASU) and be forgiven of our sins.

The argument that to the ancients evergreen trees symbolized life, and thus we should have them in our homes, is patently weak. What did the ancients do when they celebrated? The Romans held wild orgies where they would take hallucinogenic drugs, consume vast amounts of alcohol, and have elicit group sex. Following in their pattern, should we do these things when we celebrate? **God forbid!** Scripture clearly tells us "do not get drunk with wine" (Ephesians 5:18, NASU) and "the *marriage* bed *is to be* undefiled; for fornicators and adulterers God will judge" (Hebrews 13:4, NASU). Certainly we should rejoice in our Messiah Yeshua and remember Him every day of the year, but we should not knowingly participate in things that are directly forbidden in Scripture and are connected to idolatry.

We cannot judge the heart intent of those who have Christmas trees in their homes during the Winter season. Yet, Scripture does forbid this practice. Christmas trees have nothing to do with the birth of our Messiah; they are rather a prohibited custom. Certainly, **a great number of Christians who have Christmas trees do not at all worship them,** but knowing their origin should hopefully be conviction enough to change, and actually consider what God might want us to do during the Winter season. If it is acceptable to have Christmas trees in one's house, is it likewise acceptable to have a statue of Buddha, Shiva, or some other pagan god?

Santa Claus is a Child's Myth

I do not feel the need at all to address Santa Claus and the "eight tiny reindeer." Such things are as factual as the Tooth Fairy and the Easter Bunny. They are child's myths and have no place among Believers, even in seemingly "Biblical" celebrations such as Christmas. The propagation of the existence of Santa Claus during Christmas time to young children, and the revelation of him not being real in later years, has resulted in many people also denying the truth of Jesus being real as well—as both are entities we cannot see. Even

---

[9] L. Smith (2001). *The History of Christmas. Christian Study Center.* Retrieved 02 December, 2001 from <http://www.christianstudycenter.com >.

when my family celebrated Christmas many years ago as conservative, evangelical Believers, we did not play the "Santa game." Why should others?

Is Christmas mentioned in Scripture?

Is there any specific reference to Christmas in Scripture? There are certainly prophecies that speak of the virgin birth of our Messiah, His entry into the world, and the Biblical record that details the event itself—but this is *not* Christmas itself, per se.

Is the holiday we have come to know as Christmas mentioned in Scripture at all? Some Christians would actually say yes—and if it is indeed Christmas, then it is in a place that should get us all very concerned:

"And their dead bodies *will lie* in the street of the great city which mystically is called Sodom and Egypt, where also their Lord was crucified. Those from the peoples and tribes and tongues and nations *will* look at their dead bodies for three and a half days, and will not permit their dead bodies to be laid in a tomb. And those who dwell on the earth *will* rejoice over them and celebrate; and they will send gifts to one another, because these two prophets tormented those who dwell on the earth" (Revelation 11:8-10, NASU).

When I was taking a correspondence Christian prophecy course back in 1999, I was taught that after the two witnesses of Revelation are killed that then the holiday of Christmas will occur. This is based on the assumption that since the world will "make merry, and shall send gifts one to another" (KJV), that it must be Christmas time. While it is more likely that this is referring to some future ecumenical holiday where people exchange gifts—and not "Christmas" itself—suffice it to say, the fact that some Christians believe that this holiday is Christmas is extremely disturbing.

If the only reference to "Christmas" in the Bible that Christians can present us with is in a passage that speaks about the murder of God's two witnesses, then we should most certainly reevaluate our participation in it. Already, many secularists are doing their best to "eliminate Christ from Christmas," which most Christians would view as a sign of apostasy—but Christmas is not a Biblical holiday so technically it is not a sign of apostasy. But this might be what is necessary to encourage Believers to participate in the God-given festivals as specified in the Torah, rather than in substitute holidays which are tainted by some questionable practices and customs.

Should Chanukah be celebrated as an alternative to Christmas?

Many Messianic Believers who decide to give up the Christmas tree and the trappings of this holiday want to know what they should do. A valid alternative that many discover is the celebration of the Jewish holiday of *Chanukah*, which often occurs in December around the same time as Christmas. But, as has unfortunately been the case, for many, *Chanukah*

Messianic Winter Holiday Helper

presents become substitutes for Christmas presents and the birth of the Messiah is something that is readily looked down upon.

It must be readily emphasized that *Chanukah*, surprisingly to many Christians and some Messianic Believers, has not been mandated in Holy Scripture. However, unlike Christmas, *Chanukah* should be considered extra-Biblical as opposed to non-Biblical, the events of which are detailed in the Books of 1-4 Maccabees in the Apocrypha. The story of *Chanukah* is quite moving and inspiring, as it speaks of the Maccabees' defeat of the Syrian Greeks and the rededication of the Temple. *Chanukah* contains a significant message of opposing assimiliation to the ways of the world.

We encourage Messianic Believers to celebrate *Chanukah*, but emphasize that it is imperative to keep it in proper perspective. We must not uplift this celebration over the birth of our Messiah Yeshua (who some Messianics believe was conceived around the time of *Chanukah*). When you celebrate this holiday with your family, **do not forget who the Light of the World is.** Also remember that as the Lord is in the process of currently restoring His people, this should be a time that we all rededicate ourselves unto Him, and seek reconciliation with one another.

The only reference in Scripture to *Chanukah* or the Feast of Dedication **actually occurs in the New Testament**, in John 10:22-23: "At that time the Feast of the Dedication took place at Jerusalem; it was winter, and Yeshua was walking in the temple in the portico of Solomon" (NASU). These verses do not directly state that Yeshua actually celebrated *Chanukah*, but it may be safely assumed that He did. *Chanukah* is a national commemoration for Israel, much like Fourth of July celebrations for Americans, albeit with strong religious overtones. We should have no problem rejoicing in the historical triumphs of the Jewish people, but likewise we should not uplift them over the miraculous birth of our Lord and Savior.

Christmas in Perspective

It is an unfortunate predicament that many Messianics who do not celebrate Christmas, *mercilessly and vehemently* criticize Christians who do. This, in the long run, **will not work well** for the Messianic movement and will turn many Christians off to the truths that God is restoring to His people. Calling Christmas "utterly pagan" will seriously deter many sincere Believers to reexamine the holiday. It may be true that Christmas is not a Biblical holiday, but by calling it "pagan" many Christians will interpret these statements as meaning that we reject the virgin birth of Messiah Yeshua, **which we do not.** It is more appropriate to call Christmas a non-Biblical holiday, which is an accurate description that should not get as many people heated or turned off to the truth of its origins, as the term "pagan" does.

Fortunately, we serve a Creator who is much bigger than we are and He looks beyond our many shortcomings: "The LORD is slow to anger and abundant in lovingkindness, forgiving iniquity and transgression" (Numbers 14:18a, NASU). The Lord will honor those who celebrate Christmas in ignorance, who do not realize its questionable connections. During the Christmas season, many Christians will seek to please the Lord, and He who is in control of all things will use nativity scenes and the proclamation of the birth of Messiah Yeshua to bring many to Himself. During the Christmas season, the Lord will also no doubt look beyond the contentious attitudes of many Messianic Believers who unwarrantedly criticize Christians without the love, grace, or mercy which He desires us to have in our hearts.

We Need to be Careful in our Criticism

As Messianic Believers, we need to be very tactful during the Christmas season. **We should not vehemently and cruelly criticize those who celebrate Christmas**, lest they think we are denying the Messiah's birth. We must not exclusively emphasize negative aspects of the holiday.

Many Messianics who observe the Biblical festivals of Leviticus 23 have been found wanting, at times, by *excluding* Messiah Yeshua's substance in them. At a number of "Messianic" Passovers, the Last Supper and sacrifice of Yeshua may not be spoken of. A number of people fail to emphasize that *Shavuot*/Pentecost is all about the Torah *and* the Holy Spirit being given to us. At *Rosh HaShanah* and *Yom Kippur*, the gathering of the holy ones or saints, the return of Yeshua, and wrathful Day of the LORD are not usually emphasized together. And, we might just find it appropriate to talk about Yeshua's birth during *Sukkot*, the Feast of Tabernacles, instead of the Christian practice of remembering it on December 25. Furthermore, how many "Messianic" *Chanukah* celebrations will be devoid of honoring the Light of the World?

What you do during the Winter holiday season is ultimately up to you and is between you and the Lord, whether you celebrate Christmas, *Chanukah*, or do nothing at all. I certainly cannot be the Holy Spirit for you, because God Himself is the only One who can fairly judge the intentions of the human heart.

The Christmas challenge for Messianic Believers is not going away any time soon, so we must endeavor to be as loving and grace-filled as much as possible when showing Christians the problems with Christmas. We must not forget the words of our Messiah Yeshua who said, "For in the way you judge, you will be judged; and by your standard of measure, it will be measured to you" (Matthew 7:2, NASU). If we mercilessly attack people for celebrating Christmas, who in their minds are sincerely honoring the birth of the King of Kings, we could be mercilessly attacked by the same for honoring the Lord's appointed times. We will become part of the problem as opposed to the solution, and the enemy will have won once again. Contrary to this, demonstrate the great blessings of remembering a holiday such as *Chanukah*, and radiate Yeshua's light to all you encounter during the Winter holiday season!

-3-
"Christmas is Pagan"!?
How to Offend Family and Alienate Friends

J.K. McKee

reproduced from the McHuey Blog

"What! Did we just convince McKee to finally use the word pagan?"

If this is what you were thinking, **no**, you did not convince me to use the exclamation "Christmas is pagan!" Over the past ten years (1999-2009), this is what I have commonly heard declared throughout the Messianic community during the month of December. I have not only heard it proclaimed from the pulpit by teachers, but I have also heard it whispered—well, too often screamed—among the people. Those who have a problem with this approach to Christmas are viewed as either being too young or naïve in their Messianic faith, or are viewed as having succumbed to compromise in their Torah observance. Their views often get dismissed or ignored, and even if some people feel momentarily pricked to change their negative attitudes when interacting with Christians this time of year, they will generally relapse into a mean-spirited or harshly judgmental attitude. Even Messianic leaders who have a problem with the negative attitude that often manifests itself do not have the courage to speak against it.

I would like to make it perfectly and abundantly clear for those of you reading: **I have not celebrated Christmas since 1995.** Christmas is a part of my old life. From my birth until 1991 I celebrated Christmas with my family in Northern Kentucky. I grew up in the same home in which my father grew up. Kim, Margaret, John, and Jane McKee all celebrated Christmas together. It was a beautiful and ideal place. We had a glassed in porch that overlooked a lake, with trees and hills surrounding it. When it snowed you truly did have the ideal white Christmas out of story books.

Messianic Winter Holiday Helper

When my family celebrated Christmas in the past, it was not unlike your typical American celebration. We did have a tree, we did have evergreen throughout the house, and we did have mistletoe. My mother preferred to decorate in a style consistent with colonial America, so we did not have a huge place for Santa Claus, as we only had candle lights in our windows. Our church was the focal point of much of our commemoration, especially the Christmas Eve service. We did give gifts to one another, and we had a Christmas dinner not unlike what we previously had eaten at Thanksgiving. Yet our Christmas celebration more than anything else was focused on the Biblical story of Yeshua's birth, and the scene of the angelic host declaring that something profound had taken place. My Christmas memories are more of hearing Handel's Messiah and traditional hymns, than singing Rudolph the Red Nosed Reindeer.

When my father died in 1992, all of those Christmas experiences came to an end. While I did celebrate Christmas from 1993-1995, it was not at all what I remembered from before his death and it was substantially different. Just like the previous life I remember with my father with the Northern Kentucky house, my old church, even my father's office—Christmas has been consigned to a past memory. I look back fondly on those memories, remembering the good times I had with him, the good times I had going to church and participating in the Christmas play—but those are in the past and they do not make up my future. **My Christmas experience was one where I and my family worshipped the Lord, never knowing its questionable origins until we turned toward the Messianic movement.**

Because Christmas is something that was a part of my past with my late father, I do not think about it any more (even though I do think about him quite a bit). It does not bother me to not celebrate Christmas as my life has moved forward and I have embraced a Messianic lifestyle concurrent with *Shabbat*, the appointed times, and celebrations like *Purim* and *Chanukah*. It does bother me, though, when I see a mean-spirited attitude manifest itself among Messianics—who do not appear to know how to love their neighbor as themselves (Leviticus 19:18), or treat others as they would like to be treated during the holidays (Luke 6:31). This is especially true when we consider that sincere evangelical Believers celebrate Christmas thinking that they are honoring the birth of the Lord—an event attested to in the Scriptures! How are we to mature in this area, acting more like adults, and showing respect for others?

One of the publications that has encouraged a grossly unfair attitude toward Christians, that I have seen floating around the Messianic world since

1999, has been *Fossilized Customs*.[1] It is not a book that can be trusted to convey an historically accurate representation of the "facts" it purports—with very little engagement with primary sources. Its Hebrew examination is limited to Strong's Concordance. Its author, a former Roman Catholic, has a major beef with the Church *and* the Synagogue. The writing style of this publication is something more consistent with the supermarket tabloids than with reasonable Christian, Jewish, or even Messianic writing. I can criticize *Fossilized Customs* by name, because I have seen the negative impact it has had on the Messianic community over an extended period of time. Many of its sentiments have been picked up and repackaged by others.

The role of *Fossilized Customs* is to expose what its author perceives as paganism that has trickled into the Christian Church. I doubt any of us have a problem with this in principle, as we do want to rightly expose those things which have neither a Biblical basis nor are spiritually edifying (Philippians 4:8). But if we are going to say that something clearly originates from paganism, then we better have the information to back it up. This book's section on Christmas begins with the following remarks:

"The popular celebration of one's annual birth-day is acknowledged to be, by all authorities on ancient customs, a Pagan ritual from Babylon. The Babylonians served the sun, moon, planets, and constellations, a Gentile practice condemned by YHWH."[2]

No one will disagree that the Babylonians worshipped the stars,[3] but who are the "all authorities" here when it comes to the commemoration of someone's birth? **No evidence is provided.** And even though information is offered which would appear to condemn the practice of having a Christmas tree today (i.e., Jeremiah 10:2-4), the actual birth of Yeshua the Messiah as recorded in the Gospels (Matthew 1:18-2:13; Luke 2:1-20) is not examined or even referred to.

Is the birth of Yeshua a part of the Bible that we cannot trust, having been inserted by so-called lying scribes or those trying to make parallels with pagan religion? If it is, then to be consistent do recognize how liberal scholars and higher critics have long advocated that the Jewish exiles in Babylon took

---

[1] Lew White, *Fossilized Customs: The Pagan Sources of Popular Customs* (Louisville, KY: Strawberry Islands, 2001).

[2] Ibid., 29.

[3] Consult A.L. Oppenheim, "Assyria and Babylonia: Religion," in George Buttrick, ed., et. al., *Interpreter's Dictionary of the Bible*, 4 vols. (Nashville: Abingdon, 1962), 1:297-300; A. Kirk Grayson, "Mesopotamia, History of (Babylonia): Religion," in David Noel Freedman, ed. et. al., *The Anchor Bible Dictionary*, 6 vols. (New York: Doubleday, 1992), 4:773-776.

the Mesopotamian mythology of the *Enuma Elish* and Epic of Gilgamesh[4]—and rewrote it into Adam and Eve and Noah and the Flood in the Book of Genesis! When the point is made that you can seemingly trace everything in Holy Scripture to a "pagan" root, **most especially treasured accounts in the Tanach**, today's generation of ill-equipped Hebrew Roots aficionados just does not know what to do.[5]

To be fair to *Fossilized Customs*, a warning does appear in how to approach those who celebrate Christmas: "It must be done in a gentle, loving way, otherwise they will be repelled. We must help them to see we do not judge **them**, but rather the customs they have embraced since childhood."[6] Unfortunately with publications such as this, no solutions in how to communicate properly are ever offered—so the warnings are easily glossed over. Instead, people who have adopted a Messianic lifestyle resort to just saying "Christmas is pagan!" What happens is that they offend their family and they alienate their friends. Is this the testimony any of us want to have? *One of constantly being an offense?* Do we want to truly make people mad?

Some people actually want to make others mad. However, I have believed for the longest time that there is a better way to demonstrate one's Messianic faith and convictions. Several years ago I was talking to the wife of a Messianic Jewish congregational leader, who was non-Jewish, and she was recalling the experiences she had with her Jewish in-laws. Her husband's grandfather, who had come to America from Eastern Europe, would look at her in the eye, holding her hand, and simply tell her at either Christmas or Easter "I hope you have a good holiday." He was not going to celebrate either holiday, but he knew that a Christian America provided him with a freedom that he did not have in the old country. In spite of some of the problems with the origins of Christmas, God has still blessed my country and He has used it to help the Jewish people.

None of you have to celebrate Christmas or even tell people to have a good holiday season. If you are a Messianic Believer from an evangelical background, Christmas should be part of that past experience—and you should be looking to the future. This is a future where *Chanukah* should be embraced and remembered as a part of your new December experiences. (And yes, there are those who commemorate *Chanukah* in an unbalanced

---

[4] An English translation of these two mythologies is available in N.K. Sandars, *The Epic of Gilgamesh* (London: Penguin Books, 1972); Stephanie Dalley, trans., *Myths from Mesopotamia: Creation, the Flood, Gilgamesh, and Others* (Oxford, UK: Oxford University Press, 1989).

[5] For a further discussion, consult the articles "Is the Story of Yeshua Pagan?" and "Encountering Mythology: A Case Study from the Flood Narratives" by J.K. McKee (appearing in *Confronting Critical Issues*). Also consult John N. Oswalt, *The Bible Among the Myths: Unique Revelation or Just Ancient Literature?* (Grand Rapids: Zondervan, 2009).

[6] White, 38.

way—a subject for another time.) Yet surely, you should also want to be a reflection of our Heavenly Father's love and grace and mercy to our Christian brothers and sisters this time of year. **I know I do.** Many of them celebrate Christmas, believing in ignorance they are doing something Biblical. They think that the traditions of Christmas are pure and holy, not knowing where many of them originate.

How does today's Messianic movement communicate that Christmas on December 25—*not the birth of God's Son in Bethlehem*—was not our Father's original intention? Too many of the leaders and teachers of Messianic Chapter 1 have largely decided that the way to communicate is by exclaiming "Christmas is pagan!" and have given Ebenezer Scrooge a real run for his money in the anti-Christmas department. The leaders and teachers of the forthcoming Messianic Chapter 2 have to do better and have to show that there is a different way to do this. We have to communicate via our actions of faith that we are not unloving, mean-spirited, and unbalanced people for whom "pagan" is the word of choice. We have to communicate instead that we love our Lord and Savior so much, that we will not commemorate His birth on a day that was used to honor gods and goddesses and licentious revelry. We instead have an eight-day celebration of God's victory over evil to remember during this same time, where we consider resisting assimilation into the world, and His ongoing plan of salvation history yet to unfold.

This December, I challenge each one of you that if you have ever used the "Christmas is pagan!" line, and have offended family or alienated friends, **to apologize and ask for their forgiveness.** They are our brothers and sisters in the Lord who do not deserve some of the treatment that they have received from our faith community. Publicly admit that you went a little too far or were too zealous in your views of Christmas, when your intentions were not to degrade or demean the birth of our Savior. Tell your family or friends that although you might not celebrate Christmas any more, that your intention was not to unfairly condemn them. Ask them to understand that the Lord has you doing something differently now, and that you will be there to answer their *solicited* questions should they ever ask. And tell them that in the future, you will not force your new Messianic views on them unless they do ask you for your opinion. **When that time does come**, be prepared to answer "with gentleness and reverence" (1 Peter 3:15, RSV), armed with credible and fair-minded research material.

Messianic Winter Holiday Helper

-4-

The Importance of Chanukah

J.K. McKee

The subject of what Messianic Believers are to be doing for the Winter holiday season can be very controversial. On the one hand, Messianics should not be celebrating Christmas, because it is non-Biblical and was created to be one of the replacements for observing the appointed times of Leviticus 23. On the other hand, should all Messianic Believers celebrate *Chanukah*, or the Feast of Dedication? Primarily, debate surrounds the fact that often the celebration of *Chanukah* can become a replacement for Christmas, and that *Chanukah* is not a Biblically-mandated holiday, as it is not in the Leviticus 23 list.

If there is anything we must consider regarding this issue it is two things: (1) We must have an attitude that brings glory to our Heavenly Father, and (2) our actions must foster unity and understanding between Jewish and non-Jewish Believers. Sadly, like many of the issues that we face, the subject of whether or not we should celebrate *Chanukah* has two extremes. There are those who vehemently oppose its observance, and perhaps might even consider it a "gross Jewish error." And, there are those who go overboard in encouraging its celebration, in an effort to prove that they are "better" than Christians who celebrate Christmas in ignorance. Neither one of these positions is right.

In this article, we examine the historical origins of the celebration known as *Chanukah*, *Chanukah* and Yeshua, and *Chanukah* as a special time for those who who are a part of the Messianic community.

The Prophecies of Daniel and the Rise of Antiochus

Before we can examine the issues pertaining to the celebration of *Chanukah*, we must first understand its historical origins, which actually precede the time of the Maccabees in Second Century B.C.E. Israel, going back much further to the exile of the Southern Kingdom to Babylon in the 500s

B.C.E. While in Babylon, the Prophet Daniel was shown visions of the future, which included both the immediate future concerning his time as Babylon would be overtaken by Persia, as well as the far distant future. One of these prophecies included the vision of the four beasts, representative of the empires of Babylon, Persia, Greece, and Rome (and presumably revived Rome in the end-times). The third kingdom, Greece (Heb. *Yavan*), would arise and would conquer the Persians:

"The he-goat, the kingdom of Greece, and the large horn that is between its eyes is its first king" (Daniel 8:21, NASU).

Many expositors are agreed that this prophecy is a reference to Alexander the Great, the Macedonian king whose father Philip II had conquered the Greek Peloponnesus. Alexander continued his father's legacy by extending his military campaign into Asia Minor, Egypt, Persia, and all the way into India. Alexander, however, died at the age of 33 in 323 B.C.E. in Babylon. After his death, his empire was divided among his four generals who took control of Macedonia, the Greek Peloponnesus, Egypt, and Syria. It is not surprising to know that ancient history tells us that these four kingdoms became rivals and often fought among themselves:

"As for the broken one, in whose place four arose, four kingdoms will arise from one nation, but lacking its strength" (Daniel 8:22, NASU).

A notable part of Alexander's conquering of the ancient world was not only the extension of his rule, but also the exposure of the Greek language and culture into foreign areas. Macedonia itself, not really considered to be "Greek" by the Greeks, had been Hellenized during the childhood of Alexander, who was tutored by Aristotle. Part of Philip's, and later Alexander's military campaign, was to spread the way of life that had made Macedonia the great power that it was. But, not everyone in the ancient world desired to be Hellenized or forced to become like the Greeks.

Prior to Alexander the Great, the Jewish exiles had returned from Babylon to the Land of Israel. The Jewish province was a vassal of the Persian Empire, but later became engulfed into Alexander's empire and became a part of Syria. Greek culture and religion were slowly influencing the Jews, with many Jews abandoning the Torah and its commandments in favor of Greek customs and philosophies. It became increasingly more difficult for the Jews to maintain a Torah obedient lifestyle with the policies of the Syrian Greeks.

Things got out of control when Antiochus IV of the Seleucid dynasty came to power (175-164 B.C.E.). He was actually called Epiphanes or "God manifest."[1] Antiochus made it illegal for the Jews to practice the Torah,

---

[1] Grk. *Antiochos Ephiphanēs*; *epiphanēs* actually means "*coming to light, appearing, of gods*" (H.G. Liddell, and R. Scott, *An Intermediate Greek-English Lexicon* [Oxford: Clarendon Press, 1994], 306).

The Importance of Chanukah

perform circumcision, follow the kosher dietary laws, and worship in the Temple. He moved his troops into Jerusalem and had the Temple desecrated by the sacrificing of a pig, and by having a statue to the god Zeus erected. This, and the subsequent and related events following, are recorded in the Apocrypha in the Books of 1-4 Maccabees:

"And the king sent letters by messengers to Jerusalem and the cities of Judah; he directed them to follow customs strange to the land, to forbid burnt offerings and sacrifices and drink offerings in the sanctuary, to profane sabbaths and feasts, to defile the sanctuary and the priests, to build altars and sacred precincts and shrines for idols, to sacrifice swine and unclean animals, and to leave their sons uncircumcised. They were to make themselves abominable by everything unclean and profane, so that they should forget the law and change all the ordinances. And whoever does not obey the command of the king shall die" (1 Maccabees 1:44-50, RSV).

It can be rightly assumed that Antiochus was an ambitious man, and he was making a political power play, demonstrating that he was more powerful than the Ptolemaic Greeks of Egypt. After fighting Ptolemy, he sought to fully control the Land of Israel and Jerusalem:

"When Antiochus saw that his kingdom was established, he determined to become king of the land of Egypt, that he might reign over both kingdoms. So he invaded Egypt with a strong force, with chariots and elephants and cavalry and with a large fleet. He engaged Ptolemy king of Egypt in battle, and Ptolemy turned and fled before him, and many were wounded and fell. And they captured the fortified cities in the land of Egypt, and he plundered the land of Egypt. After subduing Egypt, Antiochus returned in the one hundred and forty-third year. He went up against Israel and came to Jerusalem with a strong force" (1 Maccabees 1:16-18, RSV).

The Maccabean Era

As you can imagine, the actions of Antiochus were not well received by the majority population of the Land of Israel. Led by the retired priest Mattathias, many Jews opposed the oppression of the Syrian Greek invaders and sought to see them pushed out of the Land of Israel. Many of the Jews, fearing for their lives, succumbed to not following the Torah and would not follow the rite of circumcision or eat kosher. Many of them adopted Greek religion and wanted to "blend in."

As Antiochus' army entered into the town of Modin, where Mattathias and his five sons were living, they tried to persuade them to forsake the Law of Moses and sacrifice to Greek gods. Mattathias refused to give into their demands and proclaimed his loyalty to the God of Israel and to His Instruction:

Messianic Winter Holiday Helper

"But Mattathias answered and said in a loud voice: 'Even if all the nations that live under the rule of the king obey him, and have chosen to do his commandments, departing each one from the religion of his fathers, yet I and my sons and my brothers will live by the covenant of our fathers. Far be it from us to desert the law and the ordinances. We will not obey the king's words by turning aside from our religion to the right hand or to the left'" (1 Maccabees 2:19-22, RSV).

Mattathias then declares that any Jew succumbing to these demands was a traitor to the covenants and to the God of Israel, and he calls all to join him in a revolt:

"When he had finished speaking these words, a Jew came forward in the sight of all to offer sacrifice upon the altar in Modein, according to the king's command. When Mattathias saw it, he burned with zeal and his heart was stirred. He gave vent to righteous anger; he ran and killed him upon the altar" (1 Maccabees 2:23-24, RSV).

He then began a military revolt against the Syrian Greeks, killing those who opposed him. His zeal is described like that of Phinehas in the wilderness:

"Thus he burned with zeal for the law, as Phinehas did against Zimri the son of Salu. Then Mattathias cried out in the city with a loud voice, saying: 'Let every one who is zealous for the law and supports the covenant come out with me!'" (1 Maccabees 2:26-27, RSV; cf. Numbers 26:7-8).

Mattathias would not live through his campaign to see the final victory over the Syrian Greek oppressors. The mantle would pass onto his son, Judas Maccabeus, who would lead the Jews in a revolt against the Seleucids that would take around three years. He was nicknamed *Makkabbi*, which means "hammer." During this time, a guerilla-type warfare was carried out against the Syrian Greeks, while the Jews sought allies in the Egyptian Greeks or Ptolemies, the Spartans, and the Romans. Their military challenges and triumphs are detailed and chronicled in the Apocryphal Books of 1-4 Maccabees.

The rise of Antiochus Epiphanes and the events of the Maccabean Era were prophesied by Daniel after speaking about the division of Alexander's kingdom into four regions. Daniel rightly prophesied that Antiochus would arise to expand his own kingdom, would come against the faithful ones, but would not die in battle:

"In the latter period of their rule, when the transgressors have run *their course*, a king will arise, insolent and skilled in intrigue. His power will be mighty, but not by his *own* power, and he will destroy to an extraordinary degree and prosper and perform *his will*; he will destroy mighty men and the holy people. And through his shrewdness he will cause deceit to succeed by his influence; and he will magnify *himself* in his heart, and he will destroy many while *they are* at ease. He will even oppose the Prince of princes, but he will be broken without human agency" (Daniel 8:23-25, NASU).

Antiochus was unable to stand against the Jews, many of whom faithfully resisted any attempt to Hellenize them, namely getting them to reject the Torah, circumcision, kosher eating, and the Temple service, and instead practice Greek religion. Antiochus believed himself to be a god, but later wasted away and died not in battle, but from a flesh-eating disease:

"But the all-seeing Lord, the God of Israel, struck him an incurable and unseen blow. As soon as he ceased speaking he was seized with a pain in his bowels for which there was no relief and with sharp internal tortures—and that very justly, for he had tortured the bowels of others with many and strange inflictions. Yet he did not in any way stop his insolence, but was even more filled with arrogance, breathing fire in his rage against the Jews, and giving orders to hasten the journey. And so it came about that he fell out of his chariot as it was rushing along, and the fall was so hard as to torture every limb of his body. Thus he who had just been thinking that he could command the waves of the sea, in his superhuman arrogance, and imagining that he could weigh the high mountains in a balance, was brought down to earth and carried in a litter, making the power of God manifest to all. And so the ungodly man's body swarmed with worms, and while he was still living in anguish and pain, his flesh rotted away, and because of his stench the whole army felt revulsion at his decay" (2 Maccabees 9:5-9, RSV).

The Miracle of the Oil

The Maccabees drove the Seleucids out of the Land of Israel in the month of Kislev 165 B.C.E., which is in about the month of December. They had the task of cleaning up the mess that the Seleucids had left, notably in the city of Jerusalem and in the Temple complex. Antiochus' forces had completely ransacked the Temple and made it into a haven of idolatry. The Temple needed to be cleansed of its defilement and restored to its previous sanctity so proper sacrifices could once again be performed. Of all of the items of Temple furniture that had to be cleansed and rededicated, one of the most important was the great lampstand or *menorah*. The *menorah* required special consecrated oil in order to be lit.

As many of you are no doubt aware, modern observance of *Chanukah* is commemorated by the lighting of a *chanukia*, or a special nine-branched *menorah*. This is different from the *menorah* that was in the Temple that had seven branches. It is used because when the Temple was rededicated there was only enough oil to be lit for one day. However, the oil remained lit for eight days, allowing time for newly consecrated oil to be produced. Today a ninth candle or servant candle is used to light the eight candles of the *chanukia* to commemorate the eight days the *menorah* was lit. *Chanukah*, meaning "dedication," became the nation's commemoration of this miracle. The miracle of the eight days of oil is spoken of in the Talmud:

> "*What's the point of Hanukkah? It is in line with what our rabbis have taught on Tannaite authority: On the twenty-fifth of Kislev the days of Hanukkah, which are eight, begin. On these days it is forbidden to lament the dead and to fast.*
>
> "For when the Greeks entered the sanctuary, they made all of the oil that was in the sanctuary unclean. But when the rule of the Hasmonean house took hold and they conquered them, they searched but found only a single jar of oil, lying with the seal of the high priest. But that jar had enough oil only for a single day. But there was a miracle done with it, and they lit the lamp with it for eight days. The next year they assigned these days and made them festival days for the recitation of Hallel psalms [Psa. 113-118] and for thanksgiving" (b.*Shabbat* 21b).[2]

What would have happened if the Maccabees had not stood up to Antiochus and his armies? Not only would they have succeeded in wiping out the Jewish people, either through military defeat or cultural assimilation—but Israel, *in any form*, would not have existed to give rise to Messiah Yeshua. We have ample reasons to celebrate *Chanukah* as Believers in Yeshua today— the foremost of which being that if the miracle of *Chanukah* had not taken place, **there would be no miracle of Yeshua!**

Chanukah and Yeshua

But what about Yeshua the Messiah? As *Chanukah* was established as a celebration in the mid-Second Century B.C.E., did our Lord and Savior celebrate it?

John 10:22 tells us, "Then came Hanukkah in Yerushalayim. It was winter" (CJB). The Greek source text actually uses the word *egkainia*, which in most Bibles is rendered as the "Feast of Dedication." BDAG defines it clearly as "***festival of rededication***. . .known also as Hanukkah and the Feast of Lights, beg. the 25th of Chislev (roughly=November-December) to commemorate the purification of the temple by Judas Maccabaeus on that date in 165 B.C."[3]

So what was Yeshua doing in Jerusalem during this time?

"[I]t was winter, and Yeshua was walking in the temple in the portico of Solomon. The Jews then gathered around Him, and were saying to Him, 'How long will You keep us in suspense? If You are the Messiah, tell us plainly.'

---

[2] *The Babylonian Talmud: A Translation and Commentary*. MS Windows XP. Peabody, MA: Hendrickson, 2005. CD-ROM.

[3] Frederick William Danker, ed., et. al., *A Greek-English Lexicon of the New Testament and Other Early Christian Literature*, third edition (Chicago: University of Chicago Press, 2000), 272.

The Importance of Chanukah

Yeshua answered them, 'I told you, and you do not believe; the works that I do in My Father's name, these testify of Me. But you do not believe because you are not of My sheep. My sheep hear My voice, and I know them, and they follow Me; and I give eternal life to them, and they will never perish; and no one will snatch them out of My hand. My Father, who has given *them* to Me, is greater than all; and no one is able to snatch *them* out of the Father's hand. I and the Father are one.' The Jews picked up stones again to stone Him'" (John 10:23-31, NASU).

Yeshua was present in Jerusalem during *Chanukah*. We may assume by His presence in the holy city that He was participating in whatever was commemorated at that time. Notice that during *Chanukah* some Jews ask Him if He was the Messiah. Yeshua tells them that He has already demonstrated His Messiahship to them by His actions and that they do not believe. The quintessential statement made here is "I and the Father are one" (NASU). This includes echoes of the *Shema* of Deuteronomy 6:4: "Hear, O Israel! The LORD is our God, the LORD is one!" (NASU). In proclaiming that He and the Father are one, Yeshua was proclaiming Himself to not only do the work of the Father, but to also be Divine and to be of the same substance as God. By doing so, the Jews present wanted to stone Him as they believed He was committing blasphemy.

Remembering *Chanukah* and understanding that Yeshua was in Jerusalem at this time is very important. It is especially important when we understand what Yeshua was doing and the questions that He was asked regarding His mission.

Today's Dilemma: Encountering Hellenism

One of today's serious dilemmas is how *Chanukah* is handled in certain sectors of our Messianic faith community. Because *Chanukah* often occurs in close proximity to Christmas, many people say *Chanukah* is a more Biblical celebration than Christmas, even though neither holiday is mandated in Scripture. Many, in wanting to expose the questionable nature of the Christmas tree, become vehemently opposed to commemorating the birth of Messiah Yeshua. Certainly, if Yeshua's birth is to be commemorated, it would be appropriate to remember it during the actual time of His actual birth (which some Messianics are agreed was during *Sukkot* or Tabernacles, making His conception sometime around *Chanukah*).[4] But celebration of *Chanukah* should not be viewed as a replacement for Christmas. Celebrating *Chanukah*

---

[4] Even trying to remember Yeshua's birth at Tabernacles has been met with a great deal of resistance. Indeed, probably the "safest" time to address the subject is when *Shemot* (Exodus 1:1-6:1) appears in the yearly Torah cycle, as parallels between Moses' birth and Yeshua's birth in the Gospels can be considered.

should be an occasion where we rededicate ourselves to God and to one another, as the Maccabees did to the Temple some 2,200 years ago.

Another serious problem is that *Chanukah* often becomes a time for unwarranted "Greek bashing," which oftentimes manifests itself in criticism and denial of the inspiration of the Greek Apostolic Scriptures. Hellenism, or Greek philosophy, is by no means something that we endorse, but definitions of Hellenism vary. As it concerns the time of the Maccabees, there are some very distinct definitions of Hellenism that must be taken into account that the Seleucid Greeks forced upon the Jews:

"And the king sent letters by messengers to Jerusalem and the cities of Judah; he directed them to follow customs strange to the land, to forbid burnt offerings and sacrifices and drink offerings in the sanctuary, to profane sabbaths and feasts, to defile the sanctuary and the priests, to build altars and sacred precincts and shrines for idols, to sacrifice swine and unclean animals, and to leave their sons uncircumcised. They were to make themselves abominable by everything unclean and profane, so that they should forget the law and change all the ordinances. And whoever does not obey the command of the king shall die" (1 Maccabees 1:44-50, RSV).

The Hellenism that the Maccabees fought against included:
- following the Greek religion, which included the worship of multiple gods and images, and making sacrifices to them with unclean or unfit animals
- a prohibition on animal sacrifices and prescribed offerings according to the Torah
- a prohibition on keeping the seventh-day Sabbath
- a prohibition on circumcision
- a prohibition on studying the Torah and its ordinances, so the people would forget their covenant status with the God of Israel

Hellenism, as the Maccabees understood it, included these things. Are there Christians, and indeed even some in today's Messianic world, who adhere to some of these things? Yes. There are those who believe that God's Torah is unimportant, that the seventh-day Sabbath was done away with, that eating kosher is unimportant, that circumcision is unimportant, and that the significance of the Temple service is unimportant. **I am not one of those who believes these things to be unimportant.** These things are being restored to and appreciated once again in the Body of Messiah as we approach the Lord's return.

However, in fair balance to First Century history and the time of Yeshua, the Greek language and Greek philosophy did exist in the world of the Messiah. Hebrew and Aramaic were the local languages of the Land of Israel, but Greek became the standardized language of the Eastern Mediterranean and of business on the street. *NIDB* states it correctly in saying, "The fact that Greek became the language of literature and commerce throughout the 'inhabited world,' for example, was of inestimable importance to the spread of the gospel."[5] If it had not been for Alexander the Great, the Apostles would have had a very difficult time in going out on missionary journeys, as there would have been a whole host of local languages they would have had to learn, rather than one standardized international language. A Greek translation of the Hebrew Bible, the Septuagint, was widely disseminated and was helpful in seeing many non-Jews convert to Judaism, or at least hear about the God of Israel, prior to the First Coming of Yeshua.[6]

The use of Greek in the First Century is no different than how the expansion of the British Empire in the Nineteenth Century, and American television in the Twentieth Century, have helped make English the dominant international language of today. We should be thankful that English has the widespread usage that it has today, otherwise the restorations that are being accomplished to the Body of Messiah may not be taking place as easily as they are through communication with Believers worldwide.

Our *Chanukah* celebrations should not be a time for "Greek bashing." Those who would do so need to understand the complex history of the ancient world a little better.[7] Our *Chanukah* celebrations need to instead focus on the unity of all of God's people, as we each rededicate ourselves to the Lord *and* to one another—and that individually we need to clean our personal temples of any defilements that we may have.

Commemorating Chanukah

As we focus on the Festival of Lights, we must not forget the Light of the World, Messiah Yeshua, and we must not forget the hardships and trials that the Jewish people have had to endure. We must be inspired by the dedication of the Maccabees to stand, fight, and even die for the truth of God. We must not succumb to the temptations of the popular culture, but stand for what we know is right, just, and godly.

All of us must join together and rejoice in the miracle that the Lord God performed those many centuries ago as the *menorah* remained lit for those eight special days. *Chanukah* is a great time for us to contemplate the ongoing

---

[5] Brewster Porcella, "Alexander the Great," in Merill C. Tenney, ed., *New International Dictionary of the Bible* (Grand Rapids: Zondervan, 1987), 33.

[6] The Apostle Paul, while being a Rabbinical scholar and student of the Jewish Sage Gamaliel, likely also studied Greek language and philosophy at the *same* Rabbinical school (b.*Sotah* 49b). Paul would not have studied Greek language, philosophy, and culture just for the sake of learning it, but for the sake of converting Greek-speakers to the religion of the God of Israel.

[7] For a further discussion, consult the article "The Role of History in Messianic Biblical Interpretation" by J.K. McKee (appearing in *Introduction to Things Messianic*).

Messianic Winter Holiday Helper

salvation history of our Heavenly Father, and how we should stand up for Him in the similar challenges that the world may present us with today.

-5-

A Summarization of Chanukah Traditions

Margaret McKee Huey and J.K. McKee

The holiday of *Chanukah*, or the Festival of Dedication, is full of many customs and traditions that give our celebration great life and depth. During this time of year, we have the awesome opportunity to commemorate the work of God from some 2,200 years ago during the time of the Maccabees. If they had not fought against the Seleucid invaders of Israel, the Jewish people would have either been destroyed through war, or would have disappeared via cultural assimilation. *Chanukah*, as attested in the historical record, was mandated as a national celebration so that the community could remember the sacrifice of the Maccabees, and the rededication of the Temple in Jerusalem:

"Then Judas and his brothers and all the assembly of Israel determined that every year at that season the days of dedication of the altar should be observed with gladness and joy for eight days, beginning with the twenty-fifth day of the month of Chislev" (1 Maccabees 4:59, RSV).

We have the wonderful opportunity to join with our Jewish brothers and sisters, and celebrate in the historical triumphs that are given for us in the story of the Maccabees. There is much for us to celebrate during this time, as we remember how God inspired a rag-tag army to fight a vastly superior force, and never give up until the goal of victory was achieved. We are to remember how the Maccabees fought off the cultural assimilation that they faced, which required them to deny the Torah and its commandments. We are to remember how the Maccabees rededicated the Temple to the God of Israel, restoring the vessels of worship and sacrifices to their rightful places. And, we are also to remember how Antiochus Epiphanes, the Seleucid king who thought he was a god, was ultimately judged by the One True God he was trying to destroy.

As you can imagine, many customs and traditions have developed in the centuries past when the Jewish community has remembered *Chanukah*. We have compiled the following list of elements that are included in traditional observance, followed by some things that we have adapted in our own family observance as Messianic Believers, which we believe will be helpful for you.

Lighting the Menorah

Lighting the *menorah* is probably the most common custom associated with *Chanukah*. The Temple *menorah* or lampstand was one of the most awesome and valuable pieces of worship, as well as one of the most difficult to replace. It is not agreed among Biblical historians whether or not the candelabra that the Maccabees originally lit was the actual Temple *menorah*, or something makeshift. One ancient source "states that the Hasmoneans could not use the candelabrum in the Temple since the Greeks had defiled it. They, therefore, took seven iron spits, covered them with zinc, and used them as a candelabrum (Scholium to *Megillat Ta'anit*)" (*EJ*).[1] Later traditions indicate that "upon entering the Temple, the Hasmoneans discovered that the Greeks had defiled all the oil, except for one cruse, which contained enough oil to keep the candelabrum burning for only one day. A miracle, however, happened and they kindled it for eight days" (*EJ*).[2] The reason this was a miracle is that the oil that was used to light the *menorah* took eight days to be properly consecrated. The Torah says that the oil used was to be "clear oil of beaten olives for the light, to make a lamp burn continually" (Exodus 27:20, NASU; cf. Leviticus 24:2), and the prevailing *halachah* of the day required that it took eight days for this oil to be produced. While some people today brand the miracle of the oil remaining lit for eight days only a "legend," the fact of the matter remains that Orthodox Jews, many Conservative Jews, and the vast majority of the Messianic Jewish community today, believe with great faith that it actually happened (b.*Shabbat* 21b).

While today the *chanukia*, or nine-branched *menorah* for *Chanukah*, is often decorated elaborately, and there are various styles among different Jewish communities over the world, First Century *chanukia*s would not have been as elaborate. "There was in use in talmudic times the Greco-Roman *polymixos*, a many mouthed lamp which was made of clay, stone, or bronze with eight apertures for wicks fed by a central reservoir on whose surface

---

[1] Moshe David Herr, "Hanukkah," in Encyclopaedia Judaica. MS Windows 9x. Brooklyn: Judaica Multimedia (Israel) Ltd, 1997.

[2] Ibid.

A Summarization of Chanukah Traditions

geometrical or symbolic designs often appear" (*EJ*).[3] This may have been the model for the first *chanukia*s. There is no uniform design that appears in archaeological or traditional evidence, but it is safe to assume that some kind of miniature candelabrum, either made of metal or clay, was used by Jewish families to commemorate this holiday.

We do know, based on Talmudic evidence, that the practice of kindling lights for *Chanukah* was present in the First Century world of Yeshua. In the First Century B.C.E., prior to the First Coming of Yeshua, there were *halachic* differences between the Pharisaical schools of Hillel and Shammai over when and how the *menorah* for *Chanukah* should be lit.[4] These *halachic* differences are primarily given to us in the tractates b.*Shabbat* 21b and b.*Shabbat* 23a of the Babylonian Talmud. The House of Shammai ruled that one started *Chanukah* by lighting all eight candles on the first night, and then reducing them on each successive day. The House of Hillel, however, ruled that one candle is lit for the first night, and then adding one on each successive day. It was based on the idea that holiness is something which is to steadily increase.[5]

Throughout Jewish history, there have been various ways members of the community have lit the *chanukia*. While in earlier times, olive oil was preferred to be used to light the *chanukia*, almost any oil can be used, and today the vast majority of people use candles. Many individual people in Jewish families have their own *chanukia* to light during *Chanukah*. Given the presence of women during the Maccabean crisis, it is considered mandatory for females to light the *chanukiah* (b.*Shabbat* 23a).[6] The first candle to be lit is the *shamash* candle, or "servant" candle in the center, which is then used to light the first, second, third, and whatever other candles need to be lit on the respective day(s) of *Chanukah*.

Today, the custom of lighting the *chanukia* is usually performed in the early evening. Biblically, as the day begins in the evening (cf. Genesis 1:5), the first night of *Chanukah* begins at sundown. It is notable that *Chanukah* is not a high holiday, and thus work is permitted during the eight days, except on the Sabbath. On *Shabbat* the lighting of the *chanukia* applies as though one were lighting the *Shabbat* candles, which is often performed a minimum of eighteen minutes before sundown. While simply lighting *Chanukah* candles is

---

[3] Yitzhak Einhorn, "Hannukah Lamp," in *EJ*.

[4] Some of the other theological differences and similarities between the schools of Hillel and Shammai are examined the article "You Want to be a Pharisee" by J.K. McKee (appearing in *Introduction to Things Messianic*).

[5] Ronald L. Eisenberg, *The JPS Guide to Jewish Traditions* (Philadelphia: Jewish Publication Society, 2004), 248.

[6] Ibid., 249.

often viewed as being sufficient enough to remember the holiday, it is customary to allow them to remain lit a minimum of thirty minutes.[7]

We offer this information to give you a broad perspective regarding the lighting of the *Chanukah* lights in the modern Jewish community. Some of you, as you light your *chanukia*, may only be able to leave it lit for a short time. Likewise, some of you might have several *chanukias*, and have each member of your family—or even added guests for that matter—light their own. (Some may not want to do this because of small children and the added fire hazard!) Some of you may have more traditional *chanukias*, which are somehow modeled after the Temple *menorah*, or various other classical designs. Likewise, some of you may prefer the more neo-modern looking *chanukias*, or the various other non-traditional ones available today. However you choose to kindle the *Chanukah* lights during the eight days, have fun when doing it! Remember the rededication of the Temple, and that the Maccabees may have only been using iron bars for a makeshift *menorah*, especially if your *chanukia* is not as "fancy" as those of others.

Eating Fried Foods

Feasting is a very important part of celebrating any of the holidays, be they Biblical, extra-Biblical, national Israeli holidays, or otherwise, in the Jewish community. **Eating fried foods**, in particular, is one of the great traditions surrounding *Chanukah*. More than anything else, eating fried foods has become a part of *Chanukah* so that celebrants might remember the miracle of the oil. In more Biblical times, eating foods cooked in olive oil was customary, but in more modern times, with various and diverse cooking oils, we see a wider variance of fried foods. The Ashkenazic communities in Germany and Central Europe frequently celebrated *Chanukah* by eating *latkes*, or potato pancakes fried in oil. *Latkes* are often garnished with applesauce or sour cream, although modern condiments like ketchup, or even barbeque sauce, are quite commonplace when eating them. *Sufganiot* (sing. *sufgania*) are special doughnuts fried in oil that are quite popular in the Sephardic community, and in Israel today.

Of course, concerning anyone's celebration of *Chanukah*, there are many more popular fried foods, from all over the world, that can be eaten at this time. These may also be eaten in the Jewish community during *Chanukah*, but are often more localized or regionalized. Some of our personal family "fried favorites" to eat during this time include funnel cakes, beer-battered onion rings, Southern fried chicken (not fried in lard!), and a good British fish-n-chips. Deep fried turkey is also quickly becoming a popular dish in America today. As you commemorate *Chanukah* with the more customary *latkes* and

---

[7] Ibid., 250.

A Summarization of Chanukah Traditions

sufganiot, you may wish to pull out some of your favorite "fried recipes" that can be enjoyed during this wonderful time.

Eating Cheese and Dairy Foods

An interesting custom that has grown in some segments of the Jewish community includes **eating cheese and dairy foods** during *Chanukah*. This tradition seems, in part, to be based on associations between *Chanukah* and the story of Judith, seen in the Book of Judith in the Apocrypha.[8] Relating the story of Judith to the events of the Maccabees may have been done to help include women in the celebration of *Chanukah*, and incorporate a story where a woman, Judith, was used in warfare. According to the story, Judith prepared a great feast for the general Holofernes, including cheese. When he was in a drunken stupor, Judith beheaded him and was able to help the Jews he captured escape. Some women in the Jewish community choose not to work during *Chanukah* in deference to the example of Judith.

Cheese blintzes are a very popular food at almost any holiday time in the Jewish community. These are crepes filled with a sweetened cream cheese or cottage cheese, sometimes also with fruit, and are often deep fried. In modern Israel today, eating pizza is also popular during the *Chanukah* season. Whether this is specifically because of the custom of eating cheese and dairy products during *Chanukah*, or simply because of the popularity of pizza, may never be entirely known!

Spinning the Dreidel

Spinning the *dreidel* became a popular game to play in the Jewish communities of the late Middle Ages, to deter people from playing cards and gambling, which had become the norm in some sectors. The word *dreidel* is derived from the German verb *drehen*, meaning "to turn."[9] Some believe that a form of the *dreidel* game was played by Jews during the Maccabean era when the Seleucids would inspect them to see if they were studying the Torah. The *dreidel* was played to make the Seleucids think that the Jews were gambling, instead of talking about the Scriptures among themselves.

A *dreidel* is a spinning top, based on dice that originally had the letters N, G, H, and S on its four sides, representing the German words *nichts* (nothing), *ganz* (all), *halb* (half), and *shtell arein* (put in). Jewish communities adapted the *dreidel* employing the Hebrew letter equivalents *nun*, *gimel*, *hey*, and *shin*. These four Hebrew letters also make up the acronym *nes gadol hayah sham* or "a great miracle happened there." In Israel today the *shin* is replaced by the letter *peh* for *po*, changing the meaning to "a great miracle happened

---

[8] Ibid., 247.
[9] Ibid., 251.

here." The *dreidel* game is often played using *Chanukah Gelt*, candy, or nuts as prizes.

Chanukah Gelt and Giving Presents

It has become customary for Jewish parents to give their children **Chanukah Gelt** during this time of year. *Gelt* is the Yiddish word for "money" (Ger. *Geld*), and the practice of giving money may be partially rooted in the Maccabees minting coins after restoring autonomy to Israel.[10] In Eastern Europe *Gelt* was often given to children on the fifth night of *Chanukah*, as an incentive for them to continue in Torah study, which was robbed from the Jews by the decree of Antiochus Epiphanes. In successive generations the custom of giving *Gelt* to all children was replaced by giving chocolate coins wrapped in gold foil, and by **giving presents**, one per each night of *Chanukah*, to members of one's household.

Singing the *Maoz Tzur* Hymn

One important *Chanukah* custom followed in the Jewish community is **singing the hymn *Maoz Tzur***, meaning "Rock of Ages." It is to be a song of thanksgiving to God, as He is thanked for delivering the people of Israel from the Egyptian bondage, through the Babylonian exile, Haman's plot to exterminate the Jews, and ultimately the victory of the Maccabees. An English form of *Maoz Tzur* was composed by the American Rabbis Marcus Jastrow and Gustav Gottheil in the Nineteenth Century,[11] and is the form that you will often hear on television and radio broadcasts focusing on *Chanukah*.

Reading the Books of the Maccabees

We believe that perhaps the most important *Chanukah* custom, aside from lighting the *chanukia*, is actually sitting down and familiarizing oneself with the story of the Maccabees. First of all, it is important that we in the Messianic community have a firm foundation in Biblical Studies, and that we know the history of the "elongated First Century" from the time of the Maccabees to the end of the First Century C.E. with the composition of the Book of Revelation. We have to understand that the establishment of the Hasmonean kingdom was the last time that Israel was independent until the State of Israel was founded in 1948. Furthermore, the events of the Maccabees can help us understand the position of Judea in the larger world of the First Century B.C.E., as the Roman Republic was expanding in influence and consolidating the Mediterranean basin under its control.

---

[10] Ibid., 247.
[11] Ibid., pp 251-252.

A Summarization of Chanukah Traditions

The Books of 1-4 Maccabees, found in the Apocrypha, are historical, yet are filled with important Biblical themes. We see the lives of Jewish men and women who are not afraid to die for their faith in the God of Israel. They have the confidence of knowing that they will be rewarded in the hereafter, and that those tormenting them will be punished severely and eternally by the Almighty. One group of Jews, captured and tortured by the Seleucids, had the following to say in a united voice as they faced certain death:

"Therefore, tyrant, put us to the test; and if you take our lives because of our religion, do not suppose that you can injure us by torturing us. For we, through this severe suffering and endurance, shall have the prize of virtue and shall be with God, for whom we suffer; but you, because of your bloodthirstiness toward us, will deservedly undergo from the divine justice eternal torment by fire" (4 Maccabees 9:7-9, RSV).

These are the kinds of stories that should inspire us as Messianic Believers today to not give into the peer pressures of our worldly society. We should be thankful that we do not presently face the threat of death for worshipping the God of Israel as He requires of us. **Those who lived in the period of the Maccabees did.** We have to be inspired and deeply moved by the story of the Maccabees, as we should be by any martyrs of the faith, and commit ourselves to standing for the truth of the Lord in whatever situations we may face. As you read the accounts of the Maccabees, never forget their courage and sacrifice for us, as we are all the spiritual recipients of their actions. Never forget that if they had not stood for the truth against an overwhelming force, that there would have been no people of Israel for our Messiah Yeshua to have been born into, who is the Light of the whole world.

Messianic Winter Holiday Helper

-6-

Why We Should Celebrate Chanukah

J.K. McKee

reproduced from the McHuey Blog

Chanukah is my favorite of all the holidays we get to celebrate as Messianic Believers. Why is it my favorite, you may ask? It does normally take place in December, which means it is in close proximity to my birthday. In December, I get to open a lot of presents! As a Messianic Bible teacher, *Chanukah* has the least amount of controversy associated with it, which means I get to relax (somewhat). We all know when *Chanukah* begins, the twenty-fifth of Chislev (2 Maccabees 1:18; 10:5), so there's no dispute about when it takes place. The traditions associated with *Chanukah* are fairly straightforward: light your *menorah* for eight days, on Day 1 lighting one candle, Day 2 lighting two candles, etc. Be sure to eat fried foods like latkes or doughnuts, remembering the miracle of the oil remaining lit. **Probably the biggest fight I've ever seen among people who celebrate *Chanukah* is over the menu!** Not too bad if you ask me.

Believe me, as one who often has to moderate disputes among Messianics during either the Passover season, or the time period from *Rosh HaShanah* to *Sukkot*—*Chanukah* is easy in comparison. But that does not mean that there are no questions that people ask. Generally speaking, I think those of us of the Jewish, philo-traditionalist camp, in terms of Torah observance and *halachah*, have often not explained ourselves as well as we should. (Please note that this does not mean that we are all "Orthodox.") Because of this, there are some who scratch their heads and wonder whether we should really celebrate *Chanukah*. Isn't this just "the Jewish Christmas"? While the traditionalist perspective has longevity, and brings a great deal of stability to the faithful,

Messianic Winter Holiday Helper

we do need to ask whether the custom of celebrating *Chanukah* passes the test of Philippians 4:8:

"Finally, brethren, whatever is true, whatever is honorable, whatever is right, whatever is pure, whatever is lovely, whatever is of good repute, if there is any excellence and if anything worthy of praise, dwell on these things" (NASU).

I think we will all agree that the Holy Scriptures pass the test of being holy, pure, excellent, and worthy of our attention and praise. Suffice it to say, *Chanukah* or the Feast of Dedication is mentioned in the Holy Scriptures, where John 10:23-24 speaks of Yeshua being present in Jerusalem:

"At that time the Feast of the Dedication took place at Jerusalem; it was winter, and Yeshua was walking in the temple in the portico of Solomon" (NASU).

For some, such as myself, it does not seem that difficult. Our Messiah Yeshua was present when *Chanukah* was being celebrated at the Temple complex in Jerusalem. There had to have been some kind of festivities going on, where the actions of the Maccabees in cleansing the Temple a century-and-a-half earlier were commemorated. The attention in the verses following is not spent discussing whatever celebration was going on, but instead considers the opportunity that Yeshua had to teach and demonstrate who He was as Savior (John 10:25-42). There are some critical statements made here about Yeshua's oneness with the Father and His Divinity (John 10:30, 33), worthy of exploration in other studies. Yet for some, Yeshua's presence at the porch of Solomon does not automatically mean that He celebrated—or would even endorse—the celebration of *Chanukah* today.

I agree, along with many other Messianics, that Yeshua observed all of the appointed times of Leviticus 23. But are you aware of the fact that there is no direct statement in the Apostolic Scriptures which says that the Messiah kept *Yom Teruah/Rosh HaShanah*? I haven't found it. . .(at least not yet). This does not mean that the Lord did not observe the Feast of Trumpets, but we actually have more direct evidence as seen in John 10:23-24 that the Lord observed *Chanukah*. I have heard some Messianic skeptics say that while Yeshua was present at the porch of Solomon, He was away from the Temple, as though He were standing off to the side disapproving of the celebration of *Chanukah*. However, F.F. Bruce's remarks in his commentary on the Gospel of John are more true to what is stated in the text:

"Jesus evidently had spent the two months since Tabernacles in or near Jerusalem. . .The note that 'it was winter' may be intended to explain why he was in a covered part of the temple precincts. Solomon's colonnade was the name given to the portico which ran along the east side of the outer court of Herod's temple."[1]

Yeshua's presence at the porch of Solomon is not difficult to deduce: **it was Winter when *Chanukah* was being celebrated.** There could have been cold winds, freezing rain, or maybe even snow. This was, in all likelihood, where many of the people were gathered to see what was going on for the memorial of the Feast of Dedication. If any of us live in Winter climates today, would we not be expected to celebrate *Chanukah* in some kind of an enclosed, or at least a covered, area? We would want to be shielded from the harsh elements.

I sincerely hope that during the *Chanukah* season, every one of you has taken the time to peruse through the Books of Maccabees. This is easy for me, because I have multiple study Bibles on my desk that include the Apocrypha, and even a copy of the Septuagint which includes the Greek source text used for today's English translations. As one who writes commentaries, I have to engage with literature like Maccabees on a semi-frequent basis, as verses may be referred to in the more technical commentaries that I consult in my studies. Maccabees is often considered to be martyr literature, as the Jews during the time of Antiochus Epiphanes and the Seleucid invasion had to resist assimilation and the occupation of their country. Many were tortured and killed for their faith in the God of Israel—before Yeshua even came on the scene. There is a Biblical reference to these martyrs in Hebrews 11:36:

"Others were tortured, refusing to accept release, in order to obtain a better resurrection" (NRSV).

The story of the seven brothers in 2 Maccabees 7 is something that you all need to read, if you have never read it. The second brother, before being murdered, tells his captors, "You accursed wretch, you dismiss us from this present life, but the King of the universe will raise us up to an everlasting renewal of life, because we have died for his laws" (2 Maccabees 7:9, RSV). David A. deSilva concurs in his commentary on Hebrews,

"'Those who were tortured' but who maintained their loyalty to God and trust in his reward of the faithful are frequently and rightly identified as the martyrs who suffered under Antiochus IV, whose story is vividly preserved in 2 Maccabees 6:18-7:42 and 4 Maccabees 5-18. . .That the author of Hebrews should include among his examples of faith this group of martyrs is not at all surprising. . ."[2]

Honoring those who give their lives in the service of God is something very appropriate during the season of *Chanukah*. When the Apostle Paul went

---

[1] F.F. Bruce, *The Gospel of John* (Grand Rapids: Eerdmans, 1983), 230.

[2] David A. deSilva, *Perseverance in Gratitude: A Socio-Rhetorical Commentary on the Epistle "to the Hebrews"* (Grand Rapids, Eerdmans, 2000), 419.

out into the Mediterranean and faced unwarranted arrest, imprisonment, beatings, and abuse—do you at all think that he considered the example of the Maccabean martyrs who had preceded him? Does the celebration of *Chanukah* pass his test in Philippians 4:8?

Some would say no. Some would say that the Maccabees were murderers who preyed upon Antiochus' troops and disloyal Jews, killing innocent people in cold blood. But in all honesty, if the traditions and customs of your people were based in the Torah, what else would you do when you saw gross idolatry, abominations, and collaboration with the enemy around every corner? You would stand up, fight, and resist—purging the sin and the idolaters from your midst—the exact same thing happened when the Ancient Israelites were in the wilderness. Mattathias, the father of Judah Maccabee, is testified to being of the same character as Phinehas:

"Thus he burned with zeal for the law, as Phinehas did against Zimri the son of Salu. Then Mattathias cried out in the city with a loud voice, saying: 'Let every one who is zealous for the law and supports the covenant come out with me!'" (1 Maccabees 2:26-27, RSV; cf. Numbers 26:7-8).

Some are still not convinced that honoring the Maccabees is a good thing, because some of their descendants conspired with Rome and helped set up a Hasmonean dynasty that led to the kingship of Herod, an Edomite. Yet, the celebration of *Chanukah* is not to honor those who came two to three generations *after* the cleansing of the Temple. Messianics still celebrate the Passover, even though only two adults from the Exodus generation actually made it into the Promised Land! And likewise, are the godly achievements of Joshua nullified, because things get grossly out of control in the Book of Judges after he died?

One of the problems that some skeptics have about *Chanukah* pertains to the miracle of the oil remaining lit for eight days. It is true that it is not mentioned in the historical accounts of 1-4 Maccabees, and instead appears in the Talmud (b.*Shabbat* 21b). Does this mean that it was a totally fabricated legend and that most Jews and Messianic Jews, and people such as myself, are promoting mythology? One of the advantages of reading the Scriptures in their ancient context is that you actually get to compare the Bible against the religious stories of others. You get to see what real mythology is. Some would say that Balaam's donkey speaking to him is obviously mythological (Numbers 22:28-30). Some would say that the whole Old Testament, especially things like Noah's Flood (for which there are competing stories in the Ancient Near East), is obviously mythological. But there are some major differences between mythology and the way that the Scriptures are presented. In his book *The Bible In Its World: The Bible & Archaeology Today*, K.A. Kitchen explains,

Why We Should Celebrate Chanukah

"[The patriarchal narratives] are entirely concerned with a purely human family whose lifestyle is firmly tied to the everyday realities of herding livestock (pasture, wells), yearning for children, arranging suitable marriages, and so on. We never read (for example) of animals divided up that magically rejoin and live again, or of a patriarch's path barred by blocks of lapis or gold. Rather, bearing strictly real, human names, the patriarchs move in well-defined, specific locations. . .and not in some vague, never-never land. By their names and characters, the patriarchs are a group of distinguishable individuals, neither ghosts nor stereotypes."[3]

When one compares many of the accounts of the Tanach to extant religious literature from the Ancient Near East, one compares concrete people living real lives to kings and monarchies that consort with the gods (perhaps even sexually). The contrast is so great between such mythology and the Bible that I do not know even where to begin.[4]

A candelabra of olive oil remaining lit for eight days is not an impossible miracle in which to believe—even if it is mentioned in the Talmud! We all believe in the resurrection of Yeshua the Messiah, do we not? Is that not the greatest miracle of them all? If we believe in Yeshua's resurrection, and we do not consider it mythology, why would we deny God the possibility of leaving the Temple *menorah* lit for eight days while new oil was being consecrated? Oh, do people have problems with it because it is mentioned in the Talmud and we do not trust *any* of the religious literature of Judaism? What does that say about those, involved in a Messianic movement whose shared faith heritage originates from both the Church **and** the Synagogue? Whatever happened to the Jewish people having the oracles of God (Romans 3:2)?

Certainly there have been abuses by some Messianics during the *Chanukah* season. Much of this comes from a lack of understanding, and a lack of information. Not enough attention is given to the Maccabees' story and what they faced and endured, or people do not understand the historical complexities of the era of Hellenism and specifics of Greek religion and philosophy. Some people go overboard with presents and with eating (*and* with drinking), and not enough time is spent focusing on the very serious and very sober theme of martyrdom. **Being killed in the service of God is never a popular theme at any time of year.** Yet, such a theme should be emphasized as it binds us together with men and women of God all throughout the Biblical story, through the millennia since the original Feast of

---

[3] K.A. Kitchen, *The Bible In Its World: The Bible & Archaeology Today* (Exeter: Paternoster, 1977), 64.

[4] Consult the article "Encountering Mythology: A Case Study from the Flood Narratives" by J.K. McKee for a further discussion (appearing in *Confronting Critical Issues*).

Dedication, and today as millions of Believers in the third world suffer under the threat of tyrannical regimes, not knowing if they will live another day.

Chanukah should be celebrated because it has important themes of salvation history that cannot be taken for granted, when God works through His people to accomplish His deliverance. Had the Maccabees not purged the idolatry from Ancient Judea, we may not be having this discussion today. The Jewish people would have been eliminated via cultural assimilation. Many of us might be practicing a form of neo Greco-Roman civic religion.

The Maccabees sacrificed their lives for the gospel before Yeshua was even born. While I will not justify much of the unfair criticism of Christmas by today's Messianics, *Chanukah* should not be summarily dismissed in extreme response to such criticism. It is a holiday where we all—whether Jewish or not—benefit from the actions of the Maccabees. It is a commemoration where we honor their sacrifice—**but now as Messianics we can remember them as some of the forgotten members of the Hebrews 11 Hall of Faith.**

–7–
The Message of Daniel

J.K. McKee

The Book of Daniel is not only one of the most intriguing texts of the Tanach, but it also has experienced a great deal of varied, and sometimes even colorful depictions and interpretations. Many in the history of both Judaism and Christianity have had difficulty examining Daniel, not quite knowing what to make of its words and messages. Even today, Biblical scholars are not agreed as to whether Daniel depicts events that are entirely past, events that have occurred in the past with some to occur in the future, or even if the Prophet Daniel was actually a real prophet of God in ancient times, or just a pseudo-historical figure used to critique a period in Jewish history.

Contrary to conservatives, who mostly regard Daniel as an authentic work of a real Prophet Daniel and/or his contemporaries written in the Sixth Century B.C.E., liberals often view the Book of Daniel as a late work compiled during the Second Century B.C.E. From this vantage point, Daniel does not include prophetic words delivered via a Jewish exile in Babylon and Persia, but rather some kind of religious zealot during the time of the Maccabees, an ahistorical fiction designed to bolster the resolve of the Jews who might give in to the Seleucid Greek assimilation. Views like the resurrection, then, clearly depicted in Daniel (12:2-3), are considered by such liberals to be a rather late addition to Jewish theology that were probably picked up from interactions with the Greeks.

As you can imagine, when a person hears that not all interpreters are convinced that *Daniel* is the main theme of the book that bears his name, it does not sit well. Many of today's evangelical Christians, who often know very little about the inter-Testamental period,[1] are able to easily brush it off. "Who

---

[1] That is, the approximate 400 years between the prophecies of Malachi and the birth of Yeshua.

Messianic Winter Holiday Helper

were the Maccabees, anyway?" they might ask. For those Christian traditions which accept the Apocryphal books of 1-4 Maccabees as canonical or deutero-canonical Scripture, they cannot as easily dismiss the proposal that Daniel may be a pseudo-apocalyptic work. Even though there are excellent reasons for us to consider Daniel to be the product of a real man who lived in Babylon and Persia—**and I do accept genuine Danielic involvement with the text**—the Greek period and the Maccabees will still inevitably factor into one's interpretation. How do we learn to approach the Book of Daniel properly?

Messianic Believers who consider the holiday of *Chanukah* to be a worthy celebration to consider each Winter—commemorating the rededication of the Temple—need to consider what Daniel says. We might be dealing with a book of the Bible with a great deal of symbolism and some definite future prophecies of the Last Days. Yet, when we consider what the Book of Daniel prophesied about the time of the Maccabees, perhaps we can more greatly appreciate it for what it says about the times to come, and how sometimes people do not understand prophetic fulfillment until events actually occur.

Aside from what some modern interpreters may claim, the Book of Daniel itself begins at a legitimate, and not an ahistorical point, in Jewish history. It begins when King Nebuchadnezzar besieges Jerusalem, King Jehoiakim is brought into his hands with various Temple treasures, and spoils are taken back to Babylon (1:1-2). Preparing to return to Babylon, new courtiers are to be made from members of Judah's royal family and nobility, "young men without any physical defect, handsome, showing aptitude for every kind of learning, well informed, quick to understand, and qualified to serve in the king's palace," who were to be "taught the language and literature of the Babylonians" (1:4, NIV). Among those who were to be taken from Judah to Babylon were Daniel, Hananiah, Mishael, and Azariah—who were promptly given the Babylonian names Belteshazzar, Shadrach, Meshach, and Abednego (1:6-7).

While these Jewish exiles would be trained in the ways of the Babylonians, they would never forget who they were or who their God was. Daniel and his friends were shown some favor by the chief Babylonian official who administered their training, being given some leeway for not eating the allotment of royal food and wine, which would have defiled them (1:8-10), likely having originally been first involved in idolatrous worship. Having eaten only vegetables for a period of ten days, Daniel and his friends actually looked healthier than those who had eaten the royal food (1:11-16). It was clear that even though their nation had been defeated by Babylon, "To these four young men God gave knowledge and understanding of all kinds of literature and learning. And Daniel could understand visions and dreams of all kinds" (1:17, NIV).

For some reason or another, these young men were so wise that King Nebuchadnezzar "found them ten times better than all the magicians and enchanters in his whole kingdom" (1:20, NIV). While probably being familiar with what the Babylonian arts of astrology and divination were, **there is no evidence in Daniel that they actually used them**, and instead Daniel and his colleagues were placed in Babylon to uniquely serve the interests of God and the Jewish exiles. When Babylon's officials could offer no help or provide no advice for the king, Daniel and his friends would be there to testify of the unique wisdom and insight that only came from their God. About half of the Book of Daniel (chs. 2-5) is spent with Daniel interpreting the dreams of the Babylonian kings.

King Nebuchadnezzar has a very disturbing dream, causing him not to sleep, and summoning his astrologers and magicians (2:1-3) he actually threatens them with: "This is what I have firmly decided: If you do not tell me what my dream was and interpret it, I will have you cut into pieces and your houses turned into piles of rubble. But if you tell me the dream and explain it, you will receive from me gifts and rewards and great honor. So tell me the dream and explain it for me" (2:5-6, NIV). The sorcerers ask the king to tell them his dream so that they may interpret it for him (2:7), but he recognizes "I am certain that you are trying to gain time" (2:8a, NIV). They recognize the futility of their requests of him, and "The astrologers answered the king, 'There is not a man on earth who can do what the king asks! No king, however great and mighty, has ever asked such a thing of any magician or enchanter or astrologer. What the king asks is too difficult. No one can reveal it to the king except the gods, and they do not live among men" (2:10-11, NIV).

Nebuchadnezzar is furious that his cohorts cannot help him, and so he orders their execution. This would have also included Daniel and his friends, who had been trained as apprentices of those who served the king (2:12-13). Being rounded up by Arioch of the king's guard, he is told why he and his friends are to be executed (12:14-15), and "at this, Daniel went in to the king and asked for time, so that he might interpret the dream for him" (2:16, NIV). Apparently, while considered to be of the king's astrologers, he is not depicted as one who saw him on a regular basis, and here he might have to suffer from the incompetence of those who personally serviced the king.

Daniel urges his friends to pray to God, specifically "so that he and his friends might not be executed with the rest of the wise men of Babylon" (2:18, NIV). "During the night the mystery was revealed to Daniel in a vision" (2:19, NIV), and Daniel issues a great praise to God (2:20-23). Rather than seek out the mysteries via star searching, Daniel and his friends entreat the Lord in great prayer and intercession.

Daniel goes to Arioch, who will in turn allow him to approach the king, tell him what he dreamed, and then interpret the dream for him (2:24-26).

Daniel is quite keen to open his words with, "No wise man, enchanter, magician or diviner can explain to the king the mystery he has asked about, but there is a God in heaven who reveals mysteries. He has shown King Nebuchadnezzar what will happen in the days to come. Your dream and the visions that passed through your mind as you lay on your bed are these" (2:27-28, NIV). Daniel says that Nebuchadnezzar was shown things by "the revealer of mysteries," meaning his God, and that he was shown the same things so that he "may know the interpretation and that [he] may understand what went through [his] mind" (2:30, NIV).

The vision that Daniel explains Nebuchadnezzar saw is one of a great statue. "The head of the statue was made of pure gold, its chest and arms of silver, its belly and thighs of bronze, its legs of iron, its feet partly of iron and partly of baked clay" (2:31-33, NIV). A rock was able to smash the statue into pieces with great ease, and "The wind swept" the pieces "away without leaving a trace. But the rock that struck the statue became a huge mountain and filled the whole earth" (2:35, NIV). Such a dream would have undoubtedly caused King Nebuchadnezzar some consternation.

Daniel recognizes the great power that Nebuchadnezzar possesses (2:37), in fact acknowledging him to be the head of gold on the statue (2:38). Daniel discusses how various parts of the statue represent successive kingdoms that will follow after him and rule, each becoming less prestigious than the other (2:39-41). The final kingdom that will rule is depicted as a division of not only two feet, but ten toes. Mixed of both iron and clay, it will be strong but it will also be divided (2:42-43). While these kingdoms of humanity might all wield some power to varying extents, they will all find themselves defeated:

"In the time of those kings, the God of heaven will set up a kingdom that will never be destroyed, nor will it be left to another people. It will crush all those kingdoms and bring them to an end, but it will itself endure forever. This is the meaning of the vision of the rock cut out of a mountain, but not by human hands—a rock that broke the iron, the bronze, the clay, the silver and the gold to pieces" (2:44-45a, NIV).

What Daniel assures Nebuchadnezzar of is that "The great God has shown the king what will take place in the future. The dream is true and the interpretation is trustworthy" (2:45b, NIV). All Nebuchadnezzar can do is bow to Daniel in honor, acknowledging that "Surely your God is the God of gods and the Lord of kings and a revealer of mysteries, for you were able to reveal this mystery" (2:46-47, NIV). Daniel and his friends are elevated in prestige in the Babylonian court, with Daniel being made ruler of the province of Babylon (2:48-49).

While King Nebuchadnezzar had recognized something special about Daniel and his God, by no means is he finished with making some rather rash decisions in his kingdom. Perhaps thinking that he is special because he has been shown some glimpses of the future, what does he do? He erects a 90-foot high statue of gold that all those in his realm are to bow down and worship (3:1-5). Not only are all to worship this statue, but he decrees "Whoever does not fall down and worship will immediately be thrown into a blazing furnace" (3:6, NIV). It should be no surprise why "as soon as they heard the sound of the horn, flute, zither, lyre, harp and all kinds of music, all the peoples, nations and men of every language fell down and worshipped the image of gold that King Nebuchadnezzar had set up" (3:7, NIV).

Even though they had to worship this image, some Babylonian astrologers approached Nebuchadnezzar and denounced Daniel's Jewish friends Shadrach, Mesach, and Abednego, who administered the province of Babylon (3:8-12). King Nebuchadnezzar has these men brought before him (3:13-15a), berating them that "if you do not worship it, you will be thrown immediately into a blazing furnace. Then what god will be able to rescue you from my hand?" (3:15b, NIV). These Jewish men are confident in their faith, claiming to him, "If we are thrown into the blazing furnace, the God we serve is able to save us from it, and he will rescue us from your hand, O king. But even if he does not, we want you to know, O king, that we will not serve your gods or worship the image of gold you have set up" (3:17-18, NIV). Rather than impressing Nebuchadnezzar by their tenacity, it only infuriated him more so that he had the furnace "heated seven times hotter than usual" (3:19, NIV). So hot was this furnace, that as Shadrach, Meshach, and Abednego are preparing to be thrown into it, flames blazing from it killed some of the Babylonian soldiers (3:22).

These three, who were defiant in not worshipping Nebuchadnezzar's idol, should have been instantly killed in the fire. Witnessing the event, King Nebuchadnezzar asks, "Weren't there three men that we tied up and threw into the fire?" (3:24, NIV). He observes instead, "Look! I see four men walking around in the fire, unbound and unharmed" (3:25a, NIV), with the Aramaic saying, *v'reiveih di reviaya dameh l'var-Elahin* (3:25b). Translations are not agreed on how this is to be rendered, varying from "and the appearance of the fourth is like a son of *the* gods!" (NASU) to "and the fourth looks like a divine being" (NJPS). Other versions have, "the form of the fourth is like the Son of God" (NKJV). While Nebuchadnezzar may have simply thought of this fourth being as perhaps just an angel sent by the Jewish God—many commentators and theologians are agreed that this could very well have been a pre-Incarnate manifestation of Messiah Yeshua.

King Nebuchadnezzar realizes that the three Jewish men, who rejected his demand for worshipping the gold statue, had the presence of God with them. He goes to the furnace, and shouts to them, "servants of the Most High God, come out! Come here!" (3:26, NIV). And so they come out, and both Nebuchadnezzar and his officials "saw that the fire had not harmed their bodies, nor was a hair of their heads singed; their robes were not scorched, and there was no smell of fire on them" (3:27b, NIV). What can Nebuchadnezzar do? He actually exclaims, "Praise be to the God of Shadrach, Meshach and Abednego, who has sent his angel[2] and rescued his servants! They trusted in him and defied the king's command and were willing to give up their lives rather than serve or worship any god except their own God. Therefore I decree that the people of any nation or language who say anything against the God of Shadrach, Meshach and Abednego be cut into pieces and their houses be turned into piles of rubble, for no other god can save in this way" (3:28-29, NIV). **King Nebuchadnezzar has now seen the true power of God for himself.**

One would think that after this significant display of God's great power that King Nebuchadnezzar would practically be turned over to His service. But there is still one last vignette to consider with him as the focus. Nebuchadnezzar has another dream, which begins with him being written a letter about how great the Most High God is (4:1-3). Nebuchadnezzar, narrating this scene, says "I had a dream that made me afraid. As I was lying in my bed, the images and visions that passed through my mind terrified me" (4:4-5, NIV). The Babylonian magicians and astrologers could not help him, so he instead had to turn to Daniel for help (4:6-8).

Nebuchadnezzar's dream is very strange. He sees a huge tree grow that extends itself out over the Earth, a tree that was very fruitful, where birds made their nests and where animals found shade (4:9-12). But then Nebuchadnezzar says that a messenger came from Heaven and ordered, "cut down the tree and trim off its branches; strip off its leaves and scatter its fruit. Let the animals flee from under it and the birds from its branches. But let the stump and its roots, bound with iron and bronze, remain in the ground, in the grass of the field" (4:14-15, NIV). The critical message Nebuchadnezzar is given, an obvious indication that this tree represents a person, is "Let him be drenched with the dew of heaven, and let him live with the animals among the plants of the earth. Let his mind be changed from that of a man and let him be given the mind of an animal, till seven times pass for him" (4:15-16, NIV).

Daniel (or Belteshazzar as Nebuchadnezzar addresses him) is rather perplexed at the dream, and so the king asks him not to be (4:19a). Daniel has to break the news to him that even though he would prefer the tree to represent his enemies (4:19b), it is instead, "you, O king, are that tree. You have become great and strong; your greatness has grown until it reaches the sky, and your dominion extends to distant parts of the earth" (4:22, NIV). Daniel informs him, "You will be driven away from people and will live with

---

[2] Heb. *di-shelach malakheh*; "who hath sent His messenger" (YLT).

the wild animals; you will eat grass like cattle and be drenched with the dew of heaven. Seven times will pass for you until you acknowledge that the Most High is sovereign over the kingdoms of men and gives them to anyone he wishes" (4:24-25, NIV). Nebuchadnezzar's kingdom will remain intact (4:26), but Daniel advises him to "Renounce your sins by doing what is right, and your wickedness by being kind to the oppressed. It may be that then your prosperity will continue" (4:27, NIV).

King Nebuchadnezzar apparently does not take Daniel's counsel. "Twelve months later, as the king was walking on the roof of the royal palace in Babylon, he said, 'Is this not the great Babylon I have built as the royal residence, by my mighty power and for the glory of my majesty?'" (4:29-30, NIV). It was at that point that a voice from Heaven spoke out the decree that he would lose his mind and live like an animal (4:31-32). "Immediately what had been said to Nebuchadnezzar was fulfilled. He was driven away from people and ate grass like cattle. His body was drenched with the dew of heaven until his hair grew like the feathers of an eagle and his nails like the claws of a bird" (4:33, NIV). After the designated time was over, the sanity of King Nebuchadnezzar is restored to him, and he acknowledges the Most High God (4:34-36). He testified, "Now I, Nebuchadnezzar, praise and exalt and glorify the King of heaven, because everything he does is right and all his ways are just. And those who walk in pride he is able to humble" (4:37, NIV).

The Book of Daniel portrays how King Nebuchadnezzar, who had taken away the Jewish exiles to Babylon, had an encounter with Israel's God. But he would not be the only Babylonian king who had a unique spiritual experience. His son and successor, King Belshazzar, too experiences something. During a large banquet he holds for his nobles in Babylon, Belshazzar orders that golden goblets taken from the Temple in Jerusalem be brought out. And so they drink wine from them, praising Babylon's gods (5:1-4). While they drink, a hand appears on one of the walls and writes something. "The king watched the hand as it wrote. His face turned pale and he was so frightened that his knees knocked together and his legs gave way" (5:5b-6, NIV).

Not surprisingly, the enchanters and diviners of Babylon did not know what to make of this (5:7-9), and so Daniel must be brought in to solve the king's dilemma (5:10-12). King Belshazzar recognizes that Daniel had special abilities, and promises to reward him, but Daniel simply says that he will read what was written and give him an appropriate interpretation (5:13-17). Daniel relates how Belshazzar's father, Nebuchadnezzar, was a great king who expanded his empire, and who killed whomever he wanted. Yet, King Nebuchadnezzar was humbled before the Most High God, and acknowledged Him as Supreme Sovereign (5:18-21). Quite contrary to this,

"But you his son, O Belshazzar, have not humbled yourself, though you knew all this. Instead, you have set yourself up against the Lord of heaven.

You had the goblets from his temple brought to you. . .You praised the gods of silver and gold, of bronze, iron, wood and stone, which cannot see or hear or understand. But you did not honor the God who holds in his hand your life and all your ways" (5:22-23, NIV).

The inscription that was written upon the wall included the Aramaic words "MENE, MENE, TEKEL, PARSIN" (5:25, NIV), and speak of how Belshazzar has been found wanting. Ultimately "Your kingdom is divided and given to the Medes and Persians" (5:28, NIV). Daniel was actually "proclaimed the third highest ruler in the kingdom" (5:29, NIV) at that moment, and we see "That very night [how] Belshazzar, king of the Babylonians, was slain, and Darius the Mede took over the kingdom" (5:30, NIV) as Babylon had fallen to the Persian Empire.[3]

The narrative of the Book of Daniel moves forward, and Daniel now finds himself as a high ranking official in the succeeding Persian Empire. This should not be too surprising, as the Persians had a policy of tolerance toward other peoples, and especially toward those who would be liberated from the regimes they conquered, such as the Jewish exiles in Babylon. We see how "Daniel so distinguished himself among the administrators and the satraps by his exceptional qualities that the king planned to set him over the whole kingdom" (6:3, NIV). This caused the other Persian officials to become jealous of him, because no grounds against him or corruption could be found (6:4). "Finally one of these men said, 'We will never find any basis for charges against this man Daniel unless it has something to do with the law of his God[4]'" (6:5, NIV).

Those who are jealous of Daniel convince King Darius to issue a non-repealable decree that anyone who prays to a deity other than him, for a period of thirty days, be cast into a lion's den (6:6-9). Daniel heard of it, but was not bothered. He continued as was his custom, and prayed three times a day with his windows open toward Jerusalem. When his opponents caught him praying to his God, they approached the king on the matter (6:10-12). The Persian king, because his law could not be repealed, was actually quite distressed, and "he was determined to rescue Daniel and made every effort until sundown to save him" (6:14, NIV). He is reminded that he cannot change his law (6:15), and as Daniel is thrown into the lions' den, he tells him, "May your God, whom you serve continually, rescue you!" (6:16, NIV). Knowing that Daniel was in the lions' den, the king could not eat or sleep (6:17-18).

---

[3] The Greek historian Herodotus records the fall of Babylon in his *Histories* 1.189-191. The Persian army entered into the city through the riverbed which flew through it, having receded enough for his troops to easily walk right into the city center. The Babylonians were feasting at the time, and were caught totally unaware.

[4] Ara. *b'dat Elaheh*.

The next morning King Darius goes to the lions den, and he actually speaks out, "Daniel, servant of the living God, has your God, whom you serve continually, been able to rescue you from the lions?" (6:20, NIV). Daniel acknowledges how "My God sent his angel, and he shut the mouths of the lions. They have not hurt me, because I was found innocent in his sight. Nor have I ever done any wrong before you, O king" (6:22, NIV). Daniel is lifted out of the pit (6:23), and those who had falsely accused him, along with their families, are instead thrown into it (6:24). King Darius issues a decree throughout his realm that the God of Daniel be honored, because He had delivered him from the lions' den (6:26-27).

The remainder of the Book of Daniel depicts various scenes while he is in Babylonian exile, both during and after Babylon's fall to Persia, where *he is shown* various dreams and visions by the Lord (chs. 7-12).

The first dream that Daniel experiences is one of four beasts, which he apparently writes down (7:1). "Daniel said: 'In my vision at night I looked, and there before me were the four winds of heaven churning up the great sea. Four great beasts, each different from the others, came up out of the sea'" (7:2-3, NIV). These four beasts are described as a (1) lion with eagle's wings, (2) a bear with three ribs between its teeth, (3) a leopard with four wings of a bird, and (4) a ten-headed beast with large iron teeth (7:4-7). While contemplating these beasts, a little horn enters in among the ten horns, uprooting three horns (7:8a). "This horn had eyes like the eyes of a man and a mouth that spoke boastfully" (7:8b, NIV). From this enters in a scene with the Ancient of Days, the Lord Himself, preparing to judge with books opened (7:9-10).

The little horn continues to speak boastful words, and Daniel observes it until it is slain and its rule is brought to an end (7:11). Many pre-millennial interpreters are agreed that this little horn is most likely the coming antimessiah/antichrist. In contrast to this little horn, Daniel says, "In my vision at night I looked, and there before me was one like a son of man,[5] coming with the clouds of heaven. He approached the Ancient of Days and was led into his presence. He was given authority, glory and sovereign power; all peoples, nations and men of every language worshiped him. His dominion is an everlasting dominion that will not pass away, and his kingdom is one that will never be destroyed" (7:13-14, NIV). This very much echoes the Second Coming of Yeshua in Revelation 11:15: "The kingdom of the world has become the kingdom of our Lord and of his Messiah, and he will reign for ever and ever" (NIV). The little horn or antimessiah, one whose reign will be temporary and end, **is contrasted to the Lord Yeshua whose reign will never end.**

---

[5] Ara. *k'bar enash*.

Daniel, being shown this vision of four beasts, is naturally disturbed, and so he asks an angel what all of these things mean (7:15-16). He is told, "The four great beasts are four kingdoms that will rise from the earth" (7:17, NIV), although "the saints of the Most High will receive the kingdom and will possess it forever—yes, for ever and ever" (7:18, NIV). While encouraging as the end may ultimately be, Daniel is quite curious about the fourth beast, who the ten horns are and the three horns who fell, and why this little horn is able to fight against the holy ones or saints (7:19-22). The angel only says that the fourth beast is the final kingdom that will devour the whole Earth, ten kings will come forth from this kingdom, and that three kings will be subdued from it (7:23-24). Another king will arise, speaking against the Most High and changing the laws (7:25a), and he will be able to oppress the faithful "for a time, times and half a time" (7:25b, NIV).

Many interpreters have seen a reference here to the coming antimessiah and how he will arise to power, but are not entirely agreed on what the ten kings, three kings, and what the fourth beast entirely means. Some see a revived Roman Empire in the form of today's European Union, others see a future United Nations, and some, more creative solutions are proposed. Daniel himself was troubled and did not quite know what to think (7:28). **The significant point that all should be agreed upon is that the beast's realm will be defeated by God, and all the world will fall into His everlasting dominion and worship Him** (7:27).

Daniel's vision of the ram and goat is one that is not only fascinating, but one that is so accurate there are various interpreters who think that it had to have been written *after* the fact. Given to him during Belshazzar's reign (8:1-2), Daniel describes how "I looked up, and there before me was a ram with two horns. . .and the horns were long. One of the horns was longer than the other but grew up later. I watched the ram as he charged toward the west and the north and the south. No animal could stand against him, and none could rescue from his power. He did as he pleased and became great" (8:3-4, NIV). As this ram had been charging, Daniel witnesses "a goat with a prominent horn between his eyes [coming] from the west. . .He came toward the two-horned ram I had seen. . .and charged at him in great rage. I saw him attack the ram furiously, striking the ram and shattering his two horns. The ram was powerful to stand against him; the goat knocked him to the ground and trampled on him, and none could rescue the ram from his power" (8:5-7, NIV).

Notable to understanding this symbolism is how, "The goat became very great, but at the height of his power his large horn was broken off, and in its place four prominent horns grew up toward the four winds of heaven" (8:8, NIV). It is difficult to avoid how what is being described is the ram of the Persian and Median Empire being defeated by the goat of Alexander the

Great's Macedonian Empire. At the height of its power, Alexander died and his conquered lands were split up among four of his generals.

And what became of one part of this four-way power? Daniel is shown that "Out of one of them came another horn, which started small but grew in power to the south and to the east and toward the Beautiful Land. It grew until it reached the host of the heavens, and it threw some of the starry host down to the earth and trampled on them. It set itself up to be as great as the Prince of the host; it took away the daily sacrifice from him, and the place of the sanctuary was brought low. Because of rebellion, the host of the saints and the daily sacrifice were given over to it. It prospered in everything it did, and truth was thrown to the ground" (8:9-12, NIV). This is an excellent description of how the Seleucid Greeks, led by Antiochus Epiphanes, would expand their regime over the Land of Israel, and would commit a great sacrilege in the Second Temple. They would also demand that the Jewish people turn away from God's Torah, and worship their gods and follow their customs. Fortunately, Daniel is told that this problem will only last 2,300 evenings and mornings until "the sanctuary will be reconsecrated" (8:14, NIV).

Some readers of Daniel have problems with its accuracy not necessarily because of what is said regarding the ram and goat in 8:1-15, but because the angel Gabriel is directed to give Daniel some of the specifics of what it means (8:16). Perhaps even more confusing is that Gabriel tells him, "Son of man. . .understand that the vision concerns the time of the end" (8:17, NIV), and we are living well over two millennia since these words were originally written. But perhaps this is only problematic because as mortals we often fail to view time from an Eternal God's perspective.

Gabriel continues, "I am going to tell you what will happen later in the time of wrath, because the vision concerns the time of the end" (8:19, NIV). Notable to be considered here is that not only may the time of the "end" be a little longer, but how the things described in the ram and goat vision may teach future generations about what is to befall the world at *the very end* near the Second Coming. Gabriel names the ram as Media and Persia, and the goat as Greece (8:20-21). He says, "The four horns that replaced the one that was broken off represent four kingdoms that will emerge from his nation but will not have the same power" (8:22, NIV), a clear reference to the splitting up of Alexander's empire.

What will emerge from all of this? "In the latter part of their reign, when rebels have become completely wicked, a stern-faced king, a master of intrigue, will arise. He will become very strong, but not by his own power. He will cause astounding devastation and will succeed in whatever he does. He will destroy the mighty men and the holy people. He will cause deceit to prosper, and he will consider himself superior. When they feel secure he will destroy many and take his stand against the Prince of princes. Yet he will be destroyed, but not by human power" (8:23-25, NIV). This easily describes the rise of Antiochus Epiphanes, and the terrible hardships he will force upon the Jewish people who will return to the Land of Israel. Perhaps this is why Daniel is told, "seal up the vision, for it concerns the distant future" (8:26, NIV). Daniel says that he "was exhausted and lay ill for several days" because he "was appalled by the vision; it was beyond understanding" (8:27, NIV). Fortunately for him, what was described would not take place for another four centuries.

One should not be surprised to see that with all of the terrible things that have befallen Daniel's people—his deportation to Babylon, his two brushes with death while in Babylon, and the future terrible things that are supposed to occur—that he does entreat the Lord for answers as to when the final redemption of Israel will come. Daniel says how "I. . .understood from the Scriptures, according to the word of the LORD given to Jeremiah the prophet, that the desolation of Jerusalem would last seventy years. So I turned to the Lord God and pleaded with him in prayer and petition, in fasting, and in sackcloth and ashes" (9:2-3, NIV; cf. Jeremiah 29:10). The exile would have to come to an end, right? Daniel recognizes the sin of his people, and entreats the Lord for His benevolent mercy:

"O Lord, the great and awesome God, who keeps his covenant of love with all who love him and obey his commandments, we have sinned and done wrong. We have been wicked and have rebelled; we have turned away from your commands and laws. We have not listened to your servant the prophets, who spoke in your name to our kings, our princes and our fathers, and to all the people of the land" (9:4-6, NIV).

It is not insignificant at all that Daniel recognizes the problem of exile as ***not*** only being an issue that concerns his own Jewish people. Acknowledging, "Lord, you are righteous, but this day we are covered with shame" (9:7a, NIV), he identifies those who are affected by the exile as "the men of Judah and the people of Jerusalem and all Israel, both near and far, in all the countries where you have scattered us[6] because of our unfaithfulness to you" (9:7b, NIV). Here, in his prayers to God, Daniel actually recognizes the problem of exile as affecting both his fellow Southern Kingdom Israelites, and those who had been previously scattered from the Northern Kingdom by Assyria. The judgment of exile that has come down upon them all is just, because of significant disobedience against the Lord and against the Torah (9:8-14). Daniel entreats the Lord to be merciful, and deliver his people from exile, returning them to Jerusalem just as He had guided the people out of Egypt (9:15-19).

---

[6] Heb. *l'ish Yehudah u'l'yosh'vei Yerushalayim u'l'kol-Yisrael ha'qerovim v'ha'rechoqim b'kol-ha'eratzot asher hidachtam sham.*

The Message of Daniel

The answer to Daniel's pleading is given in a very unique form of prophecy. The angel Gabriel appears to him and says, "Daniel, I have now come to give you insight and understanding. As soon as you began to pray, an answer was given, which I have come to tell you, for you are highly esteemed. Therefore, consider the message and understand the vision" (9:22-23, NIV). While many readers of Bible prophecy are familiar with the verses that follow, **what we need to pay careful attention to are the specific reasons why these things are to take place.**

What Daniel was told is that "Seventy 'sevens' are decreed for your people and your holy city to finish transgression, to put an end to sin, to atone for wickedness, to bring in everlasting righteousness, to seal up vision and prophecy and to anoint the most holy" (9:24, NIV). The purpose of *shavuim shiv'im* or "seventy weeks" (NASU) being completed is not only so that the problem of Israel's exile and dispersion can finally be solved, but also so that final atonement can be offered for sin, and that everlasting righteousness can be brought in. Some interpreters believe that *all* of these things have now come to pass, via the ministry and sacrifice of Messiah Yeshua, but other interpreters (myself included) conclude that *not all* of them are completed. While Yeshua might have been sacrificed for us, providing final atonement—**we still do not see everlasting righteousness or *tzedeq olamim* present in the Earth.**

What will take place regarding these seventy "sevens" or "weeks"? The verses that summarize them could be the most dissected and examined in the entire Book of Daniel:

"Know and understand this: From the issuing of the decree to restore and rebuild Jerusalem until the Anointed One, the ruler, comes, there will be seven 'sevens,' and sixty-two 'sevens.' It will be rebuilt with streets and a trench, but in times of trouble. After the sixty-two 'sevens,' the Anointed One will be cut off and will have nothing. The people of the ruler who will come will destroy the city and the sanctuary. The end will come like a flood: War will continue until the end, and desolations have been decreed. He will confirm a covenant with many for one 'seven.' In the middle of the 'seven' he will put an end to sacrifice and offering. And on a wing of the temple he will set up an abomination that causes desolation, until the end that is decreed is poured out on him" (9:25-27, NIV).

If you are confused after reading these verses, then be assured that you are not alone. Those who accept genuine Danielic authorship or involvement in these prophecies are not all agreed at what they mean. Many interpreters feel that what is described here is the ministry of Yeshua the Messiah, which they believe caused the animal sacrifices to come to a complete end. Others feel that while the ministry of Yeshua is a feature of the seventy-weeks prophecy, that it is the coming antimessiah/antichrist who causes sacrifices to end—in a future Seventieth Week of Israel in a future, rebuilt Temple.

While it is easy for many of my post-tribulational colleagues to totally dismiss some of the work of pre-tribulationists, I do not think that dispensational pre-tribulationists are entirely incorrect with some of their interpretations of Daniel 9:25-27. Looking at the sets of "sevens" as years, there are to be sixty-nine "sevens" (9:25, NIV) or 483 years in total from the reconstruction of Jerusalem and its walls until the Anointed One or "Messiah the Prince" (NASU)[7] arrives, who will be cut off. Beginning this count of years in 445-444 B.C.E., when Jerusalem was rebuilt during the time of Nehemiah, places one at 33 C.E., the approximate year of Yeshua's death (9:26a).[8]

Following this, the people of the ruler to come, the antimessiah/antichrist, will destroy the city of Jerusalem and its Temple (9:26b). This occurred in 70 C.E. when the Romans destroyed Jerusalem and the Temple, and was certainly followed by war (9:26c). Sometime in the future, this ruler will emerge on the scene, making or confirming an agreement for the final set of "seven," but in the middle of this seven years he will commit a great abomination (9:27). In his writing to the Thessalonicans, the Apostle Paul describes this Abomination of Desolation among a number of things that must happen before Yeshua can return:

"Don't let anyone deceive you in any way, for that day will not come until the rebellion occurs and the man of lawlessness is revealed, the man doomed to destruction. He will oppose and will exalt himself over everything that is called God or is worshiped, so that he sets himself up in God's temple, proclaiming himself to be God" (2 Thessalonians 2:3-4, NIV).

A significant part of the Prophet Daniel's visions do concern the time period of the Maccabees, as is seen in chs. 10-11. "In the third year of Cyrus king of Persia, a revelation was given to Daniel. . .Its message was true and it concerned a great war" (10:1, NIV). So serious was this, that "I, Daniel, mourned for three weeks. I ate no choice food; no meat or wine touched by lips; and I used no lotions at all until the three weeks were over" (10:2, NIV). As bad as it was for him to be in exile, what he was shown concerned what would befall his people in the future—as even more suffering and hardship would come to them.

Occurring at a season adjacent to Passover (10:4), an angel reveals himself to Daniel (10:5-9), who proceeds to speak to Daniel (10:10-11). This messenger had apparently been delayed after confronting *mal'kei Paras*, "the kings of Persia" (10:13, NASU), believed to be various Satanic agents who oversaw the

---

[7] Heb. *Mashiach nagid*.

[8] John F. Walvoord, *Every Prophecy of the Bible* (Colorado Springs: Chariot Victor Publishing, 1999), pp 253-254.

Persian realm. The archangel Michael came to his assistance (10:12-14), and now this angel is able to communicate with Daniel. While Daniel is overwhelmed, speechless, and drained of energy, the angel assures him to have strength and peace, as he will be shown important things (10:15-19). As he is told, "Do you know why I have come to you? Soon I will return to fight against the prince of Persia, and when I go, the prince of Greece will come; but first I will tell you what is written in the Book of Truth" (10:20, NIV). So, while the Book of Daniel does depict worldly forces engaged against one another—spiritual forces are very much a part of what goes on as well (10:21-11:1).

The revelation that this angel specifically shows to Daniel directly pertains to the time of the Maccabees, and it is greatly accurate when compared to 1&2 Maccabees in the Apocrypha. (This is again a reason why some doubt genuine Danielic involvement with this text.) "Three more kings will appear in Persia, and then a fourth, who will be far richer than all the others. When he has gained power by his wealth, he will stir up everyone against the kingdom of Greece" (11:2, NIV), a reference to Xerxes I and the Persian Wars. "Then a mighty king will appear, who will rule with great power and do as he pleases. After he has appeared, his empire will be broken up and parceled out toward the four winds of heaven. . .his empire will be uprooted and given to others" (11:3-4, NIV), another reference to the rise of Alexander the Great and the division of his Macedonian Empire.

A word detailing the relationship between the South and the North, the rule of the Greek-Egyptian Ptolemies and the Seleucid Antiochans in Asia Minor, is described. Even though descending from Alexander's empire, they will fight among themselves vying for superiority (11:5-15). In the midst of this fighting, a specific king from the North will arise. "The invader will do as he pleases; no one will be able to stand against him. He will establish himself in the Beautiful Land and will have the power to destroy it" (11:16, NIV). Caught in the crossfire of the Seleucid Greeks and Egyptian Ptolemies (11:17-18) will be the poor Land of Israel. Yet the North will find itself humiliated by the South (11:19).

Following the first series of conflicts, a new leader from the North will come to power (11:21-24), and "With a large army he will stir up his strength and courage against the king of the South. The king of the South will wage war with a large and very powerful army, but he will not be able to stand because of the plot devised against him. . .The two kings, with their hearts bent on evil, will sit at the same table and lie to each other, but to no avail, because an end will still come at the appointed time" (11:25, 27, NIV).

Perhaps changing his tactics on how to defeat the South, "The king of the North will return to his own country with great wealth, but his heart will be set against the holy covenant. He will take action against it and then return to his own country" (11:28, NIV). The Land of Israel will now be a major focus of his actions, as the South, Ptolemaic Egypt, will not be subdued. The angel tells Daniel, "At the appointed time he will invade the South again, but this time the outcome will be different from what it was before. . .[H]e will turn back and vent his fury against the holy covenant. He will return and show favor to those who forsake the holy covenant" (11:29, 30, NIV). The Jewish people will be opposed by this man, except those who turn from their ancestral ways.

The specific actions that this king will commit are that "His armed forces will rise up to desecrate the temple fortress and will abolish the daily sacrifice. Then they will set up the abomination that causes desolation. With flattery he will corrupt those who have violated the covenant, but the people who know their God will firmly resist him" (11:31-32, NIV). The desecration of the Temple that Antiochus Epiphanes will authorize, which would have included the sacrifice of a pig, and the corruption of many Jews into his insidious influence of Greek religion, is clearly detailed. Yet the faithfulness of those, who we now call the Maccabees, is also detailed:

"Those who are wise will instruct many, though for a time they will fall by the sword or be burned or captured or plundered. When they fall, they will receive a little help, and many who are not sincere will join them. Some of the wise will stumble, so that they may be refined, purified and made spotless until the time of the end, for it will still come at the appointed time" (11:33-35, NIV).

The personality of Antiochus Epiphanes is described in 11:36-45, although various pre-millennial expositors feel that the personality of the coming antimessiah/antichrist is also seen or echoed here. Antiochus will exalt himself, and speak great blasphemies against God (11:36), disregarding the deities that his ancestors worshipped (11:37). He will serve a foreign god instead (11:38-39). This king will engage in battle with the king of the South and be quite successful (11:40-45), but eventually "he will come to his end, and no one will help him" (11:45b, NIV).

The issue of 11:36-45, while referring to the distant past, also likely includes echoes of the future antimessiah, is how "At that time[9] Michael, the great prince who protects your people, will arise" (12:1a, NIV). The scene suddenly shifts from the several-centuries-in-the-future from Daniel's lifetime, to the very distant future. The language in Daniel 12:1b, "There will be a time of distress such as has not happened from the beginning of nations until then" (NIV), is picked up by Yeshua in His Olivet Discourse: "For then there will be great distress, unequaled from the beginning of the world until now—and never to be equaled again" (Matthew 24:21, NIV). A resurrection of deceased people will occur at this end-time, not only of righteous but also

---

[9] Heb. *u'b'et ha'he*.

unrighteous (12:2). And, "Those who are wise will shine like the brightness of the heavens, and those who lead many to righteousness, like the stars for ever and ever" (12:3, NIV).

Is the Book of Daniel confusing for you in some places? *It probably is.* It even was for Daniel, as he was told, "close up and seal the words of this scroll until the time of the end. Many will go here and there to increase knowledge" (12:4, NIV). Much of what Daniel was shown will only occur at a designated "time, times and half a time. When the power of the holy people has been finally broken, all these things will be completed" (12:7, NIV), indicating that a time of Great Tribulation will indeed await the holy ones or saints. Yet even though horrendous, "Many will be purified, made spotless and refined, but the wicked will continue to be wicked. None of the wicked will understand, but those who are wise will understand" (12:10, NIV).

The Book of Daniel portrays a period of time that begins during the Jewish exile in Babylon and Persia, it includes the assault of Antiochus Epiphanes during the time of the Maccabees, and it extends to the Great Tribulation and coming antimessiah. It concerns the distant past, and the coming future. If we understand Daniel's significance for the past, we can better understand what to expect in the future. Those of the final generation are instructed, "From the time that the daily sacrifice is abolished and the abomination that causes desolation is set up, there will be 1,290 days. Blessed is the one who waits for and reaches the end of the 1,335 days" (12:11-12, NIV)—that will ensure a person that he or she actually makes it into the restored Kingdom of God on Earth! Daniel would pass on, but was assured that he would be among those rewarded for his faithfulness (12:13).

The Book of Daniel, perhaps not that different from the other prophetic literature of the Tanach, has provoked a wide variance of interpretations. Some consider Daniel to be so accurate that it had to have been written after the fact. Others would consider Daniel to be an ancient mystic, even though all the text of Daniel says is that he was empowered by God to interpret dreams and visions—and not that he was an astrologer! Daniel was present in the right place and right time to be used by the Lord, and to testify to the kings and officials of the day of His might and power. This would be the most important of all the lessons we can learn from Daniel, so that we might be those who can not only testify of God to others—but that we can actually lead others to righteousness (12:3)! This is something all must do whether we are the last generation, approaching the last generation, or are quite some time away from the consummation of the ages.

Messianic Winter Holiday Helper

-8-

The Message of 1 Maccabees

J.K. McKee

Today's broad Messianic community often finds the season of *Chanukah* to be one of great blessing and enjoyment. More than anything else, we get to commemorate the victory of the Maccabees over the Seleucid Greek occupiers of the Land of Israel. We get to honor their courage and sacrifice in standing up for the God of Israel and His Torah, and how they were tenacious in not giving into the pressures of pagan assimilation. *Chanukah* is a season when we get to remember the rededication of the Temple in Jerusalem, and the miracle of the *menorah* remaining lit for eight days. We should all find *Chanukah* to be a very special time that teaches us many important spiritual lessons.

The historical record behind the celebration of *Chanukah* is not at all complicated, but it is often inaccessible to many Biblical readers. Why, you may ask? Because it is principally found in the Apocryphal books of 1&2 Maccabees (with associated information found in 3&4 Maccabees). These texts are not considered canonical Scripture by either Judaism or mainline Protestantism, as they form an appendix onto the Greek Septuagint. Roman Catholicism and Eastern Orthodoxy consider the Apocryphal books to be canonical Scripture, and in Anglicanism the Apocryphal books are commonly referred to as deutero-canonical. Most of today's Messianics do not principally use a Bible version (i.e., RSV/NRSV or NEB/REB) that has the Apocrypha included, and unless one is either a trained scholar in Biblical Studies or a budding amateur theologian, many of today's evangelical Christians are unfamiliar with the important role the Apocrypha plays in understanding the world of First Century Judaism.

Not all of you, fortunately, are completely unfamiliar with the Books of the Maccabees. During the season of *Chanukah*, your Messianic congregation or fellowship leader has likely made some reference to these texts. Some of you may have an edition of the *Oxford Annotated Bible*[1] or the *Oxford Study Bible*[2] (or even more recently *The New Interpreter's Study Bible*),[3] ecumenical study Bibles that include the Apocrypha, and you have been able to follow along should you hear teachings from the Books of the Maccabees. Yet even for those of you who have been able to do this, most of our attention during the week of *Chanukah* is only spent addressing 1 Maccabees chs. 1-4, the historical record that deals with the initial occupation of Judea, the defilement of the Temple, the initial zealotry of the Maccabees, and then their liberation of Jerusalem and cleansing of the Temple. Very little attention is given to the wider historical issues, including not only more of the victories of the Maccabean forces, but also how the Jewish nation interacted with the powers present in the Second Century B.C.E. Mediterranean, playing a tenuous role as it vied for its independence among shifting alliances. **I think we can all safely agree that a review of the historical record is in order.**

Most scholars are in agreement that the text known as 1 Maccabees was originally written in Hebrew, as it bears signs of original Semitic syntax and the likely preservation of various idioms, even though what we have today has survived to us in (Alexandrian) Greek translation.[4] If 1 Maccabees is considered to be a legitimate historical work (cf. 16:23-24), then its composition needed to be completed sometime during the early or middle reign of John Hyrcanus (134-104 B.C.E.), placing it near the end of the Second Century B.C.E. The author of 1 Maccabees is strictly anonymous, with it being thought that he was possibly related to Simon, a brother of Judah Maccabee. In all likelihood, though, the author of 1 Maccabees was probably a second generation admirer of the original Maccabees, and he saw the hand of Providence at work in their distinct human actions in saving the Jewish people. It is suggested by some that 1 Maccabees does show some discontent with the Hasmonean rule present among those of the author's generation, although he certainly respected the Maccabees and believed that the Jewish people could gain great inspiration by knowing about what they accomplished.[5]

---

[1] Herbert G. May and Bruce M. Metzger, eds., *The New Oxford Annotated Bible*, RSV (New York: Oxford University Press, 1977).

[2] M. Jack Suggs, Katharine Doob Sakenfeld, and James R. Mueller, eds., *The Oxford Study Bible*, REB (New York: Oxford University Press, 1992).

[3] Walter J. Harrelson, ed., et. al., *The New Interpreter's Study Bible*, NRSV (Nashville: Abingdon, 2003).

[4] Sir Lancelot C. L. Brenton, ed & trans., *The Septuagint With Apocrypha* (Peabody, MA: Hendrickson, 1999), Apocrypha pp 139-182; Alfred Rahlfs, ed., *Septuaginta* (Stuttgart: Deutsche Bibelgesellschaft, 1979), 1:1039-1099.

[5] This data is briefly summarized from "The Two Books of Maccabees," in R.K. Harrison, *Introduction to the Old Testament* (Grand Rapids: Eerdmans, 1969), pp 1260-1261.

The Message of I Maccabees

The narrator of 1 Maccabees takes us back all the way to the expanse of Alexander the Great across the ancient world in the Fourth Century B.C.E. (1:1-3a). It is said that "When at last the world lay quiet under his sway, his pride knew no limits; he built up an extremely powerful army and ruled over countries, nations, and princedoms, all of which rendered him tribute" (1:3b-4, REB). Alexander dies, and the empire he had built is split up and taken over by four of his generals (1:5-9a), generals who "brought untold miseries on the world" (1:9b, REB). Moving forward to the period of importance, "An offshoot of this stock was that impious man, Antiochus Epiphanes, son of King Antiochus" (REB), who apparently had been a prisoner in Rome (1:10). It will be important for you to keep in mind that just how certain royal dynasties in history bore many monarchs named Louis (France), George and Edward (Britain), or Friedrich and Wilhelm (Prussia), so too are the Greek kings of Syria often known by the name Antiochus. The Antiochus we are principally concerned about—who caused the whole series of problems for the Jewish people—is surnamed *Epiphanēs* or "God manifest," and was a very ambitious man who desired to be worshipped as a deity.[6]

While Antiochus Epiphanes is acceding in power, "there emerged in Israel a group of renegade Jews, who inveigled many by saying, 'We should go and make an agreement with the Gentiles round about; nothing but disaster has been our lot since we cut ourselves off from them" (1:11, REB). These Jews thought it best to become like the pagan nations at large, especially as the Seleucid Greek kingdom was expanding. They built a gymnasium in Jerusalem, removed the mark of circumcision via epispasm,[7] repudiated God's Torah, and intermarried with the heathen (1:12-15).

The original desire of Antiochus Epiphanes was not necessarily to conquer the Jewish people. The narrator describes how "Antiochus determined to become king of Egypt and so rule both kingdoms" (1:16b, REB), taking over where the Greek Ptolemies had been ruling since the time of Alexander. He amasses a great force and is able to pillage Egypt, taking great spoil (1:18-19), and now believing himself to be invisible, he begins his return home by marching with a "a strong force against Israel and Jerusalem" (1:20, REB). Much like previous conquerors before him, Antiochus Epiphanes ransacked the Jerusalem Temple, stealing whatever gold and treasure he could find (1:21-24). As one can imagine, there was great lament and mourning throughout the land (1:25-28).

---

[6] Antiochus Epiphanes is a different leader than the earlier monarch Antiochus the Great or Antiochus III (ruled 222-187 B.C.E.), who Josephus records was quite beneficent and gracious toward the Jews in Phyrgia (*Antiquities of the Jews* 12.148-153).

[7] Epispasm is a procedure by which skin is stretched over the head of a circumcised man's penis, over time effectively nullifying circumcision. Paul refers to this in 1 Corinthians 7:18: "Was a man called with the marks of circumcision on him? Let him not remove them" (REB).

"Two years later, the king sent a governor to put the towns of Judaea under tribute. When he arrived at Jerusalem with a powerful force his language, though friendly, was full of guile, for once he had gained the city's confidence he launched a sudden and savage attack" (1:29-30a, REB). As bad as the previous theft of Temple treasures had been, the Land of Israel would now be under the complete jurisdiction of Antiochus' kingdom, and even though some flowery language was used to indicate somewhat peaceful intentions—people were killed, women were captured, and livestock seized (1:32). Jerusalem itself was turned into a military fortress (1:33), "garrisoned by impious foreigners and renegades" (1:34, REB)—foreign troops and rebellious Jews. The narrator can only issue a lament similar to Psalm 79 (1:37-40).

Things get even worse for the Jews, thanks to the impetuous Antiochus Epiphanes. "The king issued an edict throughout his empire: his subjects were to become one people and abandon their own customs" (1:41, REB), presumably in a way to honor and ultimately worship him as their leader. *This would begin by adopting Greek religion.* Many of the diverse peoples in Antiochus' realm did this (1:42), "and many in Israel willingly adopted the foreign cult, sacrificing to idols and profaning the Sabbath" (1:43, REB). Written orders were sent to Jerusalem and Judea that participating in Temple worship was prohibited (1:44), and so the Temple was purposefully defiled (1:45-46). The great abomination commanded by Antiochus was:

"Pagan altars, idols, and sacred precincts were to be established, swine and other unclean beasts to be offered in sacrifice. The Jews were to leave their sons uncircumcised; they had to make themselves in every way abominable, unclean, and profane, and so forget the way and change all their statutes. The penalty for disobeying the royal decree was death" (1:47-50, REB).

The Jewish people were commanded to completely turn their back on God's Torah and His commandments, defiling themselves with sinful paganism, under the threat of death. Sadly, as this decree went forth in the towns of Judea, "Those of the people who were ready to betray the law all thronged to their side in large numbers. Their wicked conduct throughout the land drove Israel" (REB)—here presumably meaning those faithful to God—"into hiding in every possible place of refuge" (1:52-53, REB). The terrible actions committed cause the author to consider this as "the abomination of desolation" (1:54, REB), and he depicts how Torah scrolls were ripped up and burned, and how anyone—including mothers who circumcised their infant sons—were put to death (1:55-61). In spite of these atrocities, "many in Israel found strength to resist. . .They welcomed death and died rather than defile themselves and profane the holy covenant. Israel lay under a reign of terror" (1:62a, 63-64, REB).

Onto the scene emerges a certain man named Mattithias, a member of a priestly family from Jerusalem who lived in the town of Modin, who also had five sons (2:1-5). He is aghast over the terrible events happening in Jerusalem (2:6-11), expressing how "We see the temple, which is our splendour and glory, laid waste and desecrated by the Gentiles. Why should we go on living?" (2:12-13, REB). He and his sons put on sackcloth and mourn (2:14).

It is not surprising that the enforcement brigade makes its way to Modin, to make sure that the apostasy of worshipping and sacrificing to Greek gods is proceeding (2:15). When many of his countrymen comply, Mattathias stands away (2:16). The Seleucid officers actually promise Mattathias and his sons status as the king's "Friends," and great riches and honor, if as leaders of the community they comply (2:17-18). Mattathias, foaming with righteous indignation, exclaims that he will not give into such demands:

"Though every nation in the king's dominions obeys and forsakes its ancestral worship, though all have chosen to submit to his commands, yet I and my sons and my brothers will follow the covenant made with our forefathers. Heaven forbid we should ever abandon the law and its statutes! We will not obey the king's command, nor will we deviate one step from our way of worship" (2:19-22, REB).

Having declared his loyalty for God and for His Torah, an apostate Jew came forward in compliance with Antiochus' decrees to offer pagan sacrifice (2:23). Mattathias is infuriated and he kills the man (2:24), and then "At the same time he killed the officer sent by the king to enforce sacrifice, and demolished the pagan altar" (2:25, REB). The narrator connects this to the zeal of Phinehas who killed Zimri in the wilderness trek (2:26; cf. Numbers 26:7-8). Mattathias issues a plea that those who are loyal to the Law of God are to follow him, and so he and his sons escape to the hills (2:27-28).

Many Jews faithful to the Torah escaped to the desert with their families, and word makes it back to Jerusalem that there are disobedient people in Antiochus' realm (2:29-31). A group of Jews is mercilessly attacked on the Sabbath, and although they are given a chance to renounce their religion (2:32-33), they viciously refuse to profane the Sabbath (2:34). This group of Jews is mowed down and massacred for not defending themselves on *Shabbat*, up to a thousand people in total (2:35-38). When hearing about their faithfulness, Mattathias and his colleagues certainly grieve. But, they recognize that if they are not willing to defend themselves on the Sabbath, then they will certainly all be wiped out (2:39-41). Hence in Jewish law today, it is permitted to violate a ritual command to save human life, and military, police, firefighters, and doctors are all permitted to work on *Shabbat*.

Mattathias' paramilitary force grows in numbers and becomes organized, and they begin a unique guerilla campaign throughout the occupied Land of Israel (2:42-44). They turn their energies against rebellious Jews who had forsaken God's Torah and covenant, and they "swept through the country, demolishing the pagan altars and forcibly circumcising all the uncircumcised boys found within the frontiers of Israel" (2:45-46, REB). They did well, standing up for a righteous cause in defense of the Law of God (2:47-48). An aged man, Mattathias prepares to die, and he encourages his sons to continue, by recalling to them the holiness of the Torah and the examples of their forefathers in history (2:49-64). He commissions his son Simon to be a counselor to them, and his son Judah (or Judas as the REB renders it) to be their military commander (2:65-66). He admonishes, "Assemble to your side all who observe the law, and avenge your people's wrongs. Repay the Gentiles in their own coin, and give heed to what the law decrees" (2:67-68, REB). Mattathias dies and is buried in the family tomb at Modin (2:69-70).

The war with the Seleucids begins to heat up as Judah Maccabee comes forward to succeed his father. He is given extreme accolades by the author of 1 Maccabees (3:1-9). The Maccabean force experiences two quick victories. The first is against Apollonius, whose plans Judah is informed about, and who is encountered and killed (3:10-11). Judah Maccabee takes his sword "and for the rest of his life he used it in his campaigns" (3:12, REB). The second occurs when an ambitious Syrian military commander, Seron, believes that he can gain renown by putting down the Jewish rebellion. He guides a large force, reinforced by apostate Jews, to wreak vengeance on the Maccabees (3:13-15). Judah's army is overwhelmed when they see the force, fainting with hunger, but Judah is clear to say how victory does not come from numbers but from Heaven (3:16-19). The cause that they are fighting for is just. Judah issues some inspiring words to his band:

"Our enemies, inflated with insolence and lawlessness, are coming against us; they mean to kill us and our wives and children for the sake of the plunder they will get. But we are fighting for our lives and for our laws and customs, and Heaven will crush them before our eyes; you have no need to be afraid of them" (3:20-22, REB).

Following this, a surprise attack is launched which overwhelms Seron's forces (3:23-24). "Judah and his brothers came to be regarded with fear, and alarm spread among the Gentiles round about. His fame reached the ears of the king, and the story of his battles was told in every nation" (3:25-26, REB). Having had success, King Antiochus is infuriated and prepares to mobilize a massive force to crush this insurrection once and for all (3:27). He opened his treasury and gave a year's pay to his troops, with a command to be prepared to serve as required (3:28).

Ironically enough, the narrator depicts how this invincible king did not have the financial resources to enact his plan immediately. There was disaffection throughout his realm because of the Hellenistic religion he had imposed on everyone (3:29). Furthermore, he lived quite luxuriously (3:30).

The Message of I Maccabees

Antiochus goes off to Persia to collect tribute before his campaign against the Jews can begin (3:31). Lysias, a member of the royal family, is left as overseer until he returns (3:32). He is granted a sizeable military force to try to crush any rebellion in Judea and Jerusalem (3:33-37). Lysias chooses three men: Ptolemaeus, Nicanor, and Gorgias to go into Judea and try to stop the rebellion (3:38-39). A reinforced force of forty-thousand infantry and seven thousand cavalry enter into the Promised Land, and the war heats up even more.

Judah Maccabee and his guerilla army hear the news of the new Seleucid force, brought to do nothing more than bring about "the complete destruction of the nation" (3:42, REB). Even though many were distraught, "they said among themselves, 'Let us restore the shattered fortunes of our people; let us fight for our nation and for the holy place'" (3:43, REB), and rather than feel defeated, they redoubled their efforts. Arriving at Mizpah, a Maccabean force fasts, putting on sackcloth and ashes, and they take inspiration from the reading of the Torah (3:46-48). With the priestly garments by their side, and Nazirites who had recently completed their vows, these people cried out to God and asked Him to rectify the situation. They wanted God to urgently intervene so that the Jewish people and their way of life would not be destroyed (3:49-54). Judah Maccabee organizes his forces (3:55), and in accordance with the Torah those who were exempt from military service were sent home (3:56). The band then moves just south of Emmaus, where they prepare at dawn to fight against the occupying army (3:57-58), believing that it is better to die fighting than look on while the Jewish people were wiped out (3:59).

Gorgias, having a detachment of five thousand men and a thousand special cavalry, plans to launch a surprise attack on Judah's position (4:1-2), but Judah hears of it, and moves his force to attack the Seleucids in Emmaus (4:3-4). When Gorgias reaches Judah's camp, he finds it deserted and believes the Maccabean troops to be running (4:5). When day comes, the Maccabean force of three thousand can be clearly seen, and they did not have all the armaments they needed for the attack (4:6-7). Judah inspires his troops by calling them to remember God's deliverance at the Red Sea (4:8-10), and how "there is One who liberates and saves Israel" (4:11, REB). And so advancing their attack and sounding trumpets (4:12-13), "Judas and his men closed with them, and the Gentiles broke and fled into the plain...The pursuit was pressed as far as Gazara and the lowlands of Idumaea, to Azotus and Jamnia; some three thousand of the enemy were killed that day" (4:14-15, REB).

The pursuit is broken off, and Judah instructs his troops not to take any spoils, as he reminds them that Gorgias' detachment is still out there (4:16-18). At that time a patrol from Gorgias spots them, seeing that those at Emmaus had been routed (4:19-20). "They were panic-stricken as they took in the scene, and when, further, they saw the army of Judas in the plain, ready for action" (4:21, REB). Reporting back of the devastation, Gorgias' taskforce flees to Philistia (4:22), and the Seleucid camp at Emmaus is plundered (4:23-25). "Those of the Gentiles who escaped with their lives went to Lysias and reported all that had happened. He was stunned at the news, bitterly disappointed that matters with Israel had not gone as he had intended; they had turned out very differently from the king's instructions to him" (4:26-27, REB).

"The following year Lysias mustered sixty thousand picked infantry and five thousand cavalry to bring the war with the Jews to an end" (4:28, REB). The narrator describes how marching into Idumea, Judah's forces numbered ten thousand (4:29), and he prayed to the Lord as Savior of Israel, praying that his Jewish force would defeat the Seleucid army just as David had defeated the Philistines (4:30). He specifically prays, "let this army be hemmed in by the power of your people Israel, and let the enemy's pride in their troops and mounted men be humbled; so fill them with cowardice, make their insolent strength melt away, let them reel under a crushing defeat; may they fall by the sword of those who love you. And let all who know your name praise you with songs of thanksgiving" (4:31-33, REB). About five thousand of Lysias' solders are lost in hand-to-hand combat (4:34), and he was forced to withdraw to Antioch, procuring the services of mercenaries, by which he could return to Judea with a much greater army (4:35).

Seeing that Lysias has retreated, Judah and his brothers see a great opportunity. They say to themselves, "Now that our enemies have been crushed, let us go up to cleanse and rededicate the temple" (4:36, REB). The Maccabean force goes up to Mount Zion, they see how Antiochus' forces had utterly ruined the Temple and altar, and they lamented loudly before the Lord (4:37-40). The citadel garrison of Seleucids guarding Jerusalem is engaged, and select priests who were loyal to the Torah began the process of cleaning up the defilements in the Temple complex (4:41-43). The altar that had been defiled by unclean and unfit animals is demolished, and they took unhewn stones and built a new altar (4:44-47). The Temple was repaired, and all new consecrated vessels were made (4:48-49). New burnt offerings and incense could be presented before God, and "When they had set the Bread of the Presence on the table and spread out the curtains, their work was completed" (4:50-51, REB).

On the 25th of Kislev, "sacrifice was offered, as laid down by the law, on the newly constructed altar of whole-offerings. On the anniversary of the day of its desecration by the Gentiles, on that very day it was dedicated with hymns of thanksgiving, to the music of harps and lutes and cymbals. All the people prostrated themselves in worship and gave praise to Heaven for prospering their cause" (4:52-55, REB). The rededication ceremony for the

Temple and altar lasted for a total of eight days, as proper and clean sacrifices and offerings were made (4:56-57). "At the lifting of the disgrace brought on them by the Gentiles there was very great rejoicing among the people" (4:58, REB). So significant was the celebration of rededicating the Temple, after freeing Jerusalem from Seleucid occupation, that Judah Maccabee and his brothers, "and the whole congregation of Israel decreed that, at the same season each year, the dedication of the altar should be observed with joy and gladness for eight days, beginning on the twenty-fifth of Kislev" (4:59, REB).

It is at this point that most Messianics commemorating *Chanukah* and reading 1 Maccabees stop. But this is no fairy tale where all things have ended happily ever after. It is obvious that the fight against Antiochus Epiphanes and the Seleucid Greeks is by no means over. The only reason Jerusalem was captured is because Lysias had retreated to restore his army back to full strength. 1 Maccabees still has the end of ch. 4, and chs. 5-16 to go—which give us a fuller picture of how important this period is to Jewish history.

Judah Maccabee knows that the enemy is going to return, and so he has Mount Zion and Bethsura fortified (4:60-61). "The Gentiles round about were greatly incensed when they heard of the building of the altar and rededication of the temple. Determined to wipe out all of Jacob's race living among them, they set about the work of massacre and extermination" (5:1-2, REB). Knowing that the threat against his people is not only from the outside Seleucid Greeks, but also from the immediate neighbors who had sided with them, the Maccabean force needed to demonstrate that they were serious about being independent. A military campaign begins against those who had threatened the Jews, including the descendents of Esau in Idumea, the Baenites, Ammonites, and the town of Jazer (5:3-8).

A significant conflict begins to brew, as "The Gentiles in Gilead gathered against the Israelites within their territory, intent on destroying them" (5:9a, REB). A group of Jews seeks refuge in a fortress at Dathema, sending a letter to Judah for his immediate help (5:9b-13). Receiving the letter, word from Galilee reaches Judah that a force is being amassed in the north from Ptolemais, Tyre, and Sidon (5:14), along with "all heathen Galilee" (5:15, REB).

With one force amassing to the east, and another to the north, Judah has the Maccabean army divide in two. His brother Simon will take a contingent to repel those in the north, whereas Judah and his brother Jonathan will take a contingent to the east (5:17-18). Those left behind in reserve are to only defend Judea, and not engage the enemy while they were away (5:19). Both Simon's and Judah's taskforces were of eight thousand men each (5:20).

Simon is able to successfully invade Galilee, breaking the Gentile resistance, and his force kills nearly three thousand. The Jews from Galilee and Arabata are rescued, and they are taken to safety in Judea (5:21-23).

Judah and Jonathan's force crosses over the Jordan River east, and they confront friendly Nabateans, who recount to them what happened to the Jews in Gilead (5:24-25), as they are being held hostage in nearby towns and villages (5:26). They are told "Your enemies...are marshalling their forces to storm your strongholds tomorrow so as to capture them and destroy all the Jews in them in a single day" (5:27, REB). What begins is a steadily quick liberation of each town that had a significant number of Jews, including: Dathema, Alema, Casphor, Maked, and Bezer (5:28-36). Judah Maccabee's rallying cry was "Fight this day for our brothers!" (5:32, REB), and the reaction of the forces of Timotheus was fear and fleeing at seeing the Maccabean soldiers (5:34).

Timotheus gathers another force, this time opposite Raphon, and sending spies into the camp Judah is told, "all the Gentiles in the neighbourhood had rallied in very great strength to Timotheus, who had hired the help of Arab mercenaries" (5:38-39, REB). With the Maccabean detachment approaching the wadi that separated them, Timotheus observes that if they were to cross over to the other side, his force would not be able to succeed (5:40). But, if Judah were to cower, and they were to move ahead first, then they might have a chance at making them suffer (5:41). But Judah does not do this. He steadily moves his force toward the wadi, with orders that no one was to take a fixed position (5:42). The Maccabean force moves to the head of the enemy army, and it is said that "one and all they threw away their weapons and sought refuge in the temple at Carnaim" (5:43, REB). Judah has the temple burned, and "With the overthrow of Carnaim, all resistance came to an end" (5:44, REB).

With a contingent of Jews liberated, Judah Maccabee proceeds to lead them back to safety in Judea (5:45). They encounter a large and fortified town, Ephron, which was impossible to bypass (5:46), and fortified by the inhabitants (5:47). Peaceful overtures are made, but it was necessary for the Maccabean force to invade and kill the male inhabitants, razing the town, as it was obviously hostile to the Jews (5:48-51). When the group finally arrives in Judea, "With gladness and jubilation they went up to Mount Zion and offered whole-offerings, because they had returned in safety and without loss" (5:54, REB).

The fact that Judah Maccabee and his brothers had the knowledge how to fight and win is indicated by the author. Azarias and Josephus were two Jewish commanders who heard the exploits of Judah and Jonathan, and thought that they could gain some fame by routing the Gentile forces (5:55-57). They took the forces they commanded to advance on Jamnia, but were defeated by Gorgias, losing some two thousand men (5:58-60). The narrator describes, "The people suffered this heavy defeat because those in command of them, thinking to play the hero themselves, had not obeyed Judas and his brothers" (5:61, REB). Specifically it is said, "Those men were not...of that family whose prerogative it was to bring deliverance to Israel" (5:62, REB). **Those with dishonorable intentions to fight would not be met with success.** Judah and his brothers, however, gain a great reputation because of their just cause (5:63-64).

Judah's force continues to secure the safety of the Jews, as Gentile strongholds in the territory of Esau to the south, Hebron, Philistia, and Azotus are neutralized (5:65-67). We see how "he pulled down their altars and burnt the images of their gods; he carried off spoil from the towns" (5:68, REB), not unlike how figures like David had centuries earlier. And during these conflicts we see "Several priests who, from a desire to distinguish themselves, had ill-advisedly gone into action, fell in the battle" (5:67, REB). Once again, this is a reminder that those who fight to promote themselves will not succeed—especially as war and killing are not to be things that one would wish for.

While the Maccabees are purging the region of threats against the Jewish people, King Antiochus is off in Persia, the city of Elymais to be exact, collecting treasure (6:1-2). He is unsuccessful in capturing Elymais, and must withdraw to Babylon (6:3-4). Overseeing his campaign in Persia, word reaches him that Lysias has suffered defeat and has retreated, with the Jewish army gaining considerable strength and experiencing more victories (6:5-6). The narrator records how "they had pulled down the abomination built by him on the altar in Jerusalem and surrounded their temple with high walls as before" (6:7, REB). Antiochus Epiphanes is dismayed about what has happened, and retires to his bed "ill with grief at the miscarriage of his plans" (6:8, REB).

The scene of Antiochus—who having thought himself invincible, seems to be having no victory—is that "he lay for many days, overcome again and again by bitter grief, and he realized that he was dying" (6:9, REB). He calls to himself the order of Friends, and asks them why he is bereft with pain and hardship (6:10-11). He testifies that he did wrong to Jerusalem in stealing the Temple treasures (6:12). He says, "I know why these misfortunes have come upon me; and here I am, dying of bitter grief in a foreign land" (6:13, REB). Only having been to Jerusalem once, and having decreed an abomination in the Holy Place, he acknowledges this mistake as the cause of his downfall. Before dying King Antiochus appoints his friend Philip as regent over his empire, and asks him to raise his son Antiochus (6:14-15). He dies in the field a humiliated man (6:16).

Yet even while it may be tempting for us to close 1 Maccabees, as Antiochus Epiphanes is now dead—**the conflict is still not over.** "[T]he garrison of the citadel was confining the Israelites to the neighbourhood of the temple, and, by harassing tactics, giving continual support to the Gentiles" (6:18, REB). Even though the Maccabees were having military successes, they had only established a stronghold in the Temple area, and among pockets of

Jews throughout the region. There were still threats from all around that had to be dealt with—especially this citadel. "Judas determined to make an end of them; he gathered all the people to lay siege to the citadel" (6:19, REB).

The reason things are not over is fairly clear: "some of the beleaguered garrison escaped and were joined by a number of apostate Israelites. They went to the king and complained: 'How long must we wait for you to support our cause and avenge our comrades?'" (6:21, REB). They express pleasure in having followed the sinful dictates of Antiochus Epiphanes (6:22-23), and actually claim: "what was the result? Our own countrymen turned against us; indeed they put to death as many of us as they could lay hold of, and they robbed us of our property" (6:24, REB). Other peoples were attacked by the Maccabees as well, and these rebellious Jews report on how Jerusalem and the Temple have been fortified (6:25-26). Lysias, the regent, is told, "Unless your majesty quickly takes the initiative against them they will go yet to greater lengths. There will be no stopping them!" (6:27, REB).

Lysias "became furious as he listened" (6:28, REB), and so he assembles his confidants in the order of Friends, his military officials, and various mercenaries from neighboring kingdoms (6:29). So incensed is he at the rebellion in Judea, "His forces numbered one hundred thousand infantry, twenty thousand cavalry, and thirty-two war elephants" (6:30, REB). Moving in, Bethsura is laid siege (6:31), and Judah's force moves forward to a position at Bethzacharia (6:32). Marching into battle against the Jews, the narrator recounts how a war elephant was stationed with a company of a thousand men, and how five hundred horsemen were also stationed with each war elephant (6:34-36). It was an impressive sight, as each beast was guided by an Indian driver (6:37-39). Marching forward, "trembling seized all who heard the din and clash of arms of this multitude on the march, for it was indeed a very great and powerful force" (6:41, REB).

As the battle begins, Judah's army is able to take down six hundred of the king's men (6:42). A certain solider, Eleazar Avaran, saw royal armor on one of the elephants. Believing that he could gain fame should the king be riding it, he ran underneath the elephant, killing it, but he was crushed under its massive corpse (6:43-46). The Jewish forces had to give up some ground to the Seleucid army. Lysias' deploys a contingent that camped itself against Judea and Mount Zion (6:47-48), occupying Bethsura (6:49-50).

Having a garrison at Bethsura, Lysias begins a siege of the Temple. **So, as important as the rededication of the Temple was—the conflict involving the Temple is not yet over.** He "set up emplacements and siege-engines, with flamethrowers, catapults for discharging stones and barbed missiles, and slings" (6:51, REB). The Temple defenders put up massive resistance, but since there had just been a sabbatical year there were insufficient foodstuffs to last very long (6:52-54). But just as it appears that the Temple is going to be desecrated again, Lysias hears some important news. Philip, the newly appointed regent and guardian of Antiochus' son, had returned home from Persia "and was seeking to take over the government" (6:56, REB). Lysias' engagement with the Jews has to come to a quick end. "Hastily he gave orders for departure, saying...'Every day we grow weaker, our provisions are running low, the place we are besieging is strong, and the affairs of the empire are pressing'" (6:57, REB). Take important notice of what Lysias plans to say to the Maccabees:

"Let us now offer these men terms, and make peace with them and with their whole nation. Let us guarantee them the right to follow their laws and customs as they used to do, for it was our abolition of these laws and customs that roused their resentment and led to all the troubles" (6:58-59, REB).

Lysias receives the approval of his military commanders, and "an offer of peace was sent and accepted" (6:60, REB). Even more important, "The king and his commanders bound themselves by oath, and on the terms agreed the defenders emerged from their stronghold" (6:61, REB). Yet, even when Lysias recognizes that Antiochus' foolishness in wanting the Jews to abandon the Torah and follow Greek religion is the cause of all this, "when the king entered Mount Zion and saw how strongly the place was fortified, he went back on his oath, and ordered the demolition of the surrounding wall" (6:62, REB). Conflict started again, even though "with all speed he departed for Antioch, where he found Philip in possession" (6:63, REB).

The internal intrigue in the Seleucid kingdom gets more complicated. Demetrius, son of Seleucus, had been a captive in Rome, and finally makes his way back to the royal palace (7:1). Being the nephew of Antiochus Epiphanes, he believes he can take the throne, and so the army arrests the young Antiochus and opportunistic Lysias (7:2). Demetrius has them both put to death, and assumes control of the Seleucid kingdom (7:3-4). The apostate Jews who followed Antiochus Epiphanes, led by an Alcimus who wanted to be high priest, appeal to Demetrius for help (7:5-7). A man is chosen, one of the order of king's Friends named Bacchides, to wreak havoc on those living in Israel (7:8-9). Bacchides marches with a large force on Judea, but Judah Maccabee is able to see through his false offers of peace (7:10-11).

A group of Hasideans makes overtures of peace and friendship to Bacchides, who while in word is conciliatory, uses their trust to eliminate them (7:12-18). Encamped at Bethzaith, those who deserted to him were even slaughtered (7:19-20), all because of how "Alcimus put up a strong fight for his high-priesthood" (7:21, REB), rallying Jews who would be politically loyal to the Seleucid Greeks (7:22). The narrator of 1 Maccabees, in spite of some of the issues present in his later generation, is no fan of Judea being a dependent state. "When Judas saw the extent of the havoc which Alcimus and his followers had wrought among the Israelites, far worse than anything done by the Gentiles, he went throughout the territory of Judaea and its environs, punishing deserters and debarring them from access to the country districts" (7:23-24, REB). Alcimus was unable to easily fight Judah's demanding that the Jews be loyal to Israel, and returns to Demetrius (7:25).

Nicanor, a distinguished military commander and one who fiercely hated the Jews, is dispatched "with orders to wipe out that people" (7:26, REB). He "arrived at Jerusalem with a large force and sent envoys to Judas and his brothers with false offers of friendship" (7:27, REB). Nicanor greets Judah with some comradeship, but has secret plans to kidnap him (7:29). As Judah realizes what is happening, they do not meet again (7:30). His plot detected, their two armies engage near Capharsalama, with about five hundred of Nicanor's men killed (7:31-32).

The delicate nature of the Jewish independence that the Maccabees secured is seen in how Nicanor later goes up to Mount Zion, and some priests and Jewish leaders show him how they are offering up a sacrifice in the Temple for the Seleucid king (7:33-33). Nicanor does not take it seriously, demanding that Judah Maccabee and his force be turned over to them on the threat of burning down the Temple (7:34-35). The priests can do nothing more than pray to God: "take vengeance on this man and his army, and let them perish by the sword. Let their blasphemy not be forgotten; grant them no reprieve" (7:38, REB).

Nicanor moves his army away from Jerusalem and makes camp at Beth-horon, being joined by reinforcements from Syria (7:39). Judah has a force of three thousand at Adasa, and appeals for God to intervene in the same way as He defeated Sennacherib's forces that once besieged Jerusalem (7:40-42; cf. 2 Kings 19:35). The narrator records how a battle took place on the 13th of Adar, with not only Nicanor suffering great defeat, but how he was the first to fall (7:43). "Seeing Nicanor fall, his men threw away their arms and fled" (7:44, REB). Judah pursues them to Gazara, enlisting the support of Judean villages as his army moves forward (7:45). They attacked "the fugitives on the flanks, forced them back upon their pursuers, so that they all fell by the sword; not one of them survived" (7:46, REB). A great spoil is taken, and Nicanor's head and right hand are taken to Jerusalem to be displayed (7:47). So great was the victory, an annual feast of Nicanor was established to be commemorated on the 13th of Adar (7:48-49),[8] as his defeat had inaugurated a significant time of peace (7:50).

There are certainly more military battles and conflicts to be considered in 1 Maccabees chs. 8-16, **but we now get a distinct view at how the rising independent Jewish state, led by the Maccabees, interacted among the political powers of the Mediterranean.**

---

[8] This stopped being commemorated after the destruction of the Second Temple in 70 C.E.

The Message of I Maccabees

Of great interest to the narrator is the fame that Judah Maccabee had heard of a steadily rising power called the Romans, who had mustered great victories in subduing the Gauls, conquering Spain, and in defeating any of the Greeks who had tried to fight them (8:1-11). These Romans offered faithful friendship to those who desired their protection, and their Senate is praised as a model for order and discipline (8:12-16). Judah Maccabee sends two representatives, Eupolemus son of John, and Jason son of Eleazar, to Rome to conclude an offer of friendship and alliance (8:17-19). They appear before the Roman Senate, and a letter is sent back to Jerusalem on a bronze tablet (8:20-22). The treaty that is concluded includes stipulations that Rome will come to the defense of the Jewish nation should it be attacked, assuming that the Jews do not aid Rome's enemies with any supplies or war materiel (8:23-30). Furthermore, the Romans send a communication to King Demetrius, asking him why he has been attacking the Jews. With this is a threat that if they continue, they will have to face hostilities with Rome (8:31-32).

News of Nicanor's defeat had reached King Demetrius, and so he sends Bacchides and Alcimus a second time to Judea (9:1). They are successful at laying siege to Messaloth in Arbela (9:2), and they make their way further to make camp at Jerusalem, and from there march to Berea with twenty-two thousand infantry and two thousand cavalry (9:3-4). Judah was camped at Alasa with only three thousand elite troops, and then seeing the size of the enemy many desert and he is left with only eight hundred (9:5-6). With a fraction of his original force, Judah recognizes this as the time to strike, even if they must all die for their fellow countrymen (9:7-10). The fighting begins with great trumpets sounding all through the night (9:11-14), until Bacchides' right flank is able to be taken and they are pursued as far as Mount Azotus[9] (9:15). "The fighting became very heavy, and many fell on both sides" (9:17, REB). Among the fallen was Judah Maccabee himself, as the Jewish force had to finally disperse (9:18). His body was taken by his brothers Jonathan and Simon to the family tomb at Modin (9:19-20), and he is considered a champion of Israel similar to the Ancient Israelite kings (9:21; cf. 1 Kings 11:41). The narrator describes how his record of Judah's exploits and achievements were too many to be recorded (9:22).

It was only to be expected that when Judah died, "the renegades in every part of Israel emerged from hiding, and all the evildoers reappeared" (9:23, REB). Popular opinion among the Jews shifted away from being loyal to God's covenant and Torah (9:24), and the Seleucid leader Bacchides is able to exercise considerable political sway (9:25), with his forces able to reclaim Jerusalem and parts of Judea. Those who were loyal to Judah Maccabee and his close associates were hunted down (9:26). "It was a time of harsh

---

[9] This may be a scribal error for Mount Hazor.

oppression for Israel, worse than any since the days when prophets ceased to appear among them" (9:27, REB). Having to reconsider what is going on, Judah Maccabee's friends choose his brother Jonathan as his successor, to command them in battle (9:28-31).

Word gets back to Bacchides that Jonathan has been chosen as the new Maccabean leader, and so he and his brother Simon must flee to the wilderness of Tekoa (9:32-33). Bacchides and his force pursue them on the Sabbath, crossing over the Jordan. Jonathan's supplies are stolen by the Nabataens, and the Jambrites kidnap Jonathan's brother John (9:34-36), killing him (9:38). During a wedding of one of their important leaders, at Nadabath, Jonathan and his remaining brothers ambush them and avenge John, cutting many of them down and taking spoil (9:39-42). Bacchides, hearing of this, continues his pursuit, and Jonathan says that the Maccabean force is in its worst plight ever (9:43-44). They cry out to Heaven, striking Bacchides' force and killing about a thousand. They eventually make their way swimming across the Jordan River, but Bacchides does not pursue (9:45-49).

Bacchides returns to his base in Jerusalem, and fortifies a number of places in Judea: Jericho, Emmaus, Beth-horon, Bethel, Timnath-pharathon, and Tephon (9:50), strengthening his hold on Bethsura and Gazara. He has intentions of harassing the Jews, and taking some of the leading citizens away in prison (9:52). His Jewish conspirator who desired the high priesthood, Alcimus, actually "gave orders for the wall of inner court of the temple to be demolished, thereby destroying the work of the prophets" (9:54, REB). He starts to do this, but then suffers a stroke and is paralyzed from speaking, dying in great agony (9:55). Bacchides, able to subdue Judea, returns back to his king, with no major crisis ensuing for them for about two years (9:56-57). The remaining Maccabees, while not pursued, are able to return to some kind of normalcy as they try to reconsider what is to be done next.

The apostate Jews recognize that Jonathan and his band are still out there, living in some kind of peace. They propose to bring back Bacchides so that the Maccabees and all of their supporters can be seized and routed (9:58-59). Bacchides arrives back in Judea with a large force, but word gets out of the plan, and some fifty ringleaders of those who started this are killed (9:60-61). Jonathan and Simon withdraw their forces to Bethbasi in the desert, and fortified a former stronghold (9:62). Bacchides takes his army to Bethbasi, besieging it (9:63-64). During the fight, Jonathan leaves Simon in charge of the town, and takes a contingent away to attack Bacchides' allies at Odomera, then returning toward Bethbasi (9:65-67). Incensed that his assault on the Maccabees did not succeed, Bacchides is furious at the frustrations of his apostate Jewish allies, and has many of them executed before returning home in defeat (9:68-69).

Bacchides recognizes that trying to subdue Judea is a futile endeavor, and so Jonathan is able to secure terms of peace with him (9:70). "Bacchides agreed and accepted Jonathan's proposals, swearing to him that as long as he lived he would harm him no more" (9:71, REB). The Jewish prisoners of war he had taken are released, and Bacchides returns to his own country "never again to set foot on Jewish soil" (9:72, REB). The narrator records how, "So the war in Israel came to an end. Taking up residence in Michmash, Jonathan began to govern the people and root the apostates out of Israel" (9:73, REB).

Although it may be tempting to stop reading 1 Maccabees, with the significant defensive conflict over, the work of building an independent Jewish state, reconstructing what was lost, now begins. *The hope would be short lived.* Alexander Epiphanes, claiming to be the son of Antiochus Epiphanes, arrives in Ptolemais, being welcomed and proclaimed king (10:1). Hearing this, the recognized King Demetrius raises a large army to march against him (10:2). He sends a friendly and flattering letter to Jonathan, believing that by making peace with the Jews they will forget past conflicts and not support Alexander (10:3-5). Demetrius conveys upon Jonathan the title of ally, and encourages him to build up an army (10:6). Reading this letter to those of the citadel in Jerusalem, the people are naturally apprehensive (10:7-8).

Knowing that Demetrius will not move against them, Jonathan moves to Jerusalem and orders that the city be renovated and that the walls surrounding Mount Zion be fortified (10:10-11). Any remaining foreigners from the time Bacchides plagued the Jews flee, except a few apostate Jews in Bethsura (10:12-14). The pretender King Alexander hears what Jonathan is doing, and what the Maccabees had endured (10:15), asking "Where shall we ever find another man like this? Let us make him our Friend and ally at once" (10:16, REB). Alexander sends a flattering letter to Jonathan, informing him that he has been appointed as one in the order of the king's Friends (10:17-20). He sends him a purple robe and gold crown, representing the authority of the priesthood (10:20). Jonathan is able to amass an army, and stockpile a quantity of weapons (10:21).

"Demetrius was mortified at the news," saying "How did we come to let Alexander forestall us in gaining the friendship and support of the Jews?" (10:22, 23, REB). The former enemy of the Seleucid Greeks is now being courted by two rival leaders to be an ally (10:24-25). King Demetrius sends a long letter to Jonathan, promising things that his predecessors would not have even dreamed of. Demetrius says that the Jews have remained his faithful friends (10:26-28), he will not demand any tribute or certain taxes on them (10:29-30), the territory surrounding Jerusalem will be recognized as holy (10:31), he will not claim the citadel of Jerusalem as his own (10:32), any remaining Jewish prisoners of war will be immediately released (10:33), and all

Jews living within his kingdom will be free to celebrate their holidays and sacred seasons (10:34-35). Up to thirty thousand of the king's soldiers will be Jewish, made up in special Jewish units with Jewish commanders, being given the same pay and privileges as the rest of the army (10:36-37). The high priest will be given control over Judea and surrounding territory annexed from Samaria (10:38). Demetrius also promises to give funds to pay the priesthood, and to also fund the continued refurbishment of the Temple in Jerusalem (10:39-45).

Perhaps due to the overly-beneficent nature of Demetrius' proposals, neither Jonathan nor the Jews put any faith in them, remembering their long history of conflict (10:46). "They favoured Alexander, because he had been the first to make overtures of peace, and they remained his allies to the end" (10:47, REB). When Alexander and Demetrius finally engaged in battle, Demetrius' forces overwhelmed Alexander's, but Demetrius was killed in the fighting (10:48-50). This vacuum in power made Alexander the new leader, who then desires to patch things up with the Greek Ptolemies of Egypt, becoming the son-in-law of the king (10:51-54). King Ptolemy agrees to his request, desiring to meet with him at Ptolemais where Alexander's marriage with Cleopatra[10] is held (10:55-58).

While at Ptolemais, King Alexander extends his courtesies to Jonathan to meet with him in person (10:59). Jonathan agrees, and brings with him gifts of silver and gold for both Alexander, Ptolemy, and members of the king's Friends (10:60). While there were various apostate Jews who wished to bring accusations against Jonathan, Alexander would not hear of them (10:61). Instead, he sees that Jonathan is dressed in purple and sat next to him, with no more word of any complaints against the Jewish leader (10:62-64). Jonathan is made a member of the king's Friends, and appointed as a governor of Judea and ally of Alexander (10:65-66).

Three years later, the late King Demetrius' son, Demetrius, arrives from Crete and begins a campaign to retake his father's throne (10:67-68). The Jews are targeted as being the one group opposed to him, and Demetrius' military commander, Apollonius, challenges them to come and fight in battle should they dare have the courage (10:69-73). Jonathan leaves Jerusalem with ten thousand picked men, joined by his brother Simon with reinforcements (10:74). He began to lay siege to Joppa where Apollonius had staged a garrison, but then the people, being frightened, turned the city over to Jonathan's forces (10:75-76). Jonathan and Apollonius engage their armies at Azotus, with Simon's forces coming to assist (10:77-82). Apollonius' infantry

---

[10] Cleopatra is another dynastic name for female members of the Ptolemic royal family. The most famous Cleopatra (69-30 B.C.E.) would become a lover of both the Romans Julius Caesar and Mark Antony.

The Message of I Maccabees

seeks refuge in the temple of Dagon, and Jonathan has Azotus burned and a great spoil taken (10:83-84). A total of eight thousand are killed (10:85). Moving back to Jerusalem, he camps at Ascalon, where the citizens greet him (10:86-87). Hearing of the victory, King Alexander sends him a special gold clasp, and gives him Accaron and its surrounding region as a personal gift (10:88-89).

If the conflict within the Seleucid kingdom could not get any more complicated, Ptolemy sees an opportunity for his Egyptian kingdom to invade and claim it for itself (11:1-2). He is welcomed in each of their towns, as he was the father-in-law of Alexander, leaving a garrison in each town (11:3). He sees the Maccabean victory over Azotus, and confers with Jonathan at Joppa (11:4-6). King Ptolemy assumes control over various coastal towns, scheming how he might overtake Alexander (11:7-8). As a part of his plan, Ptolemy writes a letter to the new King Demetrius, promising him his daughter who is King Alexander's current wife (11:9). He regrets consenting to the marriage, and causing a schism when she marries Demetrius (11:10-12). Ptolemy is now able to claim the crown of Asia as his own (11:13). Alexander is forced to flee to Arabia, but is killed by an Arab chieftain (11:14-16). His head is sent to King Ptolemy, but shortly thereafter Ptolemy dies and King Demetrius once again controls his realm (11:17-19).

As this is happening, apostate Jews had once again claimed the citadel in Jerusalem, and so Jonathan must see that it is liberated (11:20). This news infuriates King Demetrius (11:21), who moves himself down to Ptolemais for a conference with Jonathan (11:22). They meet, and Jonathan brings with him various presents for Demetrius (11:23-24). King Demetrius does not hear the complaints lodged against Jonathan, and honors him as a member of the order of king's Friends (11:25-26), recognizing him as the high priest (11:27). Jonathan requests that Judea and the three Samaritan districts be exempted from tribute (11:28), and King Demetrius agrees (11:29-37).

A short period of quiet comes to King Demetrius' country, and so he decides to disband the army, with the exception of some foreign mercenaries (11:38). This proves to be disastrous, as those who had served him become disaffectionate, giving rise to Trypho, a former follower of King Alexander. He goes to the Arab who had been watching over Alexander's son, Antiochus, and uses him to raise unpopularity for Demetrius with the troops (11:39-40). While this is happening, Jonathan asks King Demetrius to remove his troops from Jerusalem, and he agrees (11:41). Demetrius actually asks Jonathan to send him a detachment of soldiers to Antioch (11:42). This Jonathan does.

In Antioch a revolt is stirred up against King Demetrius, who is barricaded in the royal palace. The Jewish troops are deployed, saving him, and many of the rebels are killed (11:44-48). The people of Antioch, seeing what the Jews have done in defending the king, plead for him to stop the onslaught (11:49-50). While the Jewish contingent returns to Jerusalem with fame and booty, after things return to normal King Demetrius estranges himself from Jonathan (11:51-53).

The situation works well for Trypho, as the pretender Antiochus is crowned king, and King Demetrius must flee Antioch as Trypho takes over the city (11:54-56). The new, young King Antiochus recognizes Jonathan as high priest of Jerusalem, sending to him gifts, and giving his brother Simon authority over territory along the seacoast of Israel to the Egyptian border (11:57-59). Jonathan tours the territory that he commands, having to plunder Gaza until its people sue for peace, and moving north toward Damascus (11:60-62). Moving toward Kedesh-in-Galilee, Jonathan hears that some officers from the deposed King Demetrius had arrived there with a force, to deter him (11:63). Jonathan takes an army to meet them, with his brother Simon blockading and attacking Bethsura (11:65). Simon expels the inhabitants of the town and occupies it (11:66). Jonathan successfully engages the enemy at Hazor, even though many of his men panicked (11:67-74).

The complicated political situation and shifting of alliances in the region make it obvious that if the Jewish nation were to have any major partner that would not (immediately) turn on them, such a partner would need to be someone other than the Seleucid Greeks (Syria) or Ptolemaic Greeks (Egypt). "Jonathan considered that the time was now opportune to select representatives and dispatch them on a mission to Rome to confirm and renew the treaty of friendship with that city. He also sent a letter to the same effect to Sparta and elsewhere" (12:1-2, REB). The Romans afford the Jews the proper courtesies (12:3-4).

The narrator then finds it important to include the text of the letter sent by Jonathan to the Spartans. In this letter is included a reference "to our brothers of Sparta" (12:6, REB), and included in it a reference to a previous communication about a century-and-a-half earlier between Onias the high priest and Sparta's King Arius (12:7-8). The Jews wish to renew their ties (12:10), and note that "We never neglect any opportunity, on festal and other appropriate days, of making mention of you at our sacrifices and in our prayers, as it is right and proper to remember kinsmen; and we rejoice at your fame" (12:11-12, REB). Various commentators feel that these are literary devices of a "diplomatic fiction of a common ancestry,"[11] only designed to flatter the Spartans. The letter acknowledges that the Jewish people "have been under the constant pressure of attacks on every side, as the surrounding kings have made war upon us" (12:13, REB). They have chosen not to appeal to the Spartans for help, until now (12:14, 18).

---

[11] Neil J. McEleney, "The First Book of the Maccabees," in *The Oxford Study Bible*, 1224.

The narrator of 1 Maccabees also finds it necessary to include a copy of the original letter that the high priest Onias had sent to Arius of Sparta (12:19-20). This letter attested, "A document has come to light which shows that Spartans and Jews are kinsmen, both being descended from Abraham. Now that we have learnt of this, we beg you to write and tell us how your affairs prosper" (12:21-22, REB), extending great courtesies to the Spartans (12:23). Many interpreters of 1 Maccabees are inclined to think that this letter was not genuine. Yet even if it were not originally sent to Sparta, and is only some kind of an add-on to the letters of Jonathan, R.K. Harrison notes how it "may conceivably have been of Jewish origin."[12] The author of 1 Maccabees, or a later editor, included this letter—whether originally sent or not—and by doing so reflected a view that the Ancient Spartans were descended from Abraham, logically meaning that they had among them descendants of the exiled Northern Kingdom. What would have been the rhetorical effect for including this in the text? What would it have communicated to Jewish readers of 1 Maccabees?

The narrator moves us back to the conflict taking place. Demetrius' forces come back to attack Jonathan's forces again, this time with a much larger army (12:24). Jonathan is determined that Demetrius will not set foot on Jewish soil, and sends out spies to survey for a night assault (12:25-26). The enemy withdraws upon hearing that Jonathan's army is ready to attack them at night (12:27-28). The enemy flees leaving their fires lit (12:29), and although Jonathan orders a pursuit, they are unable to be overtaken (12:30). Jonathan instead orders his force to rout some Zabadaean Arabs, moving toward Damascus (12:31-32). Upon returning to Jerusalem, Jonathan summons his council and efforts are made to repair the walls of Jerusalem, and build various fortresses throughout Judea (12:33-38).

With Demetrius' forces engaging in conflict in Judea, Trypho now plans to assume control of Asia, and usurp the King Antiochus he had helped to install (12:39). He fears that Jonathan will be a major deterrent to his plans, and so he plots to have him captured and killed (12:40). Jonathan moves a force of forty-thousand to Beth-shan, and Trypho is reluctant to attack (12:41-42). Jonathan is instead received by Trypho with full honors, and is given great gifts (12:43). Trypho asks him why he has moved his army forward, because they are not at war. Jonathan is asked to not only send his army home, but to accompany Trypho to Ptolemais where it will be given to Jonathan along with a great number of troops (12:44-45). Jonathan believes the word of Trypho, leaving three thousand men mobilized (12:46). But having reached Ptolemais, he is seized, and those with him are killed (12:47-48).

---

[12] Harrison, *Introduction to the Old Testament*, 1262.

Messianic Winter Holiday Helper

Trypho sends a taskforce to wipe out the troops that Jonathan had not demobilized, but learning that he had been taken, they march ahead for battle, and Trypho's soldiers turn back (12:49). "Though all came safely home to Judaea, they were greatly afraid and mourned for Jonathan and those who were with him; the whole of Israel was plunged into grief. The Gentiles round about were all bent on destroying them root and branch. 'The Jews have no leader or champion,' they said; 'so now is the time for us to attack and we shall blot out all memory of them from among men'" (12:52-53, REB).

Simon, Jonathan's brother and one of the original Maccabees, takes leadership. Word reaches him that Trypho is amassing a huge invasion force that is to destroy Judea, and so he must gather the assembly of Jewish leaders (13:1-2). He tries to encourage them by declaring, "I do not need to remind you how much my brothers and I and my father's house have done for the laws and the holy place, what battles we have fought, what hardships we have endured. All my brothers have fallen in this cause, fighting for Israel; only I am left" (13:3-4, REB). Simon is not one to complain, but will rather stand up and defend his people (13:5-6), and the people instill in him their confidence (13:7-9). Fortification of the walls of Jerusalem continues (13:10), and Jonathan son of Absalom is sent to occupy Joppa (13:11).

Trypho marches his army from Ptolemais, taking with him Jonathan who is still alive, meeting Simon's force at Adida (13:12-13). Trypho demands one hundred talents of silver and two of his sons as hostages to let him go (13:14-16). Although believing it to be a trick, Simon has the necessary monies brought to him and concludes the transaction, knowing that his fellow Jews would demand Jonathan's safe return (13:17-18). The ransom is paid, but Jonathan is not let free (13:19).

Trypho marches his army through the country to ravage it, and Simon's force follows it on a parallel course (13:20). The garrison of his citadel needed supplies, though, but is deterred by a snowstorm (13:21-22). Withdrawing to Bascama, Jonathan is executed, and Trypho returns home to Asia (13:23-24). Jonathan's remains are taken back to the family tomb at Modin, and Simon has the mausoleum ornately decorated to honor his family members who had fallen (13:25-30). Meanwhile, having returned to Asia, Trypho assumes the throne of the Seleucid kingdom, and has the young King Antiochus put to death (13:31-32).

Simon sees to it that the fortresses in Judea are rebuilt, along with high towers and barred gates, stocked with provisions (13:33). Simon also seeks to form better relations with Demetrius, the rival of Trypho (13:34-35), who sends back a letter indicating that there will be peace between him and the Jewish people (13:36-40). "Israel was released from the gentile yoke; the people began to write on their contracts and agreements: 'In the first year of Simon, the great high priest, general, and leader of the Jews'" (13:41-42,

REB). The narrator recounts Simon's feat of occupying Gazara, which had been one of the last hostile strongholds in Judea (13:43-46). While besieging the city, Simon shows mercy on its inhabitants and allows many to leave, removing it of idolatry (13:47). "Everything which was polluted he threw out, and he settled there men and women who would keep the law. He strengthened the fortifications, and he built himself a residence in town" (13:48, REB). The final hostile stronghold was the citadel at Jerusalem, whose occupants were allowed to surrender after a famine, and not receiving any relief supplies (13:49-50). At this point, the conflict had been going on for a total of twenty-five years (13:51), and the citadel at Jerusalem was made Simon's principal base (13:52). His own son, John, was appointed commander of his forces, making Gazara his headquarters (13:53).

King Demetrius still has his eyes on retaking his kingdom away from Trypho, and so he moves his forces into Media to elicit supplies and support from the Persians (14:1). Hearing about this, the Persian monarch Arsakes has one of his generals engage him in battle and take him alive (14:2-3).

"As long as Simon ruled, Judaea was undisturbed. He sought his nation's good, and they lived happily all through the glorious days of his reign" (14:4, REB). Simon had captured the port of Joppa, to secure an overseas communication line (14:5). He extended the borders of the country (14:6), and former prisoners of war were able to be repatriated home (14:7a). Control over Gazara, Bethsura, and the citadel were assured, "from which he removed all pollution. None could withstand him" (14:7b, REB). Life returned to normal for the Jews, with people planting crops and eating well (14:8-9). "Simon supplied the towns with food in plenty and equipped them with weapons for defense, so that his renown spread to the ends of the earth. Peace was restored to the land and throughout Israel there was great rejoicing" (14:10-11, REB). Everyone had a part in the prosperity that came (14:12), with security established (14:13). The poor were protected, the Torah was honored, and apostates were removed (14:14). The Temple was once again brought back to high standing, properly furnished with the right materials (14:15).

The narrator records how when word of Jonathan's death reached the Jews' allies in Sparta and Rome, they were deeply saddened (14:16). They were, however, pleased that Simon had succeeded his brother (14:17), and a renewal of the friendship treaty was sent on bronze tablets, to be read to those in Jerusalem (14:17-19). A copy of the message from the Spartans is reproduced by the author of 1 Maccabees (14:20-23). Simon, to confirm for the treaty of alliance, sends an envoy, Numenius, to Rome with a large gold shield (14:24).

Knowing about all of the sacrifices and accomplishments of Simon and his family, especially in defending the rights of Israel, the Jews had special bronze tablets commissioned, as well as a monument built for the Maccabees on

Mount Zion (14:25-27). The message that recounts the lives of Jonathan and Simon is long, as it instills a significant degree of absolute authority in the dynasty that their family had established (14:28-47). Copies of the message were to be placed in the precincts of the Temple, and placed on record with the Jewish treasury (14:48-49).

King Antiochus, the son of the deposed King Demetrius, has it in his heart to take back his father's kingdom (15:1-4). He writes a letter to Simon, and in it promises to release the Jewish people from any debts or tribute that was owed to his father's kingdom (15:5-8). The Jews were totally free to mint their own currency (15:6), and he promises to make their two realms close friends when his throne is established (15:9). The new King Antiochus is able to put Trypho to flight (15:10). Trypho flees all the way to Dor, with one-hundred twenty-eight thousand soldiers on his back (15:11). Antiochus establishes a blockade of both troops and ships to prevent his escape (15:12).

At this point, the narrator interrupts, as the Jewish envoy Numenius had returned from Rome, along with letters to deliver to the various regional kings (15:13). Lucius, the Roman consul, writes King Ptolemy of Egypt and informs him that an alliance with the Jews has been renewed. He says not to threaten the Jews, and to turn over any apostate Jews who have escaped back to them (15:14-21). The same letter was sent to the other regional kings (15:22-24), indicating that a rising power was on the Jews' side.

Problems erupt for Simon as this next King Antiochus launches a siege on Trypho on Dor (15:25). Simon sends a battalion of two-thousand to him, along with gifts of gold and various supplies. Antiochus refuses them, and breaks off diplomatic contact. He sends a member of his order of Friends, demanding that Simon withdraw from *his cities* of Joppa, Gazara, and the citadel in Jerusalem (15:26-28). This new monarch accused Simon, "you have made yourselves masters of many places in my kingdom" (15:29, REB), and he demands appropriate compensation for *his* losses (15:30). Furthermore, if proper tribute is not paid, then war will begin (15:31).

Athenobius, the king's Friend, relays the message to Simon, and makes notice of the wealth that the Jews possess (15:31). All Simon can tell him in response is, "We have neither occupied other people's land nor taken possession of other people's property; we have taken only our ancestral heritage, unjustly seized for a time by our enemies. We have grasped the opportunity to reclaim our patrimony" (15:32-34, REB). Simon acknowledges, though, the problems with Joppa and Gazara, and offers them for sale (15:35).

Athenobius returns to Antiochus in anger, and the king is furious at what he hears. Athenobius also recounts to him the wealth of Simon that he had seen (15:36). As this is happening, Trypho escapes by ship to Orthosia (15:37). Antiochus gives orders to Kendebaeus to occupy the coastal zone, blockade

Judea, and rebuild and fortify Kedron (15:38-39). This he does, and he begins to harass the Jews by capturing and killing many (15:40-41).

John, in charge of the Maccabean army, reports back to his father what Kendebaeus has been doing (16:1). Simon summons John and Judas, who are his oldest sons, and gives them an important commission: "My brothers and I and my father's family have fought Israel's battles from our youth until this day, and many a time have we been successful in rescuing Israel. Now I am old, but mercifully you are in the prime of life. Take my brother's place and mine, and go out and fight for our nation. And may help from Heaven be with you!" (16:2-3, REB). John amasses a great army of twenty-thousand men and cavalry, and marches against Kendebaeus (16:4). While his force is reluctant to fight at first, they strike Kendebaeus' army, and many are killed (16:5-8). Even though Judas is wounded in the fighting, Kendebaeus flees to Kedron, and others flee to forts built around Azotus. John sets fire to Azotus, with two thousand of the enemy killed (16:9-10).

An ambitious, wealthy Jew from Jericho, named Ptolemaeus, sees a chance for Simon and his sons to be put "out of the way" (16:13, REB), and for himself to be made high priest (16:11-12). Sadly, on a tour of the region, Simon and his sons Mattathias and Judas are brought to the home of Abubus at Dok. There, Ptolemaeus sets his trap and has them all killed (16:13-16). The narrator says, "It was an act of base treachery in which evil was returned for good" (16:17, REB).

Ptolemaeus intends to declare his loyalty to King Antiochus, and asks him for troops and for assistance (16:18). Support comes to him, and "He ordered some of his men to Gazara to make away with John" (16:19a, REB) as well, giving gold and gifts to the senior officers (16:19b). Other troops would be sent to occupy Jerusalem (16:20). John, however, gets word that his father and brothers have been murdered, and that assassins are out to get him (16:21). "The news came as a great shock to John, and, learning of the plot against his life, he arrested and put to death the men who came to kill him" (16:20, REB). The author ends 1 Maccabees in describing that he had accomplished many feats himself, worthy of a son of one of the original Maccabees (16:21-22). While as the succeeding priest, John Hyrcanus, he did make some controversial decisions during his tenure as Jewish leader, the author of 1 Maccabees is not concerned about them in his work.

Most of our attention during the season of *Chanukah* is often focused around 1 Macccabees chs. 1-4, but as it should be obvious, there is so much more to learn about the complicated history of the period. We see poor, tiny Judea, stuck in the middle of major powers. There are complicated and entangling alliances. The Maccabean leaders simply want their people to survive, worshipping God at the Temple, and following His Torah. They do what is necessary to ensure that the Jewish people are not wiped out. They are first guerilla fighters, then they learn to lead a professional army, and they try their hand at diplomacy. They gain respect in the region, and from far-off allies like Sparta and Rome. *They do what they have to do.*

Much is learned from this period of Jewish history, how Antiochus Epiphanes thought himself invisible, but was ruined for defiling the Temple. Those who come after him, perhaps not thinking themselves to be as divine as he, certainly were ambitious and wreaked more havoc on the Jewish people. They certainly thought themselves to be vastly superior to tiny little Israel.

So having seen some of what the Jews were up against in 1 Maccabees, with their peace and livelihood threatened *even after the Temple was rededicated*—is it surprising that by the time of the Apostles, non-Jewish inclusion among the Jewish Believers *as their equals* (Galatians 3:28), was so controversial? Would not thoughts of all the persecutions that the generation of the Maccabees endured, the broken and failed promises by the Jews' pagan neighbors, and still being stuck in the midst of hostile Gentiles—be something that affected your worldview? It is fairly easy to see how many of the Jewish Believers had some prejudices to overcome.

What can we learn from a record of history like 1 Maccabees as today's Messianic movement? What might it teach us about Jewish attitudes to the nations' salvation in the Book of Acts and Apostolic letters? What might it teach us about the need to be sensitive to unique Jewish needs in our faith community, and how we should not at all dismiss the importance of *Chanukah?* Indeed, if we are to learn anything from this—not only should we rejoice in the rededication of the Temple, but non-Jewish Messianics should learn to be honest and truthful to their (Messianic) Jewish brothers and sisters. They should be shown true respect and honor, as *we are all recipients* of the sacrifices of the Maccabean leaders from over two millennia ago!

-9-

The Message of 2 Maccabees

J.K. McKee

There is a huge amount of difference between the style and approach of 1 Maccabees, when compared to 2 Maccabees. Whereas 1 Maccabees attempts to be a relatively objective historical analysis of the events that befell the Jewish people, the compiler of 2 Maccabees attempts to show his audience a theological perspective of what took place. In 1 Maccabees, while we may encounter Judah Maccabee, and his brothers Jonathan and Simon, as appealing to past Israelite history for inspiration—in 2 Maccabees we see the omnipotence of God working directly through the Jewish people. They are His servants, put in dire straights, who will be vindicated throughout eternity because of their faithfulness to Him and to His Torah. The Maccabees appeal to God to intervene when hope appears lost. We get a glimpse into the lives of some of the "normal people" who suffered under the tyranny of the Seleucid Empire.

Unlike 1 Maccabees, 2 Maccabees covers a much shorter historical period of about fifteen years, from right before the ascension of Antiochus V, son of Antiochus Epiphanes, to about 160 B.C.E. 2 Maccabees 4:7-15:36 parallels much of 1 Maccabees chs. 1-7. 2 Maccabees claims to have originally been part of a larger, five volume work no longer extant, that had been written by a Jason of Cyrene. 2 Maccabees was condensed by an editor or Epitomist, who certainly interjects his thoughts as he summarizes what he considered to be the main points of Jason's original work. The original audience of 2 Maccabees is the Jewish community of Egypt (1:1-2:18), and so because of this, the editor or Epitomist of 2 Maccabees is sometimes thought to be a contemporary of the Jewish philosopher Philo,[1] placing 2 Maccabees'

---

[1] R.K. Harrison, *Introduction to the Old Testament* (Grand Rapids: Eerdmans, 1969), 1273.

composition sometime in the late First Century B.C.E. or early First Century C.E.

The emphasis of the editor is to focus on the people who fought and were martyred during the Seleucid period, something he does quite well. Yet because of this, it may be that he was more concerned with his literary abilities than with attention for the historical detail originally laid out in Jason's work. Some interpreters of 2 Maccabees feel that the Epitomist may have exaggerated some of the facts and figures, superimposing his own religious ideas onto the actual events, as he details that his focus was "on the main points of my outline, [and] I shall leave to the original author the minute discussion of every particular" (2:28, REB). Reading 2 Maccabees as a literary work first, and not necessarily historical, will aid us for understanding the people of the time—even if the events have been clouded in flowery language. Unfortunately, we do not have Jason's work to make a proper comparison, so the accuracy of whether various miracles or supernatural works actually took place, will need to be considered *by you* as you read the text for yourself.

Let us remember, though, as R.K. Harrison observes, "the Epitomist performed a valuable service in preserving the bulk of a work that is no longer extant. His condensation was admittedly meant for popular consumption, and the gratitude with which it was received"[2] led to the Greek text of 2 Maccabees translated into other contemporary languages. The accounts preserved in 2 Maccabees undeniably affected First Century Jewish theology, and the worldview of many Jews during the ministry of Yeshua. For that reason alone, today's Messianic community needs to be familiar with it.

A main purpose of 2 Maccabees is to persuade the Jewish community in Egypt to continue to remember the Festival of Dedication, which they had forgotten to do. The editor begins his work by writing two letters, the first being a general letter to the Egyptian Jews, expressing a desire for their well being (1:1-6). He also appeals to the past crises experienced by the Judean Jews, and even how the original author Jason took up arms against his own people who had defected to the Seleucids (1:7). God intervened on their behalf, as "We prayed to the Lord and were answered; we brought a sacrifice and an offering of fine flour, we lit the lamps, and laid out the Bread of the Presence" (1:8, REB). **The role that the Temple plays is quite important for the Epitomist of 2 Maccabees.** Reminding the Egyptian Jews of the faithful actions of their Judean brethren, he says, "Now we instruct you to observe the celebration of a feast of Tabernacles in the month of Kislev" (1:9, REB), as what would become the eight-day celebration of *Chanukah* was partially modeled after *Sukkot*, something they would have been familiar with from the Torah.

---

[2] Ibid.

The Message of 2 Maccabees

The second, and much longer letter, is written to Aristobulus (1:10), who was some kind of a Jewish teacher or philosopher to Ptolemy IV Philometor (180-145 B.C.E.) of Egypt. Thanks are issued to God for saving the Jews from the invaders (1:11-12). The Epitomist records an interesting death, or at least fall, of Antiochus Epiphanes, much different than that recorded in 1 Maccabees 6:1-17. While in Persia, Antiochus had "a force that seemed invincible," but "they were cut to pieces in the temple of the goddess Nanaea[3] through a stratagem employed by her priests. On the pretext of a ritual marriage with the goddess, Antiochus, escorted by his Friends, had come to the temple to secure the considerable treasure by way of dowry...As soon as he was inside, the priests shut the sanctuary; then, opening a secret trapdoor in the panelled ceiling, they hurled stones at them, and the king fell as if struck by a thunderbolt. They hacked off limbs and heads and threw them to those outside" (1:13-16, REB). In the Epitomist's words: "Blessed in all things be our God, who handed over the godless to death!" (1:17, REB).

He also goes into describing to Aristobulus how significant it would be for the Egyptian Jewish community to observe the Festival of Dedication "on the twenty-fifth of Kislev, so that you may celebrate a feast of Tabernacles" (1:18a, REB), as *Sukkot* would again serve as an appropriate prototype for what would become *Chanukah*. (It may be that references to *Sukkot* are made, so that the Egyptian Jews would have a frame of reference for remembering the much newer commemoration of *Chanukah*.) A considerable part of the Epitomist's letter is spent discussing how the sacred fire that was to be used in the Temple had been preserved during the period of the Babylonian exile, invoking a sense of nostalgia for the Temple worship that had continued in spite of the hardship that the Jews had faced (1:18-2:12).[4] He affirms that the account of how the fire was preserved during the Exile is available for the Egyptian Jews to see, no differently than the chronicles of Israel's kings and the works of David (2:13), as well as the relevant documents that concerned the recent conflict between the Jews and Seleucid Greeks (2:14-15). The Epitomist summarizes the importance of what he is about to deliver, writing,

"Since we are about to celebrate the purification of the temple, we are writing to impress upon you the duty of holding this festival. God has rescued his whole people and granted to all of us the holy land, the kingship, the priesthood, and the consecration, as he promised by the law. We have confidence that God will soon show us compassion and gather us from

---

[3] Identified with the Greek goddess Artemis.

[4] In reading 2 Maccabees 1:18b-2:12, you will have to decide if this is a legendary story concocted by the Epitomist, an exaggerated account of how the fire was preserved, or something more-or-less historically accurate.

everywhere under heaven to the holy place, for he has delivered us from great evils and purified that place" (2:16-18, REB).

The Epitomist's opening commentary is over with these two letters, and he can now begin his summary of Jason of Cyrene's original five-volume work (2:19a). He records how Jason not only compiled a history of Judah Maccabee and his brothers, but also the war that the Maccabees fought against Antiochus Epiphanes and his successors (2:19b-20). Apparently, Jason's work also included supernatural encounters that the Maccabees had. Jason is said to have "described the apparitions from heaven which appeared to those who, in the cause of the Jewish religion, vied with one another in heroism. Few though they were, they ranged through the whole country, taking booty and routing the foreign hordes; they recovered the world-renowned temple, liberated the city of Jerusalem, and reaffirmed the laws, which were in danger of being abolished. All this they achieved because the Lord showed them clemency and favour" (2:21-22, REB).

In reviewing the Epitomist's work, he reminds those reading that his is a condensed summary for which he slaved over day and night: "The task which I have taken on myself in making this summary is no easy one; it means hard work and late nights" (2:26, REB). And we are reminded again, we no longer have access to Jason of Cyrene's original volumes (2:28), to which we can compare. The Epitomist proceeds, comparing himself not to the architect of a house, but rather one who (artfully) paints inside it (2:29).

Unlike 1 Maccabees, which begins principally with the rise of Alexander the Great and the division of his empire following his death, the narrative of 2 Maccabees tells us more of the internal issues going on in Judea. Apparently, Antiochus Epiphanes' ordered defilement of the Temple was not the first action taken by a Seleucid monarch. The Epitomist details how during the administration of the Jewish high priest Onias, "the Holy City enjoyed unbroken peace and prosperity, and there was exemplary observance of the laws, because he was pious and hated wickedness. The kings themselves held the sanctuary in honour and embellished the temple with the most magnificent gifts; King Seleucus of Asia even met the whole cost of the sacrificial worship from his own revenues" (3:1-3, REB). Apparently, there had been a time when there were excellent relations between the Jews and their various Greek neighbors.

The first problems erupt when a certain Simon, administrator of the Temple, has a quarrel with Onias over the Jerusalem city market. Perhaps envious of power, he goes to Apollonius, governor of Coele-Syria and Phoenicia (3:4-5), telling them that the treasury of Jerusalem was filled with untold riches, riches that could belong to the Seleucid king (3:6). Apollonius informs the king of what he has been told, who then sends an official named Heliodorus to remove the Temple riches (3:7). Heliodorus embarks on an inspection tour of the region, and is received warmly by the Jews when he reaches Jerusalem (3:8-9). He asks about the allegations of the Temple treasury hording tax monies, and so the high priest explains how the funds are largely held for disbursement to orphans and widows (3:10). Heliodorus, however, informs that because the king has given orders, the Temple funds must be turned over to the royal treasury (3:13).

When the day came for the Temple funds to be tallied and taken away, the Epitomist records there was great distress throughout the city—the high priest not only in agonizing pain, but also people offering significant prayers in sackcloth and ashes (3:14-19). "[W]ith outstretched hands all made solemn entreaty to Heaven. It was pitiful to see the crowd lying prostrate in utter disarray and the high priest in agony and apprehension" (3:20-21, REB). As Heliodorus prepares to appropriate the Temple funds for the king, the prayers of the people are heard (3:22-23). The Epitomist says, "just as he was arriving with his escort at the treasury, the Ruler of spirits and of all power sent a mighty apparition, so that everyone who had dared to accompany Heliodorus collapsed in terror, stricken with panic before the might of God" (3:24, REB). Angelic beings then appear to beat Heliodorus, so that he might stay away from the Temple treasures:

"There also appeared to Heliodorus two young men of surpassing strength and glorious beauty, magnificently attired. Taking their stand on either side of him, they flogged him, raining on him blow after blow. Suddenly, overwhelmed by a great darkness, he fell to the ground, and his men quickly took him up and placed him on a stretcher. This man, who so recently had entered the treasury accompanied by his whole bodyguard and an attendant crowd, was now borne off utterly helpless, publicly compelled to acknowledge the sovereignty of God" (3:27-28, REB).

The Jews who witnessed this praised God for His intervention (3:30), and Heliodorus' various companions appealed to Onias the high priest to pray for him, so that the Lord would spare his life (3:31). Knowing how the king might react, Onias offered a sacrifice for Heliodorus on behalf of the Jewish nation (3:32). "As the expiation was being made, the same young men, dressed as before, again appeared to Heliodorus, and standing over him said: 'You should be very grateful to Onias the high priest; it is for his sake the Lord has spared your life. You have been scourged by God; now proclaim his mighty power to all men.' With these words they vanished" (3:33-34, REB). Heliodorus, having been visited by two of God's angels, then proceeds to make "lavish freewill-offerings to the Lord who had spared his life" (3:35, REB), and "To everyone he bore witness of the miracles of the supreme God which he had seen with his own eyes" (3:36, REB). Returning to the king, Heliodorus reports how the presence of God filled the Jewish Temple, opposing those with evil intent (3:37-39).

The incident in the Temple treasury begins a series of unfortunate events for the Jewish nation. Simon, who had originally told Apollonius of the great Temple riches, is incensed, spreading rumors about Onias the high priest (4:1). The Epitomist comments, "He had the effrontery to accuse of conspiracy against the government one who was a benefactor of the city, a protector of his fellow-Jews, and a staunch upholder of the law" (4:2, REB). His supporters resort to murder (4:3), likely killing various opponents. Apollonius continued to encourage Simon on his course of action (4:4), and things got so bad that Onias feels he has no choice but to appeal to the king himself for the sake of all the Jews (4:5). "He saw that unless the king intervened there could be no peace in public affairs, nor would Simon be stopped in his mad course" (4:6, REB).

King Seleucus dies and is succeeded by his brother Antiochus, who would also be known as Epiphanes (4:7a). As this takes place, "Jason, Onias's brother, procured for himself the office of high priest by underhanded means" (4:7b, REB). Jason, the new high priest, promises Antiochus great sums of money (4:8-9a). Add to this how Jason actually asks the new king for permission "to set up a gymnasium for the physical education of young men, and to enrol in Jerusalem a group to be known as 'Antiochenes'" (4:9b, REB), as though they were citizens of the capitol Antioch. We see that "The king gave his assent; and Jason, as soon as he had secured the high-priesthood, made his fellow-Jews conform to the Greek way of life" (4:10, REB).

The previous allowances for the Jews, which had been negotiated by John, the father of Eupolemus,[5] were set aside by Jason (4:11a). The Epitomist records all of the dastardly deeds done by this new "high priest," which were anti-Torah and which affected many of the Jews who looked to the Temple for spiritual guidance:

"He abolished the institutions founded on the law and introduced practices which ran counter to it. He lost no time in establishing a gymnasium at the foot of the citadel itself, and he made the most outstanding of the young men adopt the hat worn by Greek athletes. So with the introduction of foreign customs Hellenism reached a high point through the inordinate wickedness of Jason, an apostate and no true high priest. As a result, the priests no longer showed any enthusiasm for their duties at the altar; they treated the temple with disdain, they neglected the sacrifices, and whenever the opening gong called them they hurried to join in the sports at the wrestling school in defiance of the law. They placed no value on dignities prized by their forefathers, but cared above everything for Hellenic honours. This brought misfortune upon them from every side, and the very people

---

[5] Eupolemus would later negotiate the Maccabees' treaty of alliance with Rome (1 Maccabees 8:17).

whose way of life they admired and tried so hard to emulate turned out to be vindictive enemies. To act profanely against God's laws is no light matter, as will in due course become clear" (4:11b-17, REB).

Jason was quite zealously inclined toward Hellenistic religion and culture. For the games held at Tyre, he sent a group of his Antiochenes with three hundred drachmas of silver to be offered in the sacrifice to Hercules (4:18-19a). These Antiochenes, Jewish citizens of Antioch, thought this to be improper, and so the money was instead spent to outfit various triremes[6] (4:19b-20).

The politics of the region begin to play a role in how the new King Antiochus acts toward the Jewish people. Upon the coronation of the new King Philometor of Egypt, he learns that Egypt is "hostile to his interests" (4:21, REB). Antiochus comes to Jerusalem, being greatly welcomed by the people (4:22), and then he moves himself to Phoenicia, obviously wanting to take a closer look at what is happening to the south.

As bad as Jason was as high priest, he could not hold onto his office indefinitely. Menelaus, a brother of the Simon who had informed Apollonius of the great Temple treasure, is sent by Jason to the king on important business (4:23). "Menelaus, once in the king's presence, flattered him with an air of authority, and diverted the high-priesthood to himself, outbidding Jason by three hundred talents of silver. He arrived back with the royal mandate, but with nothing else to make him worthy of the high-priesthood; he had the passions of the cruel tyrant and the temper of a savage beast. Jason, who had supplanted his own brother, was not supplanted in his turn and forced to seek refuge in Ammonite territory" (4:24-26, REB). The Epitomist records how things get even more complicated with this new high priest, Menelaus, who has no intention of paying King Antiochus what he had promised (4:27). The funds are continually demanded, though, and so Menelaus is summoned to meet with the king (4:28-29).

King Antiochus is not there when Menelaus arrives, due to a revolt in Tarsus and Mallus that must be put down (4:30), and so he leaves an Andronicus behind as his regent (4:31). Thinking that he can manipulate Andronicus, Menelaus presents him with some special gold from the Temple treasure (4:32). The deposed high priest Onias had heard about this, coming to Daphne, right outside Antioch (4:33). Onias denounces Menelaus, and because of this Menelaus persuades Andronicus that he needs to be eliminated. A meeting is arranged between Andronicus and Onias, and although Andronius appears to greet him and gives him various assurances of safety, "Then at once, with no respect for justice, he made away with him" (4:34, REB).

---

[6] A trireme was an ancient class of warship, with three banks of oars.

The murder of the high priest Onias, who had been a Torah-faithful Jew, "caused indignation and resentment not only among the Jews but among many from other nations as well" (4:35, REB). When King Antiochus returns from the west, a petition protesting Onias' murder is sent to him by the Jews of Antioch, also considered to be "a crime detested equally by the Gentiles" (4:36, REB). King Antiochus is actually described as being "moved to pity and tears" (4:37, REB), and he becomes so angry that Andronicus is not only stripped of his high position, but he is led to the very place where Onias was murdered, and is executed there himself (4:38).

Back in Jerusalem, Lysimachus, brother of Menelaus and the one left to oversee the Temple, "entered on a career of sacrilege and plunder in Jerusalem" (4:39a, REB). But as this occurs, and as news reaches the people of how much gold had been taken away and given to Andronicus, popular opinion falls against Lysimachus (4:39b). Lysimachus, the acting high priest, actually assembles a force of three thousand and orders an attack against those in opposition (4:40). This only incenses the people more against him. "Recognizing that Lysimachus was behind the attack, some of the crowd seized stones, others blocks of wood, others again handfuls of burning embers that were lying about, and they hurled them indiscriminately at Lysimachus and his men. The result was that many were wounded, some were killed, and the rout was complete; the temple robber himself they put to death near the treasury" (4:41-42, REB).

When King Antiochus comes to Tyre, charges are pressed against Menelaus in regard to this incident (4:43-44). Menelaus, however, is quite conniving and manipulative, and promises a Ptolemaeus a large sum of money if he will persuade Antiochus to change his intent toward him (4:45-46). What happens? The Epitomist writes, "Menelaus, the author of all the mischief, was acquitted and the charges brought against him were dismissed, but the king condemned to death the unfortunate accusers, men who would have been let go entirely as innocent had they appeared even before Scythians" (4:47, REB).[7] He can only further observe how bad Menelaus was for the Jewish nation, stating,

"At once those who had pleaded for their city, their people, and their sacred vessels, suffered this undeserved penalty. It caused even some of the Tyrians to show their detestation of the crime by providing a splendid funeral for the victims. Yet thanks to the cupidity of those in power, Menelaus, this arch-plotter against his fellow-citizens, continued in office and went from bad to worse" (4:48-50, REB).

---

[7] The Scythians were a nomadic people from north of the Black Sea who were known for their considerable cruelty. The Apostle Paul makes specific reference of them in Colossians 3:11, and how the power of Yeshua has the capacity to change even the most barbaric of people.

King Antiochus undertakes a second military expedition against Egypt (5:1), and during this time the Epitomist relates how there were various supernatural signs "seen in the sky all over Jerusalem" (5:2a, REB) for forty days. These included "galloping horsemen in golden armour, companies of spearmen standing to arms, swordsmen at the ready, and squadrons of cavalry in battle order. Charges and countercharges were made in this direction and that; shields were brandished, spears massed, javelins hurled; breastplates and golden ornaments of every kind blazed with light. That the phenomenon might portend good was the prayer of everyone" (5:2b-4, REB).

A false report is heard that King Antiochus was killed in battle (5:5a), and so the deposed high priest Jason uses it as an opportunity, leading a surprise attack on Jerusalem with one thousand men (5:5b). The Epitomist observes how "Jason embarked upon an unsparing massacre of his fellow-citizens, for he did not grasp that success against one's own kin is the greatest of failures" (5:6a, REB). His attack against Jerusalem is a failure, though, and he had to return to Ammonite territory for asylum (5:7). He had to move from place-to-place, eventually making his way to Egypt, and then having to cross over to Sparta[8] where he dies in exile (5:8-9).

King Antiochus, not having died in Egypt, hears what is going on in Judea. What he does should be no surprise. "It was clear to the king, when news of those happenings reached him, that Judaea was in a state of insurrection, and he set out from Egypt in a savage mood. He took Jerusalem by storm" (5:11, REB). Over a period of three days, the Epitomist says that eighty-thousand were slaughtered, with about the same number sold into slavery (5:12-14). Yet this is not enough. "Not satisfied with this, and guided by Menelaus, who had turned traitor to both religion and country, the king had the audacity to enter the most holy temple on earth. The villain laid his polluted hands on the sacred vessels, and profanely swept up the votive offerings which other kings had made to enhance the splendour and fame of the shrine" (5:15-16, REB). Do note, however, **that this is not the significant defilement that the Maccabees would later have to cleanse;** this is only a ransacking of the Temple with King Antiochus taking massive spoil away. But while this utterly inflames the Epitomist, he is forced to conclude that what took place was Divine punishment from God:

"The pride of Antiochus passed all bounds. He did not understand that the sins of the people of Jerusalem had for a short time angered the Lord, and that this was the reason why the temple was left to its fate. Had they not been guilty of many sinful acts, Antiochus would have fared no better than Heliodorus, who was sent by King Seleucus to inspect the treasury; like him,

---

[8] The Epitomist says that he went to Sparta "because of the Spartans' kinship with the Jews" (5:9, REB), *dia tēn sungeneian*.

he would have been flogged and his presumption foiled at once. But the Lord did not choose the nation for the sake of the sanctuary; he chose the sanctuary for the sake of the nation. That was why the sanctuary itself had its part in the misfortunes that befell the nation, and afterwards shared its good fortune; it was abandoned when the Almighty was roused to anger, but restored again in all its splendour when the great Master was reconciled with his people" (5:17-20, REB).

King Antiochus makes his way back to the capitol at Antioch, along with eighteen hundred talents of treasure from the Temple (5:21a). The Epitomist offers an editorial comment, "Carried away by arrogance he thought that he could make ships sail on dry land and men walk over the sea!" (5:21b, REB). Seleucid Greek overseers are left to watch over Jerusalem and Mount Gerizim where the Samaritans convened (5:22-23a). Menelaus is viewed as a total turncoat Jew, "who was more brutally overbearing than the others" (5:23b, REB). The king sends a large force into Judea to quell any chance of rebellion, although some literary exaggeration is likely seen in the Epitomist's summary: "he sent Apollonius, commander of the Mysian mercenaries, with an army of twenty-two thousand men; his orders were to slaughter all the adult males and to sell the women and children into slavery" (5:24, REB). An incident of how this Apollonius deceives the Jews by coming in peace is recalled, murdering a great number of people on the Sabbath (5:25-26). From this incident enters Judah Maccabee onto the scene, who escaped with nine others into the desert, where he and his companions had to feed on wild animals and sparse vegetation (5:27).

Shortly after, "King Antiochus sent an elderly Athenian to compel the Jews to give up their ancestral customs and to cease regulating their lives by the laws of God" (6:1, REB). As Antiochus' agent of evil, "He was commissioned also to pollute the temple at Jerusalem and dedicate it to the Olympian Zeus" (6:2a, REB). Even the sanctuary of the Samaritans at Mount Gerizim was also to be dedicated to Zeus, god of Hospitality (6:2b)—quite something to be recorded, considering how the Jews and the Samaritans did not get along!

What happened to the Temple of God on Mount Zion was a hard scene indeed to bear, and what is described in 2 Maccabees is much more detailed than simply pigs being slaughtered on the altar. The Epitomist summarizes how "This evil onslaught bore hard on the people and tried them grievously, for the Gentiles filled the temple with licentious revelry: they took their pleasure with prostitutes and had intercourse with women in the sacred precincts. Moreover, they introduced things which the law forbade, and heaped the altar with offerings prohibited as impure. No one was allowed to observe the sabbath or to keep the traditional festivals or even to admit to being a Jew at all" (6:3-6, REB). King Antiochus' birthday had to be honored every month (6:7a), and the Jews were forced to participate in the feast of Dionysius, god of revelry (6:7b). Jews living throughout the region were ordered to do the same (6:8), on the threat that "they should put to death everyone who refused to conform to the Greek ways" (6:9a, REB).

Two horrific examples immediately considered are the deaths of two women who had their infant sons circumcised (6:10), and how a group of Jews who had observed the Sabbath in caves were burned alive, after failing to defend themselves (6:11). The Epitomist of 2 Maccabees is very reluctant to mention any specific examples, observing, "I beg my readers not to be disheartened by those tragic events, but to reflect that such penalties were inflicted for the discipline, not the destruction, of our race" (6:12, REB). Perhaps this is an observation that simply destroying the Jews would not be enough to convey the greatness and superiority *and divinity* of King Antiochus and his Greek culture, as the Jews should have just followed his decrees. At the same time, what has taken place to the Jews, as the Epitomist thinks, may be the discipline of God upon His people, who knew His ways and failed to resist sin (6:13-17).

One of the most significant incidents to consider is the example of the aged Torah teacher, Eleazar, who refused to forcibly eat pork (6:18). His story is one that aptly summarizes the continued Jewish animosity to this day toward the swine. This often hatred toward pigs is by no means pigs' fault; it is because the Seleucid Greeks demanded that the Jewish people eat pork to prove that they had turned their backs on their God. The Epitomist recounts, "[B]ut preferring death with the honour to life with impiety, [Eleazar] spat it out and voluntarily submitted to the torture. So should men act who have the courage to reject food which despite a natural desire to save their lives it is not lawful to eat" (6:19-20, REB). Eleazar's associates tried to persuade him that all he needed to do was to pretend to eat pork, escaping death (6:21-22), but Eleazar refused (6:23). Eleazar says that to do this, at his old age, would be quite hypocritical for the young people to witness:

"If I went through with this pretense at my time of life, many of the young might believe that at the age of ninety Eleazar had turned apostate. If I practiced deceit for the sake of a brief moment of life, I should lead them astray and stain my old age with dishonour. I might for the present avoid man's punishment, but alive or dead I should never escape the hand of the Almighty. If I now died bravely, I shall show that I have deserved my long life and leave to the young a noble example; I shall be teaching them how to die a good death, gladly and nobly, for our revered and holy laws" (6:24-28a, REB).

After asserting this, Eleazar was taken off to be tortured (6:28b), with his former associates considering him to be mad (6:29). At the point of death after being beaten senseless, Eleazar would groan, "To the Lord belongs all holy knowledge; he knows what terrible agony I endure in my body from this flogging, though I could have escaped death; yet he knows also that in my soul I suffer gladly, because I stand in awe of him" (6:30, REB). Eleazar then dies a martyr's death, the Epitomist's eulogy being, "So he died; and by his death he left a noble example and a memorial of virtue, not only to the young but also to the great mass of his countrymen" (6:31, REB).

Another example of martyrdom is considered by the Epitomist, one of seven brothers and their mother who were tortured, for failing to eat pork in violation of the Torah (7:1). Their tenacity in not giving in is seen in how one speaks out, "What do you expect to learn by interrogating us? Rather than break our ancestral laws we are prepared to die" (7:2, REB). This account is written as though King Antiochus himself is present (7:3a), leading some scholars to actually question its validity. No location of this scene is given in the text, so it is not impossible for the seven brothers and their mother to have been taken to a place, outside of Judea, where Antiochus could personally see some of the so-called "Jewish rabble." Consequently, King Antiochus orders that this brother, speaking for his family, have his tongue cut out, and then be scalped and mutilated in front of everyone (7:3b-4). He is then roasted alive in the presence of his family (7:5). All they could say to each other was, "The Lord God is looking on...and we may be sure that he has compassion on us. Did not Moses say to Israel in the song plainly denouncing apostasy, 'He will have compassion on his servants'?" (7:6, REB).[9]

The second brother is asked whether or not he will eat pork, and he refuses to not only partake of it, but is quite blunt in refusing to speak the torturer's language (7:7-8a). As he is dying, all he can say is, "Fiend though you are, you are setting us free from this present life, and the King of the universe will raise us up to a life everlastingly made new, since it is for his laws that we are dying" (7:8b-9, REB). He expected a life of resurrection to come, a reward for his steadfastness to God.

The third brother is tortured to eat pork (7:10), but refuses with the words, "his [God's] laws mean far more to me than they [the brother's hands] do, and it is from him that I trust to receive them again" (7:11, REB), meaning in the resurrection. The Epitomist observes, "Both the king himself and those with him were astounded at the young man's spirit and his utter disregard for suffering" (7:12, REB). After dying, the fourth brother is also tortured (7:13). All he can say before dying is, "Better to be killed by men and to cherish God's promise to raise us again! But for you there will be no resurrection" (7:14, REB). He either reflected a Jewish view that the resurrection was only for the righteous, *or* that the resurrection he was to experience was one of being ushered into God's future Kingdom on Earth—something the Seleucid Greek oppressors were certainly not going to experience.

---

[9] Deuteronomy 32:36.

The fifth brother is dragged forward (7:15), and what he says is very important: "Mortal as you are, you have authority among human beings and can do as you please. But do not imagine that God has abandoned our nation. Wait, and you will see how his mighty power will torment you and your descendants!" (7:16-17, REB). What the sixth brother has to say when he is brought forward is important to consider. He acknowledges that the Jewish people are being punished for their crimes against God, in denying His Torah, but also that the punishers are not going to get away with what they are doing:

"Do not delude yourself: it is through our own fault that we suffer these things; we have sinned against our God and brought these appalling events on ourselves. But do not suppose you yourself will escape the consequences of trying to contend with God" (7:18-19, REB).

The Epitomist, while expressing high regard for these brothers, also expresses high regard for their mother. He says, "The mother was the most remarkable of all, and she deserves to be remembered with special honour. She watched her seven sons perish within the space of a single day, yet she bore it bravely, for she trusted in the Lord" (7:20, REB). She had encouraged each of her sons *in their native language*, no less (7:21), and recognized that God as their Creator would bring them back to life again in the resurrection, because they have been steadfast in not giving up on His Torah (7:22-23).

King Antiochus is sitting there, observing these things, suspecting that although he could not understand her words, he was being insulted (7:24a). Knowing how far he has gone with killing six of seven sons, Antiochus changes his tactics from one who tortures. With only one brother left alive, the Epitomist describes, Antiochus "assured him on oath that once he abandoned his ancestral customs he would make him rich and enviable by enrolling him as a king's Friend and entrusting him with high office" (7:24b, REB). King Antiochus urges the mother to tell her surviving son to accept (7:25), and so she finally agrees to try (7:26). What she actually tells her son in front of the tyrant can never be forgotten:

"I implore you, my child, to look at the heavens and the earth; consider all that is in them, and realize that God did not create them from what already existed and that a human being comes into existence the same way. Do not be afraid of this butcher; accept death willingly and prove yourself worthy of your brothers, so that by God's mercy I may receive back both you and them together" (7:28-29, REB).

She barely finishes her words, and the seventh and her final son speaks out (7:30a). His zeal for the God of Israel is difficult to overlook:

"What are you all waiting for? I will not submit to the king's command; I obey the command of the law given through Moses to our forefathers. And you, King Antiochus, who have devised all manner of atrocities for the

Messianic Winter Holiday Helper

Hebrews, you will not escape God's hand. It is for our own sins that we are suffering, and, though to correct and discipline us our living Lord is angry for a brief time, yet he will be reconciled with his servants. But you, impious creature, most villainous of the human race, do not let vain hopes buoy you up or empty delusions carry you away when you lay hands on Heaven's servants. You are not safe from the judgement of the omnipotent, all-seeing God. My brothers, after a short period of pain, have under God's covenant drunk of the waters of everlasting life; but you by God's verdict will pay the just penalty of your brutal insolence. I, like my brothers, surrender my body and my life for our ancestral laws. I appeal to God to show favour speedily to his people and by whips and scourges to bring you to admit that he alone is God. May the Almighty's anger, which has justly fallen on our race, end with me and my brothers!" (7:30a-38, REB).

The result of this apologetic speech to King Antiochus causes him to just rage, and so the seventh brother is punished far worse than the previous six (7:39). The Epitomist can only say, "the young man, putting his trust in the Lord, died without having incurred defilement" (7:40, REB). The mother also dies, and the editor closes his recalling of those who were tortured for their faithfulness to God's Law (7:41-42).

Much of what is seen in 2 Maccabees chs. 8-15 is paralleled by the war accounts in 1 Maccabees. Judah Maccabee and his brothers now enter the literary scene. Forced into the wilderness, Judah Maccabee and his companions recruit a force of six thousand men, people who had remained loyal to God and to the Torah (8:1). "They appealed to the Lord to look with compassion on his people whom all were trampling underfoot, to take pity on the temple now profaned by apostates, and to have mercy on Jerusalem, which was being destroyed and would soon be levelled to the ground. They prayed him also to give ear to the blood and cried blood that cried out to him for vengeance, to keep in mind the infamous massacre of innocent children and the blasphemous deeds against his name, and to show his hatred of wickedness" (8:2-4, REB). They all appealed to God for His deliverance, and for discernment in how they were to proceed.

The Epitomist considers the growing Maccabean force to be an important tool of God, asserting, "Once [Judah's] band of partisans was organized, the Gentiles found Maccabaeus invincible, now that the Lord's anger had changed to mercy" (8:5, REB), as it was time for the Jewish people to be vindicated. "Maccabaeus came on towns and villages without warning and burnt them down; he recaptured strategic positions, and inflicted many reverses on the enemy, choosing the night-time as being especially favourable for these attacks. Everywhere there was talk of his heroism" (8:6-7, REB).

The Seleucid commissioner, Philip, was very worried about what had started, writing to Ptolemaeus, governor of Colele-Syria and Phoenicia, for help (8:8). He sends Nicanor, a member of the king's Friends, and with him twenty-thousand troops, in the Epitomist's estimation, "to exterminate the whole population of Judaea" (8:9, REB), and with him the general Gorgias. Profits from selling Jews as slaves could be used to pay off some tribute that King Antiochus still owed the Romans (8:10-11).

When Judas and his men heard that Nicanor was coming, many of them deserted and fled (8:12-13), but those who stayed, "disposing of their recent possessions, joined in prayer to the Lord for deliverance from the godless Nicanor, who had put them up for sale even before any fighting took place" (8:14, REB). They appealed to God for His intervention, not for what they had done, but rather "on the ground of the covenants God had made with their forefathers, and because they bore his holy and majestic name" (8:15, REB). Judah Maccabee appealed to his force not to fall into panic, because they had a just cause to fight for, and for them to remember the desecration of the Temple and suppression by Gentiles of the Jewish religion (8:16-17). He appealed to his army, "They rely on weapons and deeds of daring...but we put our trust in Almighty God, who is able with a nod to overthrow our present assailants and, if need be, the whole world" (8:18, REB). Judah reminded the Maccabean army of previous times when God had intervened, such as the defeat of Sennacherib (8:19; 2 Kings 19:35), and a massive defeat of the Galatians with the Macedonians (8:20).[10] As the Epitomist says, "His words put heart into his men and made them ready to die for their laws and their country" (8:21a, REB).

In this first major engagement recorded, Judah divides his army into four groups, with three of his brothers—Simon, Josephus, and Jonathan—commanding a division of fifteen hundred (8:21b-22). A man named Eleazar delivers a Scripture reading "from the holy book," crying out "God is our help" (8:23, REB). The Epitomist details how "With the Almighty fighting on their side they slaughtered over nine thousand of the enemy, wounded and disabled the greater part of Nicanor's forces, and routed them completely" (8:24, REB). The money that the slavetraders were going to buy them with is also seized, and the remaining enemy is pursued until dark (8:25). They stop fighting because of the Sabbath, then offering appropriate praise and thanksgiving to God for the victory (8:26-27). When the Sabbath is over, some of the spoils they had collected are distributed among their fellow Jews who had been persecuted, various widows and orphans, and among the Maccabees' own

---

[10] This is a conflict that may have involved Jewish mercenaries, alluded to in Josephus *Antiquities of the Jews* 12.148-153; cf. John R. Bartlett, "2 Maccabees," in James D.G. Dunn and John W. Rogerson, eds., *Eerdmans Commentary on the Bible* (Grand Rapids: Eerdmans, 2003), 841.

families (8:28). "This done, all together made supplication to the merciful Lord, praying him to be fully reconciled with his servants" (8:29, REB).

The momentum of victory continues, as "The Jews now engaged the forces of Timotheus and Bacchides, killed over twenty thousand of them, and gained firm control of some of the high strongholds" (8:30a, REB). The Maccabees are sure to distribute the booty that they capture to Jewish victims of the Seleucids, orphans, widows, the elderly, and their own growing army (8:30b). The weapons that are captured are "carefully collected and stored at strategic points" (8:31, REB). The Epitomist records the execution of an officer who was in charge of Timotheus' bodyguard, who "was an utterly godless man who had caused the Jews great suffering" (8:32, REB). One can certainly detect that the pains and torture inflicted upon the Jews are returned to the Seleucid Greeks. The Epitomist recounts, "During the victory celebrations in their ancestral capital, they burnt alive the men who had set fire to the sacred gates, including Callisthenes, who had taken refuge in some small house; so he received the due reward of his impiety" (8:33, REB).

Nicanor, described as "that double-eyed villain who had brought along the thousand traders to buy the Jewish captives" (8:34, REB), has to scurry away in utter defeat. The Epitomist of 2 Maccabees has this to say about him:

"[Nicanor] was with the Lord's help humiliated by the very people whom he had dismissed as of no consequence. He threw off his magnificent garment, and all alone made his escape across country like a runaway slave; he was, indeed, exceedingly fortunate to reach Antioch after the destruction of his army. He who had undertaken to secure tribute for the Romans by taking prisoner the inhabitants of Jerusalem now proclaimed to the world that the Jews had a champion and were invulnerable, because they kept the laws that this champion had given them" (8:35-36, REB).

While the Seleucid Greek occupiers of Judea are experiencing defeat at the hands of Judah Maccabee and his forces, things are not going well for Antiochus Epiphanes in his Persian campaign. The Epitomist records how he tried to plunder the temples of Persepolis and gain control, but the local population rose up against him, forcing him "into a humiliating withdrawal" (9:2, REB). (Apparently, the death described earlier in 1:13-17 is of Antiochus' companions, and not that of himself, as will be seen in ch. 9). Retreating to Ecbatana, a report reaches King Antiochus of how the forces of Nicanor and Timotheus had been defeated (9:3), "and this so roused his anger that he proposed to make the Jews suffer for the injury inflicted by those who had routed him" (9:4a, REB). Antiochus Epiphanes was so arrogant, that he actually thought that he would make the Jewish people pay not for the forces he had sent to fight them, *but* on account of the Persians who had just defeated him.

Antiochus is so angry, that he pushes his charioteer not to stop until they reach their destination (9:4b), but as the Epitomist records, "riding with him was the divine judgement! In his arrogance he said: 'Once I reach Jerusalem, I will make it one big Jewish graveyard'" (9:4c, REB). **Antiochus Epiphanes would never make it to Jerusalem, or even that far out of Persia.** "[T]he all-seeing Lord, the God of Israel, dealt him a fatal, invisible blow. No sooner had he uttered the words than he was seized with incurable pains in his bowls and acute internal suffering" (9:5, REB), in the Epitomist's view, "a punishment entirely fitting for one who had inflicted many unheard-of torments on the bowels of others" (9:6, REB). Yet, even in such pain he insisted that the journey speed on, and became even more vengeful and threatening against the Jews (9:7a). This only made things worse, because "as the chariot hurtled along he fell from it, and so violent was his fall that he suffered agony in every limb" (9:7b, REB). King Antiochus was never to be the same again, as his body would be ravaged and he would succumb to a flesh-eating disease. The Epitomist's literary skills should not be overlooked in his description:

"He, who in pretension to be superhuman had been thinking that he could command the waves of the sea and weigh high mountains on the scales, was brought to the ground and had to be carried on a stretcher. The power of God was thus manifest to all. Worms swarmed from the body of this godless man and, while he was still alive and in agony, his flesh rotted off, and the whole army was overwhelmed by the stench of decay. It was so unbearably offensive that no one was able to convey the man who only a short time before had seemed to reach to the stars in the heavens" (9:8-10, REB).

Humiliated not only by a recent military defeat, but now broken in body, "Antiochus began to moderate his monstrous arrogance; scourged by God and racked with incessant pain, he was coming to see things in their true light" (9:11, REB). The Epitomist ably describes how "He was unable to endure his own stench," and so he cries, "It is right for mortals to submit to God and not claim equality with him" (9:12, REB). **Antiochus Epiphanes was having to recognize the superiority of God, and how significantly presumptuous he was in his exploits.**

Antiochus Epiphanes would not be granted any significant mercy by God, and he was going to die (9:13), but the Epitomist records how he recognized his error, and reversed his approach to the Jews on his deathbed. Antiochus vowed "that the Holy City, which he had been hurrying to level to the ground and transform into a graveyard, he would publicly declare to be free; to all the Jews, a people he had considered not to be worthy of burial but fit only to be thrown out with their children as carrion for birds and beasts, he would now give privileges equal to those enjoyed by the citizens of Athens; the holy temple, which he earlier had plundered, he would adorn with the most

Messianic Winter Holiday Helper

magnificent gifts, and would replace all the sacred vessels on a much more lavish scale, and he would meet the cost of the sacrifices from his own revenues. In addition, he would even turn Jew and visit every inhabited place to proclaim God's might" (9:13-17, REB).

Is some of this exaggerated? That King Antiochus would not only give the Jews citizenship rights only enjoyed by Athenians, but that he would convert to Judaism himself? *What we know for certain is that he lamented his mistake against Israel's God.* King Antiochus sends a letter to the Jewish people, what the Epitomist considers "as a kind of olive branch" (9:18, REB). In this letter, he wishes the Jews well (9:19-20), and actually says that he keeps "an affectionate remembrance of your respect and goodwill (9:21a, REB). Antiochus describes his physical illness (9:21b), and how he has chosen a successor for himself (9:22-26). His son, another Antiochus, will be encouraged to follow the new policies of "moderation and benevolence" (9:27, REB) toward the Jews. But even though he may have seen the proverbial "light" in his final days, the Epitomist by no means considers his sins atoned for. His epitaph of Antiochus Epiphanes is, **"So this murderer and blasphemer, suffering the greatest agony, such as he had made others suffer, met a pitiable end in the mountains of a foreign land"** (9:28, REB). His body was brought back, but his close friend Philip feared the successor Antiochus (9:29).

You can definitely get a sense from examining the remaining chapters of 2 Maccabees that the Epitomist is jumping over a great deal of data, which Jason of Cyrene likely elaborated on more fully. The Epitomist summarizes how Jerusalem and the Temple precinct were recovered by Judah Maccabee (10:1). The pagan altars are demolished, the sanctuary is purified, sacrifices are offered for the first time in two years, and the worship vessels are restored to their rightful place (10:2-3). When the Temple practices are restored, prayer is offered to the Lord, "that he would never again allow them to fall into such disasters but, were they ever to sin, would discipline them himself with clemency rather than hand them over to blasphemous and barbarous Gentiles" (10:4, REB). The Epitomist asserts how on the 25th of Kislev, the same day on which the Temple had been previously defiled, it was now restored to proper order (10:5). Following the rededication, a commemoration of what the Maccabees had done took place, lasting eight days, not too dissimilar from the prior remembered Feast of Tabernacles:

"The joyful celebration lasted for eight days, like the feast of Tabernacles,[11] and they recalled how, only a short time before, they had kept that feast while living like wild animals in the mountains and caves. So carrying garlanded wands and flowering branches, as well as palm-fronds,

---

[11] Grk. *skēnōmatōn tropon*; "in the manner of the feast of booths" (RSV).

they chanted hymns to the One who had so triumphantly achieved the purification of his own temple. A decree was passed by the public assembly that every year the entire Jewish nation should keep these days holy" (10:6-8, REB).

We see here the establishment of *Chanukah* as a unique and special national holiday for the Jewish people. This new Feast of Dedication originally used the Feast of Tabernacles as a prototype for celebration, but was to remember the liberation and dedication of the Temple from the Seleucid Greek occupiers of Jerusalem. Yet we are reminded, simply because the Temple has now been rededicated before the Lord, and is back in working order, the conflict with the Seleucids *is by no means over*. While there is debate among interpreters whether or not the material that follows is actually in historical order, it still gives the reader an important picture of how the Jewish nation was encroached upon by adversaries.

The Epitomist moves his readers forward, having just described the death of Antiochus Epiphanes (10:9), now intending to discuss the evil that his son and successor, Antiochus Eupator, performed (10:10). Upon becoming king, Antiochus appointed Lysias as governor of Colele-Syria, who succeeded Ptolemaeus (10:11). The Epitomist makes the important observation that "Because of the injustice formerly done to the Jews, Ptolemaeus had taken the lead in treating them with justice and endeavoured to maintain amicable relations with them. For this he was denounced to Eupator by the king's Friends; on every side he heard himself called traitor...He still enjoyed power, but no longer respect, and he ended his own life by taking poison" (10:12-13, REB). This official, who had favorable policies toward the Jews, was not trusted and eventually committed suicide.

When a man named Gorgias becomes governor of the region, "he hired mercenaries and seized every opportunity of attacking the Jews" (10:14, REB). The same was true of the nearby Idumeans, who saw an opportunity "to foment hostilities" (10:15, REB). The Idumeans make themselves a prime target of the Maccabees, as Judah Maccabee issues "public prayers entreating God to fight on their side" (10:16, REB), then launching an assault on the Idumeans. According to the Epitomist, "They pressed the attack vigorously and captured them, driving off those who manned the walls and cutting down everyone they encountered. No less than twenty thousand of the enemy were killed" (10:17, REB).

Nine thousand took refuge in two forts able to withstand a siege (10:18). Judah leaves his brothers Simon and Josephus, along with a Zaccheus, behind to attack, as he leaves for other areas that needed help (10:19). The Epitomist records that "Simon's men were avaricious, and when they were offered some seventy thousand drachmas by some of those in the forts, they accepted the bribe and let them slip through their lines" (10:20, REB). There is some serious controversy about this statement because of what follows: "On being informed of this, [Judas] Maccabaeus denounced the men before the assembled leaders of the army for having sold their brothers for money by letting their enemies escape to fight again, and he had them executed as traitors" (10:21-22a, REB). While the Idumean fort is destroyed, and "his military operations were crowned with complete success" (10:23a, REB), it could appear that Simon as his brother (and later successor) is a complete failure. Yet, John R. Bartlett suggests, "If Simon here is Judas's brother, 2 Maccabees discredits him utterly; but if this Simon is included among the traitors killed, the identification falls."[12] It is not impossible that this is another Simon.

Timotheus, who had been previously humiliated by the Maccabees, returns to attack the Jews, this time with a force of mercenaries and cavalry (10:24). The piety of the Maccabees is lauded: "At his approach, [Judas] Maccabaeus and his men made their prayer to God; they sprinkled dust on their heads and put sackcloth around their waists, prostrated themselves on the altar-step and entreated God to show them favour—in the words of the law: 'to be an enemy of their enemies and an opponent of their opponents'" (10:25-26, REB; cf. Exodus 23:22). The Maccabean force moves a considerable distance from Jerusalem to meet Timotheus' army (10:27), and as put by the Epitomist, "For the Jews success and victory were assured, not only because of their courage but still more because they had recourse to the Lord, whereas the other side had only their own fury to lead them into battle" (10:28, REB).

The battle ensues, and growing more fierce the Epitomist describes how "there appeared to the enemy five magnificent figures in the sky, each riding a horse with a golden bridle. Placing themselves at the head of the Jews, they formed a circle round Maccabaeus and kept him unharmed under the protection of their armour, while they launched arrows and thunderbolts at the enemy, who, confused and blinded, broke in complete disarray" (10:29-30, REB). Because of this supernatural military intervention, it is recorded that twenty-five thousand infantry and six hundred cavalry of the enemy are killed (10:31).

Timotheus flees to Gazara in defeat, to a stronghold with a heavy garrison (10:32). He is pursued by Judah Maccabee, who lays siege to the place for four days (10:33). As the Jews attack, "The defenders, confident in the strength of their position, hurled horrible and wicked blasphemies at them until, at dawn on the fifth day, twenty young men from the Maccabaean force, burning with rage at the blasphemy, bravely stormed the wall and in savage fury cut down all they encountered" (10:34-35, REB). This serves well for the rest of the Maccabees who attack, as the stronghold is taken and many are burned alive,

---

[12] Bartlett, in *ECB*, 843.

with the city occupied (10:36). Timotheus himself, hiding in a cistern, too meets his end (10:37). The Epitomist can say, "In celebration of their achievement, the Jews praised with hymns and thanksgivings the Lord who showers benefits on Israel and gives them the victory" (10:38, REB).

This great victory does not go without a backlash from the Seleucids (11:1). The viceregent Lysias, musters an army of eighty thousand, and a large amount of cavalry, to march against the Jews. His intention was to make Jerusalem a fully Gentile city (11:2), including "the temple subject to taxation like all gentile shrines and the high-priesthood up for auction each year" (11:3, REB). The Epitomist observes, "Reckoning not at all with the might of God, he was carried away by the thought of his tens of thousands of infantry, his thousands of cavalry, his eighty elephants" (11:4, REB). Invading Judea, he fortifies himself about twenty miles from Jerusalem (11:5).

The Epitomist narrates how "When Maccabaeus and his men were informed that Lysias was besieging their strongholds, they and all the people, wailing and weeping, prayed the Lord to send a good angel to deliver Israel" (11:6, REB). Judah Maccabee took up arms, and urged his companions to do so to rescue their fellow Jews (11:7). The Epitomist describes how "While they were still in the neighbourhood of Jerusalem, there appeared at their head a horseman arrayed in white and brandishing golden weapons" (11:8, REB). The Maccabees' only response to seeing this is one of joy: "With one voice they praised their merciful God and felt so strong in spirit that they could have attacked not only men but also the most savage animals, or even walls of iron" (11:9, REB). When the battle commences, to the Epitomist, defeat of the enemy is just inevitable:

"Under the Lord's mercy and with their heavenly ally they came on in battle array. Like lions they hurled themselves on the enemy, laid low eleven thousand foot-soldiers, as well as sixteen hundred cavalry, and put the remainder to flight. Most of those who escaped had lost their weapons and were wounded, and Lysias himself saved his life, if not his honour, by ignominiously taking to his heels" (11:10-12, REB).

Lysias had to escape from the devastating defeat described by the Epitomist. He was a man who "was no fool, and as he took stock of the defeat he had suffered he realized that the Hebrews were invincible, because God in his power fought on their side" (11:13, REB). Lysias sends representatives to the Jews to broker a peace agreement, promising that the king will be favorable to them (11:14). Judah Maccabee agrees, especially because "the king had accepted whatever written terms Maccabaeus had forward to Lysias from the Jewish side" (11:15, REB). The Epitomist includes the Maccabees' letter to Lysias, which mostly includes how the two sides were trying to wish one another well, in the hope of cordial relations for the future (11:16-21).

Messianic Winter Holiday Helper

The king's letter, delivering instructions to Lysias, is also included (11:21). It is perhaps of no small importance that King Antiochus first writes, "Now that our royal father has joined the company of the gods..." (11:22a, REB). Within the instruction to Lysias includes a reference to how the Jews were obviously not prepared to adopt Greek ways (11:24a), and how it is best that they remain allowed to observe their own religion and laws (11:24b). He says, "We hereby decree that their temple be restored to them and that they be allowed to regulate their lives in accordance with their ancestral customs" (11:25, REB). Lysias is expected to convey this good intention to the Jewish people (11:26). King Antiochus also sends a letter to the Jewish people themselves, granting a period of amnesty for Jews to return home (11:27-30). Quite notable is the stipulation, "The Jews may follow their own food-laws..." (11:31a, NEB). Another interesting part of this section of 2 Maccabees is the interjection of the Romans Quintus Memmius and Titus Manilius, who were apparently active diplomats in the East overseeing Roman interests.[13] They too are informed of the new policies of the Seleucid regime, and have apparently served as intermediaries on behalf of the Jews (11:32-38).

Simply because a peace between the new King Antiochus and the Jews has been established on paper, by no means is an indication that it is going to be enacted. The Epitomist is forced to tell his audience more accounts of where the Jews' safety was threatened. After this peace agreement is brokered, "The Jews busied themselves on their farms, but they were prevented from leading stable and tranquil lives by some of the governors of the region" (12:1b-2a, REB). The exploits of the Maccabees that are described—even though the Temple has already been rededicated—communicate to the Jews' neighbors that they will defend themselves and their interests.

"A dastardly atrocity was perpetuated by the inhabitants of Joppa: they invited the Jews living among them to embark with their wives and children in boats they had provided, giving no indication of any animosity towards them" (12:3, REB). Apparently, being a largely non-Jewish city, the people of Joppa wanted the Jews to peacefully leave, given the complicated history of recent events. "As it was a public decision by the whole town and because they wished to live in peace and suspected nothing, the Jews accepted; but once out at sea the people of Joppa sank the boats, drowning no fewer than two hundred of the Jews" (12:4, REB). Judah Maccabee hears of this, and orders up his troops (12:5). Being righteously indignant, he was "invoking God the just judge," falling "upon the murderers" (12:6a, REB). The port of Joppa was

---

[13] Neil J. McEleney, "The Second Book of the Maccabees," in M. Jack Suggs, Katharine Doob Sakenfeld, and James R. Mueller, eds., *The Oxford Study Bible*, REB (New York: Oxford University Press, 1992), 1250.

The Message of 2 Maccabees

lit on fire during the night (12:6b). Judah was unable to return to attack the city itself, as he learned that the people of Jamnia were planning a similar ploy to the Jews there. So, Judah attacks Jamnia, lighting its port and ships on fire—such a sight that the flames were able to be seen in Jerusalem (12:7-9).

While the attack on Jamnia had been a success, the Epitomist describes that they were set upon by five thousand Arabs, and five hundred horsemen (12:10). Only with God's help in battle were the Jews victorious (12:11a). Interestingly enough, seeing the futility of trying to fight the Jews in the future, "The defeated nomads begged Judas to make an alliance with them, promising to supply cattle and to furnish the Jews with all other assistance" (12:11b, REB). Judas agrees, and allows the Arabs to return to their tents (12:12).

Judah Maccabee continues his campaign of establishing Jewish dominance over the region. He attacks Caspin, a walled city (12:13). The people are confident that their town is sufficiently fortified, treating "Judas and his men with insolence, abusing them and uttering the most wicked blasphemies" (12:14, REB). The Maccabees, though, call upon "the great Ruler of the universe" who had defeated Jericho "without the aid of battering-ram or siege-engine" (12:15, REB). Caspin was rushed and captured. The Epitomist describes, "The carnage was indescribable; the nearby lake, a quarter of a mile wide, appeared to be overflowing with blood" (12:16, REB).

Judah Maccabee has every intent on capturing Timotheus, the governor of the region, who alludes them. His force makes its way to Charax, a place inhabited by Tubian Jews (12:17). Timotheus had withdrawn from the district, yet he did leave behind a strong garrison (12:18), which the Maccabean generals Dositheus and Sosipater quickly destroyed, killing ten thousand (12:19). Judah Maccabee himself, though, divides his forces into various sub-units, hurrying in pursuit of Timotheus, who had a hundred and twenty thousand infantry and twenty-five hundred cavalry (12:20). As the Maccabees advance on Timotheus' force, the Epitomist recounts how "panic seized the enemy, who were terrified at a hostile manifestation of the all-seeing One. In headlong flight they rushed in all directions, so that frequently they were injured by their own comrades and run through by the points of their swords" (12:22, REB). Judah's forces take advantage of their confusion, killing thirty thousand (12:23). Timotheus was captured by the Maccabean forces commanded by Dositheus and Sosipater, but was actually able to convince them to let him go. He was a man of influence, after all, and could use his power to set free some of the Jewish family members who had been taken prisoner (12:24-25). Whether he actually did this is not stated.

Another stronghold is attacked at Carnaim, where twenty-five thousand are killed (12:26). The next target is Ephron, a city heavily fortified with "a great supply of engines of war and missiles" (12:27, REB). The Jewish force once again invoked "the Ruler whose might shatters the enemy's strength," and "made themselves masters of the town and laid low as many as twenty-five thousand" (12:28, REB). The Maccabean forces move again to Scythopolis, seventy-five miles from Jerusalem (12:29). There, they are actually told by the Jews that there was "goodwill shown them by the people and the kindness with which they had been treated in times of misfortune" (12:30, REB). Appreciating this, "Judas and his men thanked them, charging them to be no less friendly to the Jews in the future" (12:31a, REB), returning to Jerusalem to celebrate the Feast of Weeks (12:31b).

When their observance is over, the Maccabees march against Gorgias, who was in control of Idumea (12:32). In battle, he comes out with a force of three thousand men and four hundred cavalry (12:33), with only a small number of Jews killed (12:34). In the battle, a Tubian Jew, Dositheus, "caught hold of Gorgias by his cloak and was dragging the villain off by main force, with the object of taking him alive" (12:35a, REB). Instead, a Thracian horsemen bore down on him, cutting off his arm, enabling Gorgias to escape (12:35b).

The fighting against Gorgias' force proved exhausting for the Maccabees, in particular those commanded by Esdrias (12:36a). So, Judah "appealed to the Lord to show himself their ally and leader in battle" (12:36b, REB), and so he issues a battle cry of hymns in Hebrew to God, launching a surprise attack (12:37). Later, regrouping his forces, Judah settles for the Sabbath at Adullam (12:38). Following this, the bodies of those who had died were collected for burial (12:39). As they collect the dead, idolatrous amulets of Jamnia, forbidden by the Torah, are found, and this is believed to be the very reason that these soldiers died (12:40).

Some very interesting words are then provided by the Epitomist, as praise is actually issued to God for revealing this secret (12:41). The Maccabees turn to praying, especially so that this sin of them carrying idols can be erased (12:42a). "The noble Judas exhorted the people to keep themselves free from wrongdoing, for they had seen with their own eyes what had happened because of the sin of those who had fallen" (12:42b, REB). Monies are collected so that a sin-offering could be made back in Jerusalem (12:43a). This is considered to be "a fit and proper act in which he took due account of the resurrection" (12:43b, REB). The challenging words to understand are where the Epitomist describes,

"Had he not been expecting the fallen to rise again, it would have been superfluous and senseless to pray for the dead; but since he had in view the splendid reward reserved for those who die a godly death, his purpose was holy and devout. That was why he offered the atoning sacrifice, to free the dead from their sins" (12:44-45, REB).

Some later Catholic theologians would take these words and around them develop the doctrine of Purgatory, a temporary place of holding for the righteous dead until their final sins are extirpated, enabling them to enter Heaven. Because of the difficulty of the situation witnessed here in 2 Maccabees, and the literary style of the Epitomist in summarizing Jason of Cyrene's original work, readers need to be cautious in the conclusions they draw. Was it really the intention for Judah Maccabee to atone for the sins of these Jews who had fallen? *Or is this a conclusion of the Epitomist?* Could the original intention of Judah Maccabee—in at least trying to atone for these sins—actually been to serve as a warning to the rest of his living force who had not (at least to him) used idolatrous amulets?

While we can be thankful that the editor of 2 Maccabees affirms the doctrine of resurrection, his hamartology or theology of sin may be too clouded in his unique writing style. He may also reflect an ancient Jewish view that only the righteous were to experience the resurrection and be welcomed into the world to come, whereas the Apostolic Scriptures affirm Daniel 12:2 and the condemned also experiencing a resurrection unto judgment (Revelation 20:6). **This is ultimately why 2 Maccabees is a part of the Apocrypha or deutero-canon.**

The Epitomist's record continues, as Judah Maccabee hears that Antiochus Eupator is marching with a large army against Judea (13:1), accompanied by Lysias. This force included one hundred ten thousand infantry, five thousand three hundred cavalry, twenty-two elephants, and three hundred special chariots (13:2). Also joining them was the high priest Menelaus: "This he did most disingenuously, not for his country's good, but because he believed he would be established in office" (13:3, REB). It is observed, though, "The King of kings...stirred up the anger of Antiochus against this wicked man, and when Lysias produced evidence that Menelaus was responsible for all the troubles, the king ordered him to be taken to Beroea and there executed in the manner customary at that place" (13:4, REB). This opportunist, who had committed heinous deeds against his own people, is finally rewarded for his sins. The unique method of death that Menelaus experiences does not go unnoticed:

"In Beroea there is a tower some seventy-five feet high, filled with ashes; it has a circular device sloping down sheer on all sides into the ashes. This is where the citizens take anyone guilty of sacrilege or any other heinous crime, and thrust him to his doom; and such was the fate of the renegade Menelaus, who, in accordance with his just deserts, was not even given burial in the earth. Many a time he had desecrated the sacred ashes of the altarfire, and by ashes he met his death" (13:5-8, REB).

The high priest Menelaus is apparently thrown into a cremation cauldron, where in this town, criminals were executed. Without doing a thorough background study, suffice it to say this was one of the worst methods of dying that a Jew—even an unfaithful one—could experience. Historically, the Jewish people have extensively frowned on cremation, believing that God will not be able to resurrect a body from ashes. According to the Epitomist, Menelaus was so evil, he had even desecrated a place where criminals were dishonored in death.

Simply because Menelaus is vacated, does not mean that the Maccabees will have an easy time against Antiochus Eupator. The Epitomist says, "In savage arrogance the king came on, aiming to inflict sufferings on the Jews far worse than they had endured under his father. When Judas learnt of this, he ordered the people to invoke the Lord day and night, and pray that now more than ever he would come to their aid, since law, country, and holy temple were all at risk" (13:9-10, REB). **Even though the Temple had been rededicated, more sustained conflict was on the scene.** Judah Maccabee was insistent that the Jewish nation not fall into the hands of idolaters, just as they were starting to rebuild themselves (13:11). It is stated that at his orders "They all complied: for three days without respite they prayed to their merciful Lord, they wailed, they fasted, they prostrated themselves" (13:12a, REB).

Judah convenes a council of war, and it is decided not to wait for the enemy to invade Judea, taking Jerusalem—but with the help of God to march out and fight (13:13). The Epitomist lauds, "He committed the outcome to the Lord of the universe, and exhorted his troops to fight nobly to the death for the law, temple, and city, for their country and their way of life" (13:14, REB). Setting camp at Modin, Judah gives his army the watchword "Victory with God!" and then launches a secret night attack (13:15a, REB). Two thousand in the enemy camp are killed, including the death of the leading elephant (13:15b). This operation succeeds in creating panic throughout the enemy camp, with the Epitomist recognizing how the Maccabees had received help from the Lord (13:16-17).

It is indicated that the king "had a taste of Jewish daring" (13:18a, REB), and so he had to alter his tactics, specifically by "probing their positions" (13:18b, REB). Antiochus Eupator advances on Bethsura, a strong fort, first being repulsed and then being defeated (13:19). Judah Maccabee sends supplies to the garrison (13:20), but while this is happening, a Jewish soldier named Rhodocus is caught passing secret information to the enemy, for which he is executed (13:21). Antiochus then engages with Judah Maccabee's force directly, "but had the worse of it" (13:22, REB). Furthermore, he must quickly return back to the capitol at Antioch, as Philip, who was administrating the empire, was trying to fully gain the reigns of power (13:23a). Being concerned about his throne, "In consternation the king summoned the Jews, agreed to their terms, and took an oath to respect all their rights. After reaching this settlement he offered a sacrifice, paid honour to the sanctuary and its precincts, and received Maccabaeus in a friendly manner" (13:23b-24, REB). Hegemonides is left as the governor of the region (13:25a), and Antiochus must quickly retreat for Antioch (13:25b-26).

The Epitomist narrates that after three years, Judah Maccabee and his company hear that Demetrius son of Seleucus had taken over the country, with a large fleet arriving at Tripolis with a powerful army (14:1-2). A certain Alcimus, who had once been high priest, and who is said to have "willingly submitted to defilement at the time of the revolt" (14:3a, REB), takes advantage of Demetrius' arrival as an opportunity. He goes to King Demetrius, along with a gold crown and palm, and special olive branches from the Temple (14:3b-4). Meeting with Demetrius, Alcimus hatches his scheme (14:5), informing him that "Those Jews called Hasidaeans who are led by Judas Maccabaeus are keeping the war alive and fomenting sedition; they refuse to let the kingdom have peace. Thus, although I have been deprived of my reditary dignity, by which I mean the high-priesthood, I have two motives in coming here today" (14:6-7, REB). What Alcimus intends to do is stated to King Demetrius:

"[F]irst, I have a genuine concern for the king's interests; and secondly, a regard for my fellow-citizens, since our whole race is suffering considerable hardship as a result of the senseless conduct of those people I have mentioned. My advice to your majesty is to get to know the details of these matters and then, as befits your universal kindness and goodwill, make provision for our country and our beleaguered nation" (14:8-9, REB).

Alcimus' opportunism can easily be seen by his word, "For as long as Judas remains alive there can be no peace for the state" (14:10, REB). Saying this, other members of the order of king's Friends spoke up, adding "fresh fuel to Demetrius's anger" (14:11, REB). King Demetrius selects Nicanor, a commander of the elephant guard, and makes him the governor of Judea (14:12). Nicanor is granted a commission to rout out the Maccabean forces, and see that Alcimus is installed as high priest (14:13). Any of the Gentiles in the region, having suffered by the military actions of Judah Maccabee, joined to support Nicanor, "supposing that defeat and misfortune for the Jews would spell prosperity for them" (14:14, REB).

The Epitomist is still quite concerned about the religious piety of the Maccabees, speaking of how "When the Jews heard of Nicanor's offensive and the onset of the Gentiles, they sprinkled dust over themselves and prayed to him who has established his people for ever, who never fails to manifest himself and afford help when his chosen are in need" (14:15, REB). Having appealed to God for help, the Maccabean force moves out and meets the enemy at Adasa (14:16). Simon, Judah's brother, had fought with Nicanor, but was deterred (14:17). Interestingly enough, even though he had a large military force, the Epitomist can record: "In spite of this, when Nicanor learnt how brave Judas and his troops were and how courageously they fought for their country, he shrank from deciding the issue by the sword" (14:18, REB). Emissaries are sent to negotiate a peace agreement (14:19).

Hearing the proposals, Judah and his men have a favorable disposition to accepting them (14:20). When the day comes to finalize the agreement, special seats are placed in the middle of the two armies (14:21). Judah was sure to place "armed men at strategic points ready to deal with any sudden treachery on the enemy's part" (14:22a, REB), but the Epitomist instead observes how "The discussion between the two leaders was harmonious. Nicanor stayed some time in Jerusalem and behaved correctly. Dismissing the crowds that had flocked from round about, he kept Judas close to himself at all times, for he had developed a real affection for him" (14:22b-24, REB). The Epitomist even says how Nicanor "urged him to marry and have children; so Judas married and settled down to the quiet life of an ordinary citizen" (14:25, REB). Some kind of peace between the Jewish nation and their Seleucid Greek neighbors was able to be concluded.

Alcimus, the one who convinced King Demetrius that the Maccabees were a threat to him, gets a copy of the peace settlement (14:26a). He goes to King Demetrius "and claimed that Nicanor was pursuing a policy detrimental to the interests of the state by appointing Judas, a man guilty of conspiracy, as king's Friend designate" (14:26b, REB). King Demetrius, infuriated, sends Nicanor an order that Judah Maccabee is to be arrested and sent to the capitol at Antioch (14:27). The Epitomist relays how "The instructions dismayed Nicanor, and he took it hard that he should have to go back on his agreement when the man had committed no offence" (14:28, REB). Yet, we find the old axiom "orders are orders" at work, because "since there was no gainsaying with the king, he watched for an opportunity of carrying out the order by some stratagem" (14:29, REB). Judah Maccabee notices that Nicanor's original friendly disposition toward him had waned, and so he goes into hiding (14:30).

What can Nicanor do in enacting the royal order? "Recognizing that he had been outmanoeuvred by the resolute action of Judas, Nicanor appeared before the great and holy temple at the time when the priests were offering the regular sacrifices, and ordered them to surrender Judas" (14:31, REB). The priests swear that they do not know where he is (14:32), but that is not good enough. "Nicanor stretched out his right hand towards the shrine and swore this oath: 'Unless you surrender Judas to me in chains, I shall level this sanctuary of God to the ground and destroy the altar; on this spot I shall build a temple to Dionysus for all the world to see" (14:33, REB). Hearing this severe threat, and knowing that only shortly before the Temple had been cleansed of defilement, the priests call out to the Almighty:

"Lord, you have no need of anything in the world, yet it was your pleasure that among us there should be a shrine for your dwelling-place; now, holy Lord from whom all holiness comes, keep this house, so recently purified, free from defilement for ever" (14:35-36, REB).

In order to demonstrate how serious Nicanor is about Judah Maccabee being found, he makes an example of a Jewish man named Razis. He is a distinguished Jewish leader, for whom the Epitomist issues some high words: "He was a patriot and very highly spoken of, one who for his loyalty was known as Father of the Jews. In the early days of the revolt he had stood trial for practicing the Jewish religion, and with no hesitation had risked life and limb for that cause" (14:37b-38, REB). So severe did Nicanor want to make an example of him, five hundred troops are sent to arrest Razis (14:39), with the intention of this being "a severe blow to the Jews" (14:40, REB). Troops pressed against his home compound, with calls even to burn it down (14:41). Razis prepares to actually fall on a sword, rather than being captured, as it was better "to die nobly rather than fall into the hands of evil men and be subjected to gross humiliation" (14:42, REB). With things happening quickly, though, Nicanor's troops then poured into his house. Razis decides on a whim to run up to the wall around the house, and then throw himself down into the crowd (14:43-44).

When Razis is found "He was still breathing and still ablaze with courage; streaming with blood and severely wounded as he was, he picked himself up and dashed through the crowd" (14:45a-b, REB). Apparently, the fall had not killed him as he intended, and the Epitomist records a very gruesome scene indeed: "Finally, standing on a sheer rock, and now completely drained of blood, he tore out his entrails and with both hands flung them at the crowd" (14:45c-46a, REB). To the Epitomist, Razis died a godly death, "invoking him who disposes of life and breath to give them back to him again" (14:16b, REB). Certainly, while Razis' self-martyrdom is something that we can respect, as he by no means gave up his faith in God or loyalty to the Torah, it is safe to say that it asks more questions than it answers as Razis died of causes he created.

The Book of 2 Maccabees ends, as we should expect it to, on a high note, with one last victory accomplished. Nicanor receives a report that Judah Maccabee is in the vicinity of Samaria, and so he plans to attack him on the Sabbath (15:1). The Epitomist relays how "Those Jews who were forced to accompany his army begged him not to carry out so savage and barbaric a massacre" (15:2a, REB). They cry, "Have regard for the day singled out and made holy by the all-seeing One" (15:2b, REB). Nicanor has no respect for the Jewish religion, taunting back, "Is there some ruler in the sky who has ordered the sabbath-day observance?" (15:3, REB). The Jews he pressed into service respond, "The living Lord himself is ruler in the sky, and he

Messianic Winter Holiday Helper

commanded the seventh day to be kept holy" (15:4, REB).[14] Nicanor's arrogance prevents him from considering their claim: "And I am ruler on earth...I order you to take up arms and do your duty to the king" (15:5a, REB). For the Epitomist, though, "he did not succeed in carrying out this outrage he had planned" (15:5b, REB).

Nicanor's plan was to actually "erect a public trophy from the spoils taken from Judas's army" (15:6, REB). Yet would he be able to do this? The Epitomist issues a great laud for Judah Maccabee, both his piety and tenacity, in standing up to God-less aggression:

"But Maccabaeus's confidence never wavered, and he had not the least doubt that he would obtain help from the Lord. He urged his men to have no fear of the gentile attack, but to bear in mind the aid they had received from Heaven in the past and look with confidence to the Almighty for the victory he would send them on this occasion also. He drew encouragement for them from the law and the prophets and, by reminding them of the struggles they had already come through, filled them with a fresh ardour. When he had roused their courage, he issued his orders, reminding them at the same time of the Gentiles' broken faith and perjury. He armed each one of them, not so much with shield and spear for protection, as with brave and reassuring words; and he cheered them all by recounting a dream he had had, a waking vision worthy of belief" (15:7-11, REB).

The Epitomist details how Judah Maccabee had seen a motivating vision, by which Divine approval was given to the Maccabees' cause in fighting the Seleucid Greeks:

"What he had seen was this: there had appeared to him the former high priest Onias, a good and noble man of modest bearing and mild disposition, a ready and apt speaker, an exemplar from childhood of every virtue; with uplifted hands Onias was praying for the whole Jewish community. Next there appeared in the same attitude a figure of great age and dignity, whose wonderful air of authority marked him as a man of the utmost distinction. Onias then spoke: 'This is God's prophet Jeremiah,' he said, 'one who loves his fellow-Jews and constantly offers prayers for the people and for the Holy City.' Extending his right hand Jeremiah presented a golden sword to Judas, saying as he did so, 'Take this holy sword, a gift from God, and with it shatter the enemy'" (15:12-16, REB).

Judah Maccabee's words had a significant influence on his troops, especially with the Prophet Jeremiah, a devoutly righteous man, appearing in his dream. Boys were able to be as courageous as men (15:17a). They would all fight decisively, not in a long campaign, but "by fighting in close combat with

---

[14] Is this an indication that these Jews thought that the Sabbath was only something for Israel, or something that had wider implications for all people?

all their courage. This they did because Jerusalem, their religion, and the temple were in peril" (15:17b-c, REB). The fear that the Maccabean soldiers demonstrated was not for their wives and children, or even their fellow brothers, but for the sanctity of the Temple (15:18)—in spite of how those bunkered down in Jerusalem "were anxious about the outcome of a battle on open ground" (15:19, REB).

You can definitely tell that the Epitomist crafts the battle with Nicanor as a fitting conclusion to his work. He builds up the intensity, as "All were awaiting the decisive struggle which lay ahead. The enemy had already concentrated his forces: his army drawn up in battle order, the elephants strategically positioned, and the cavalry ranged on the flanks. Maccabaeus observed the deployment of the troops, the variety of their weapons, and the ferocity of the elephants" (15:20-21a, REB). All Judah Maccabee can do is what he has done in previous conflicts: **call out to the Lord.** He appeals to God's previous intervention, especially as He assisted King Hezekiah of Judah in fighting the Assyrian Sennacherib (15:21b-22; cf. 2 Kings 19:35; Isaiah 37:36). Judah appeals, "Now, Ruler of heaven, send a good angel once again to go before us spreading fear and panic. May these blasphemers who are coming to attack your holy people be struck down by your strong arm!" (15:23-24, REB).

Somewhat more than the previous battles, the Epitomist invokes that this is as much a spiritual fight, as it is a physical fight. "Nicanor and his forces advanced to the sound of trumpets and war-songs, but Judas and his men engaged the enemy with invocations and prayers on their lips. Praying to God in their hearts and greatly cheered by his care, they killed no fewer than thirty-five thousand in hand-to-hand fighting" (12:25-27, REB). Of course, the results of the battle, include not only a significant number of the enemy dead, but Nicanor himself is discovered "lying dead in full armour" (12:28, REB). The Maccabees rejoice in Hebrew praises (12:29). Judah Maccabee orders that Nicanor's head and arm be severed, and taken to Jerusalem for display (12:30-31). This is specifically done because of "the hand which the bragging blasphemer had stretched out against the Almighty's holy temple" (12:32, REB). Nicanor's tongue is cut out, and Judah orders that evidence of what he had done be hung up adjacent to the Temple (12:33).

Great praise is issued to the Lord in the defeat of Nicanor (12:34-35), so much so that a decree was issued that this day would go remembered with a commemoration occurring in the 13th of Adar (12:36). All the Epitomist can say is, "Such then, was the fate of Nicanor, and from that time Jerusalem has remained in the possession of the Hebrews" (12:37, REB), an obvious indication that he is compiling his work during a time of a significant Jewish presence in Jerusalem.

The Book of 2 Maccabees then comes to an abrupt close, indicating that the events it recounts stop just short of the record of Judah Maccabee's death (1 Maccabees 9:1-22). The Epitomist tells his audience, "If [my work] is found to be well written and aptly composed, that is what I myself aimed at; if superficial and mediocre, it was the best I could do" (15:38, REB). He actually compares his summarization work to being like wine mixed with water, something he considers to be "a pleasant and delightful taste" (15:39b, REB), perhaps a reflection of how in his mind, Jason of Cyrene's original work was either too potent, or too dull. His closing remark is, "so too variety of style in a literary work charms the ear of the reader. Let this, then, be my final word" (15:39c, REB).

Similar to the Epitomist of 2 Maccabees, I have done my best *to summarize* his work, narrating it in a way that will help you appreciate what 2 Maccabees communicates not only to us as Bible students—but more specifically Messianic Believers who see importance in remembering the Festival of Dedication, *Chanukah*. Do you think his Egyptian Jewish readership would have been convinced that honoring the Festival of Dedication was a good thing, reflective of not only Jewish nationalism, but more importantly of holiness and piety toward God? Were the Maccabees people who should have been honored, fighting for the right of the Jewish nation to survive? Should we remember how God intervened, or should we treat these things as legends to be discounted?

The Epitomist of 2 Maccabees is undeniably an artful writer, and he is more concerned with the spiritual and social dynamics of the war with the Seleucids than the author of 1 Maccabees. But no different than 1 Maccabees, 2 Maccabees too records the hard realities of war. The licentious nature of the sacrilege committed in the Temple is explained in more detail than 1 Maccabees. Most importantly, the religious zeal of the Maccabean forces is lauded, as opposed to the Maccabees just being an army trying to repel invaders from their homeland.

As you read and compare 2 Maccabees with 1 Maccabees, there are certainly historical issues to be considered. The accounts detailed in both books are given from different vantage points. 2 Maccabees is more of a literary work than an historical piece, and we do have to be reminded that we no longer have Jason of Cyrene's original five-volume work for comparison. More than anything else, although there may be some issues to examine here or there—somewhat critically perhaps—2 Maccabees did affect the worldview of the Jewish people in the First Century C.E. The terrible hardships and martyrdoms that the Maccabees endured, influenced how the Jewish people of Yeshua and the Apostles' time interacted with outsiders. The Maccabean martyrs fought and died for God's Torah, and would have rather given up their lives than eat pork. **How did this sentiment affect the spread of the gospel among the nations in the First Century?**

The long-lasting ramifications of 2 Maccabees cannot be overlooked for their impact on the Jewish social scene as witnessed in the Apostolic Scriptures.

Messianic Winter Holiday Helper

-10-

The Impact of the Maccabees on First Century Judaism

J.K. McKee

For most Messianics I know who celebrate *Chanukah*, they hear a great deal about the military exploits of the Maccabees and the rededication of the Temple. Many of them honestly take the time to flip through the Books of 1&2 Maccabees in the Apocrypha, the principal historical record that influences our understanding of the wars fought by the Maccabees. When Jerusalem was recaptured and the Temple was rededicated, much more really did take place. *This goes beyond the lives of Judah Maccabee and his brothers.* Sadly, too many congregations and fellowships which honor *Chanukah* are not that familiar with this period of complicated history—not only for what took place in the Second Century B.C.E., **but how it would influence the First Century C.E.**

Good Relations that the Jews Had With the Seleucids

When surveying 1&2 Maccabees, one easily finds how Judea has been encroached between two divisions of Alexander the Great's divided Greek Empire. The Ptolemaic Greeks dominate Egypt to the south, and the Seleucid Greeks dominate Syria to the north. Originally, it seems that the Jewish nation had fairly good relations with the Seleucid regime, and had no problems serving as a vassal state. Two of the preceding monarchs to Antiochus Epiphanes, Antiochus the Great or Antiochus III (222-187 B.C.E.), and Seleucus IV (187-175 B.C.E.), are recorded to have been favorable toward the Jews.

King Antiochus III actually writes a letter, indicating how a population of Jews are to be moved out of Mesopotamia and Babylon, into Lydia and Phrygia. These are people, he attests, who will be loyal to the state, if they are simply left alone to worship their God and observe their religious laws. They will be productive and honorable citizens. As the historian Josephus recorded,

> "King Antiochus to Zeuxis his father, sends greetings. 'If you are in health, it is well. I also am in health. Having been informed that a sedition has arisen in Lydia and Phrygia, I thought that matter required great care; and upon advising with my friends what was fit to be done, it has been thought proper to remove two thousand families of Jews, with their effects, out of Mesopotamia and Babylon, to the citadels and places that lie most convenient; for I am persuaded that they will be well disposed guardians of our possessions, because of their piety toward God, and because I know that my predecessors have borne witness to them, that they are faithful, and with alacrity do what they are desired to do. I will, therefore, though it be a laborious work, that you remove these Jews; under a promise that they shall be permitted to use their own laws; and when you shall have brought them to the places before mentioned, you shall give everyone of their families a place for building their houses, and a portion of the land for their husbandry, and for the plantation of their vines; and you shall discharge them from paying taxes of the fruits of the earth for ten years; and let them have a proper quantity of wheat for the maintenance of their servants, until they receive grain out of the earth; also let a sufficient share be given to such as minister to them in the necessities of life, that by enjoying the effects of our humanity, they may show themselves the more willing and ready about our affairs. Take care likewise of that nation, as far as you are able, that they may not have any disturbance given them by anyone.' Now these testimonials which I have produced are sufficient to declare the friendship that Antiochus the Great bore to the Jews" (*Antiquities of the Jews* 12.148-153).[1]

Some Colossians commentators note how, even though there were Jews in the region of Phrygia and Lydia going back from much earlier, this group that was transplanted may have been the more immediate forbearers of any Jews in Colossae and the Lycus Valley, which either would have recognized Yeshua as Messiah[2]—or who would have errantly influenced the Colossian Believers.[3]

Seleucus IV did not rule as long as Antiochus the Great, but the Epitomist of 2 Maccabees certainly does issue some complimentary words of him. He remarks, "the kings themselves honored the place and glorified the temple

---

[1] Flavius Josephus: *The Works of Josephus: Complete and Unabridged*, trans. William Whiston (Peabody, MA: Hendrickson, 1987), pp 317-318.

[2] The gospel made it to Colossae via the preaching of Epaphras (Colossians 1:7), who presumably had heard it during Paul's tenure in the neighboring city of Ephesus (Acts 19:9-10).

[3] F.F. Bruce, *New International Commentary on the New Testament: The Epistles to the Colossians, to Philemon, and to the Ephesians* (Grand Rapids: Eerdmans, 1984), pp 8-13.

with the finest presents, so that even Seleucus, the king of Asia, defrayed from his own revenues all the expenses connected with the service of the sacrifices" (2 Maccabees 3:2-3, RSV). The Jewish nation by no means always had bad relations with the Seleucid Greek Empire. As long as they were allowed to worship in the way that the Torah required, things stayed somewhat cordial. Things may have not exactly been perfect, especially since the Babylonian exile—but having to pay tribute to a nearby great power was certainly better than another exile. The office of high priest may have become a political appointment that needed to be approved by a nearby governor or Seleucid monarch—but that was certainly preferable to having no Temple or priesthood.

Bad Relations that the Jews had with the Seleucids

The fact that Judea had become a vassal of the Seleucid Empire, with the high priesthood often up for sale to the highest bidder, meant that sooner or later things were going to get complicated. This is exactly what we see in the opening chapters of 2 Maccabees. The Epitomist records how a certain Simon had told the Seleucid governor Apollonius, that the Temple treasury "was full of untold sums of money" (2 Maccabees 3:6, RSV), which were being withheld from the royal tribute. While these funds were found out to be mainly in trust for widows and orphans (2 Maccabees 3:10), and via angelic intervention they were not stolen (2 Maccabees 3:22-30), a trend of incidents began. The high priest Onias was slandered by Simon (2 Maccabees 4:1-5), and so Onias goes to Apollonius and pleads how "without the king's attention public affairs could not again reach a peaceful settlement" (2 Maccabees 4:6, RSV)—with Simon actually being considered a threat to peace in the region.

When Antiochus Epiphanes succeeds his brother, King Seleucus, Onias' brother, Jason, "obtained the high priesthood by corruption" (2 Maccabees 4:7, RSV). Significant actions promoting Hellenism also are seen, with the founding of a gymnasium (presumably where men would train nude) and an order of Antiochenes (2 Maccabees 4:9). The author of 1 Maccabees considers these things to be considerable acts of renegade apostasy, describing,

"In those days certain renegades came out from Israel and misled many, saying, 'Let us go and make a covenant with the Gentiles around us, for since we separated from them many disasters have come upon us.' This proposal pleased them, and some of the people eagerly went to the king, who authorized them to observe the ordinances of the Gentiles. So they built a gymnasium in Jerusalem, according to Gentile custom, and removed the marks of circumcision, and abandoned the holy covenant. They joined with the Gentiles and sold themselves to do evil" (1 Maccabees 1:11-15, NRSV).

Take important notice of how these acts of Hellenism were willfully imposed by a corrupt high priest who wanted to curry favors with the

Seleucid Empire. Yet the corruption ran deeper, because when the high priest Jason sends Menelaus, a brother of the Simon who had informed Apollonius of the Temple treasury, to King Antiochus—he loses his high priesthood. The Epitomist of 2 Maccabees recounts, "But he, when presented to the king, extolled him with an air of authority, and secured the high priesthood for himself, outbidding Jason by three hundred talents of silver" (2 Maccabees 4:24, RSV). Menelaus is not at all a person whom the Epitomist of 2 Maccabees approves of, recognizing how he used his high priesthood to appropriate gold objects from the Temple for bribes, and then selling them for personal profit (2 Maccabees 4:32).

Onias, the previously respected and Torah-faithful high priest (2 Maccabees 3:1), now deposed from that office, makes his way to Antioch to protest the crimes Menelaus has committed (2 Maccabees 4:33). Antiochus Epiphanes is away putting down a rebellion in Tarsus and Mallus, and so Menelaus convinces his deputy, Andronicus, to have Onias put away—which he does (2 Maccabees 4:34-35). The murder of Onias, the former Jewish high priest, is met with a great deal of anger, so much so that "many also of other nations, were grieved and displeased at the unjust murder of the man" (2 Maccabees 4:35, RSV). When Antiochus returns, he is actually saddened, and has Andronicus humiliated, and then executed on the very spot where Onias was killed (2 Maccabees 4:37-38).

Simply because King Antiochus does briefly show a moment of human feeling, by no means is an indication that he was not an opportunistic leader. A mob scene takes place when Menelaus is away from the Temple in Jerusalem, caused by the sacrilege committed by his brother Lysimachus, creating a huge uproar among the people with Lysimachus himself killed near the Temple treasury (2 Maccabees 4:39-42). Charges are brought against Menelaus over this mob riot, when King Antiochus comes to Tyre (2 Maccabees 4:43-46). Yet as the Epitomist of 2 Maccabees says, "through the covetousness of them that were of power Menelaus remained still in authority, increasing in malice, and being a great traitor to the citizens" (2 Maccabees 4:50, KJV). The relationship that the Jewish nation has with the Seleucid Empire gets increasingly more difficult, due to bribery, corruption, and the desire for certain men to be in positions of power.

Preceding some of the events that we commemorate at *Chanukah*, visions of horsemen and soldiers had appeared over the skies of Judea (2 Maccabees 5:1-4), as Antiochus Epiphanes is overseeing his second invasion of Egypt. A rumor is circulated that he has fallen dead in battle, and so the deposed high priest Jason uses this as an opportunity to attack Jerusalem and retake his prior office (2 Maccabees 5:5-6). All that can be said is that he utterly failed, and then he has to flee—first to Egypt, and then onto Sparta, where he dies in exile (2 Maccabees 5:7-10).

What happens when there is all of this internal fighting and politicking among the Jews? First, Jewish religious leaders embrace various ungodly ways from Hellenism. Secondly, different men vie for the office of the high priest. And although not entirely unsuccessful in Egypt, Antiochus Epiphanes hears that Judea is in revolt, and he feels compelled to come and "intervene" in what is happening—asserting Seleucid Greek dominance.

Things Fought and Died For

After the failed attempt by Jason to reclaim his priesthood, Antiochus Epiphanes invades Jerusalem, kills many people, and then ransacks the Temple. Sadly enough, the high priest Menelaus is said to have actually collaborated with him, as Antiochus took a great spoil from the Temple:

"Not content with this, Antiochus dared to enter the most holy temple in all the world, guided by Menelaus, who had become a traitor both to the laws and to his country. He took the holy vessels with his polluted hands, and swept away with profane hands the votive offerings which other kings had made to enhance the glory and honor of the place" (2 Maccabees 5:15-16, RSV).

This was not the later, and much more serious defilement that the Maccabees would have to come and clean up—but just a matter of Antiochus Epiphanes wanting to demonstrate his supremacy, as well as make up for an unsuccessful military campaign elsewhere. Even though all Antiochus did here was steal a great deal of sacred objects (1 Maccabees 1:20-24), the Jews were absolutely distraught over it. The author of 1 Maccabees describes how there was great mourning and despair among the people:

"Taking them all, he departed to his own land. He committed deeds of murder, and spoke with great arrogance. Israel mourned deeply in every community, rulers and elders groaned, maidens and young men became faint, the beauty of women faded. Every bridegroom took up the lament; she who sat in the bridal chamber was mourning. Even the land shook for its inhabitants, and all the house of Jacob was clothed with shame" (1 Maccabees 1:24-28, RSV).

As terrible as this is, however, the Epitomist of 2 Maccabees observes how because of the sin present, this was considered to be rightful punishment from the Lord:

"But the Lord did not choose the nation for the sake of the holy place, but the place for the sake of the nation. Therefore the place itself shared in the misfortunes that befell the nation and afterward participated in its benefits; and what was forsaken in the wrath of the Almighty was restored again in all its glory when the great Lord became reconciled" (2 Maccabees 5:19-20, RSV).

Following this sacrilege, the author of 1 Maccabees further details how Jerusalem was transformed into a military citadel, where the Seleucid Greeks stationed "sinful people, lawless men" (1 Maccabees 1:34, RSV). Several years after the sacking of the Temple, Antiochus Epiphanes issues a decree that his entire kingdom "should be one people, and that each should give up his customs" (1 Maccabees 1:41, RSV). Many obey his orders (1 Maccabees 1:42), but the Jewish people would prove to be a very serious problem. This would require the Jews to give up various Torah practices, including the Temple sacrifices and worship (1 Maccabees 1:45a-b), the weekly Sabbath and appointed times (1 Maccabees 1:45c), they would have to build idolatrous idols and shrines (1 Maccabees 1:47), and they would have to leave their sons uncircumcised (1 Maccabees 1:48). The decree issued by Antiochus Epiphanes meant that the Jerusalem Temple would itself be desecrated. The author of 1 Maccabees, and the Epitomist of 2 Maccabees, describe what takes place from their two vantage points:

> "Now on the fifteenth day of Chislev, in the one hundred and forty-fifth year, they erected a desolating sacrilege upon the altar of burnt offering. They also built altars in the surrounding cities of Judah" (1 Maccabees 1:54, RSV).

> "Not long after this, the king sent an Athenian senator to compel the Jews to forsake the laws of their fathers and cease to live by the laws of God, and also to pollute the temple in Jerusalem and call it the temple of Olympian Zeus, and to call the one in Gerizim the temple of Zeus the Friend of Strangers, as did the people who dwelt in that place. Harsh and utterly grievous was the onslaught of evil. For the temple was filled with debauchery and reveling by the Gentiles, who dallied with harlots and had intercourse with women within the sacred precincts, and besides brought in things for sacrifice that were unfit. The altar was covered with abominable offerings which were forbidden by the laws. A man could neither keep the sabbath, nor observe the feasts of his fathers, nor so much as confess himself to be a Jew. On the monthly celebration of the king's birthday, the Jews were taken, under bitter constraint, to partake of the sacrifices; and when the feast of Dionysus came, they were compelled to walk in the procession in honor of Dionysus, wearing wreaths of ivy. At the suggestion of Ptolemy a decree was issued to the neighboring Greek cities, that they should adopt the same policy toward the Jews and make them partake of the sacrifices, and should slay those who did not choose to change over to Greek customs. One could see, therefore, the misery that had come upon them" (2 Maccabees 6:1-9, RSV).

Yeshua's later words to the moneychangers, "It is written, 'MY HOUSE SHALL BE CALLED A HOUSE OF PRAYER' [Isaiah 56:7]; but you are making it a ROBBERS' DEN [Jeremiah 7:11]" (Matthew 21:13, NASU; cf. Mark 11:17; Luke 19:46), on how people were being shortchanged—as serious as they were—

The Impact of the Maccabees on First Century Judaism

actually seem pretty light compared to what was going on a century-and-a-half earlier. When the decree of Antiochus Epiphanes was enacted, God's House *literally became* a whorehouse!

The considerable bulk of the Books of 1&2 Maccabees is spent detailing how Judah Maccabee and his brothers stood against what was happening, raising an army, and fighting against the Seleucid invaders of Judea. At *Chanukah*, we remember how they were able to cleanse and rededicate the Temple (1 Maccabees 4:36-59; 2 Maccabees 10:1-8). We rightfully commemorate their tenacity and sacrifice. **But do we really think about what they were fighting for?** We know they were fighting for the rights of the Jewish people, and for a religion based in God's Torah, to survive. But do we really understand how the Maccabees fought and died for the injustices delivered against normal, everyday Jews? These were people who did not allow themselves to be engulfed by the corruption of the different priests, or the decrees of the Seleucid Empire. They were people who loved God, obeyed God, and simply wanted to do what was required of God's chosen people.

There are a number of religious issues that are given attention in 1&2 Maccabees, for which the Jewish fighters, who followed Judah Maccabee, were willing to die. Antiochus Epiphanes' decree that the Jews should dismiss both God's Torah and their ancestral customs was very much designed to see them eventually assimilated into the religious and cultural milieu of his empire. You have probably already noticed how many of the Jews appearing in the Books of 1&2 Maccabees have Greek names.[4] But this would even go further—eventually because of Antiochus' polices *there was to be no recognizable Jewish people*. The identity of the Jewish people was understandably tied up in God's Torah and the Temple. And so, as the author of 1 Maccabees asserts, Antiochus Epiphanes wanted them to "forget the law and change all the ordinances" (1 Maccabees 1:49, RSV). If Jews in the Holy Land itself willingly gave up on God and the Temple, what would that signal? Could the Jewish people survive?

The overarching insult for any faithful Jew at the time would be to not only see the scrolls of God's holy Torah torn up and burned, but also people killed for obeying God's Law:

"The books of the law which they found they tore to pieces and burned with fire. Where the book of the covenant was found in the possession of any one, or if any one adhered to the law, the decree of the king condemned him to death" (1 Maccabees 1:56-57, RSV).

While it is easy for us to simply think of the Torah as being a spiritual document, describing how God wanted His people to live their lives in

---

[4] I.e., the Menelaus of fame was the estranged husband of Helen of Troy, and brother of King Agamemnon, from Homer's *Iliad*.

obedience to Him, the period of the Maccabees shows us how it very much became a national symbol—**perhaps mores than ever before**—of Jewish identity. Jews faithful to God could be rounded up and slaughtered if they obeyed His commandments, not turning their back on Him and worshipping the gods and goddesses of the Greeks. There are a number of specific areas of the Torah that are targeted by the Seleucid Greeks that needed to be put down, beyond just general obedience. Both 1&2 Maccabees record instances how various Jews were martyred because they refused to give into the decrees of a wicked king.

Circumcision

It is not difficult to see that circumcision is a major issue of importance to the time period of the Maccabees. Before the desecration of the Temple by the order of Antiochus Epiphanes, there were already Jewish men who "removed the marks of circumcision" (1 Maccabees 1:15, RSV). How did they do this? *IDB* observes, "When Hellenistic influence grew strong in Palestine, the Jews came into contact with Greeks who did not practice circumcision. Some Jews sought to overcome the effect of circumcision by epispasm, making foreskins for themselves."[5] According to Josephus, when the gymnasium had been established in Jerusalem, the Jewish men "hid the circumcision of their genitals, that even when they were naked they might appear to be Greeks" (*Antiquities of the Jews* 12.241).[6] The Apostle Paul, speaking of a Jewish man first being called to faith in Yeshua, says, "Let him not seek to remove the marks of circumcision" (1 Corinthians 7:18, NRSV).

Apparently in ancient times there did exist a (primitive) medical procedure that could remove the marks of circumcision. The verb *epispaō*, appearing in 1 Corinthians 7:18, can mean "**to pull the foreskin over the end of the penis**" (*BDAG*).[7] To the author of 1 Maccabees, Jewish men who would go through the hassle of having to stretch over and grow a new foreskin, "abandoned the holy covenant. They joined with the Gentiles and sold themselves to do evil" (1 Maccabees 1:15, RSV).

Even though there were Jewish men who abandoned the rite of circumcision, and were effectively considered traitors to God—the real attention in 1&2 Maccabees is given to those who continued to circumcise their sons. 1 Maccabees 1:60-61 describes the brutal murder of those who practiced circumcision: "According to the decree, they put to death the

---

[5] J.P. Hyatt, "Circumcision," in George Buttrick, ed., et. al., *The Interpreter's Dictionary of the Bible*, 4 vols. (Nashville: Abingdon, 1962), 1:629.

[6] *The Works of Josephus: Complete and Unabridged*, 323.

[7] Frederick William Danker, ed., et. al., *A Greek-English Lexicon of the New Testament and Other Early Christian Literature*, third edition (Chicago: University of Chicago Press, 2000), 380.

women who had their children circumcised, and their families and those who circumcised them; and they hung the infants from their mothers' necks" (RSV). 2 Maccabees 6:10 further says, "two women were brought in for having circumcised their children. These women they publicly paraded about the city, with their babies hung at their breasts, then hurled them down headlong from the wall" (RSV). For simply obeying the Torah's requirement that male children be circumcised (Leviticus 12:3), these women were murdered as criminals against the state.

So serious was this to the Maccabees, that when Mattathias, Judah Maccabee's father, begins his campaign with those "who offered [themselves] willingly for the law" (1 Maccabees 2:42, RSV)—they not only smash down idolatrous shrines, but they also see that uncircumcised Jewish boys are promptly circumcised:

"And Mattathias and his friends went about and tore down the altars; they forcibly circumcised all the uncircumcised boys that they found within the borders of Israel" (1 Maccabees 2:45-46, RSV).

Circumcision became an issue that the Maccabean Jews considered to be one worth dying for, especially if Jewish women were unjustly murdered by the Seleucid regime for only obeying God.

Keeping the Sabbath

Another major sign, of Jewish apostasy against the Torah, is considered to be how "Many even from Israel...profaned the sabbath" (1 Maccabees 1:43, RSV). While a Creation ordinance (Genesis 2:2-3; Exodus 20:9, 11), the Sabbath was also to be a special sign of how God led the Ancient Israelites out of slavery from Egypt (Deuteronomy 5:15), and how His people could now rest one day each week, being free. Keeping the Sabbath was an integral part of obedience to God, and so it is not at all surprising how when faithful Jews continued to keep the Sabbath—in spite of Antiochus' decrees against it— they often died. 1 Maccabees 2:31-38 records an incident of how many Jews, who had fled into hiding, were slaughtered because they refused to defend themselves on the Sabbath:

"And it was reported to the king's officers, and to the troops in Jerusalem the city of David, that men who had rejected the king's command had gone down to the hiding places in the wilderness. Many pursued them, and overtook them; they encamped opposite them and prepared for battle against them on the sabbath day. And they said to them, 'Enough of this! Come out and do what the king commands, and you will live.' But they said, 'We will not come out, nor will we do what the king commands and so profane the sabbath day.' Then the enemy hastened to attack them. But they did not answer them or hurl a stone at them or block up their hiding places, for they said, 'Let us all die in our innocence; heaven and earth testify for us that you are killing us unjustly.' So they attacked them on the sabbath, and they died, with their wives and children and cattle, to the number of a thousand persons" (RSV).

The soldiers who tracked these people down actually gave them the option of recanting on their convictions, letting them keep their lives. These faithful Jews retorted back that they would not profane the Sabbath, and so they were attacked and were killed. When Mattathias and the other Maccabees heard of this "they mourned for them deeply" (1 Maccabees 2:39, RSV), recognizing how they died for their piety. Yet at the same time, acknowledging the severe gravity of the circumstances, the Maccabees all agreed that if they were attacked on the Sabbath, that they would defend themselves, lest their entire cause be lost:

"And each said to his neighbor: 'If we all do as our brethren have done and refuse to fight with the Gentiles for our lives and for our ordinances, they will quickly destroy us from the earth.' So they made this decision that day: 'Let us fight against every man who comes to attack us on the sabbath day; let us not all die as our brethren died in their hiding places'" (1 Maccabees 2:40-41, RSV).

Today in Judaism, because of examples like this, it is considered appropriate to violate any ritual commandment—save committing idolatry—to save a life. This is why in modern Israel, the military, police, and doctors, can all work on *Shabbat*. The historical record does include a reference to how, when faced with an opposing force, the Maccabees did fight on the Sabbath (1 Maccabees 9:43-49). At the same time, the Maccabees' faithfulness to the Torah is recognized, in that they did keep the Sabbath when they could (2 Maccabees 8:24-29).

The record in 2 Maccabees similarly describes how the holy institution of the Sabbath was turned against the Jews. In the two-year time period between Antiochus Epiphanes' ransacking of the Temple, and his later decree for all to Hellenize which saw the Temple defiled, an Apollonius, captain of some Mysian mercenaries, came to inflict considerable damage on the people (2 Maccabees 5:24). The Epitomist describes how he waited for the Sabbath, when the Jews would not be working, to attack:

"When this man arrived in Jerusalem, he pretended to be peaceably disposed and waited until the holy sabbath day; then, finding the Jews not at work, he ordered his men to parade under arms. He put to the sword all those who came out to see them, then rushed into the city with his armed men and killed great numbers of people" (2 Maccabees 5:25-26, RSV).

The Epitomist also records how, along with the women who were murdered for circumcising their sons, "Others who had assembled in the caves near by, to observe the seventh day secretly, were betrayed to Philip and were all burned together, because their piety kept them from defending themselves, in view of their regard for that most holy day" (2 Maccabees 5:11, RSV). In

The Impact of the Maccabees on First Century Judaism

the later fighting against Nicanor, occurring after the rededication of the Temple but still in a tenuous time, Nicanor mocks the Jews among his army who ask him to remember the Sabbath day:

"When Nicanor heard that Judas and his men were in the region of Samaria, he made plans to attack them with complete safety on the day of rest. And when the Jews who were compelled to follow him said, 'Do not destroy so savagely and barbarously, but show respect for the day which he who sees all things has honored and hallowed above other days,' the thrice-accursed wretch asked if there were a sovereign in heaven who had commanded the keeping of the sabbath day. And when they declared, 'It is the living Lord himself, the Sovereign in heaven, who ordered us to observe the seventh day,' he replied, 'And I am a sovereign also, on earth, and I command you to take up arms and finish the king's business.' Nevertheless, he did not succeed in carrying out his abominable design" (2 Maccabees 15:1-6, RSV).

Suffice it to say, it is not difficult to see how important the Sabbath would become to later Jewish generations—including the imposition of many extra-Biblical rulings and regulations designed to protect its sanctity. Since people departing from Sabbath remembrance was believed to be a partial cause of Antiochus' desecration, guarding the Sabbath would have to be enacted to see that a catastrophe would not take place again. While some of the Rabbinical views of guarding the Sabbath might go overboard here or there (m.*Shabbat* 7:2), we should at least understand *why* such regulations would be formulated.

Eating Pork

One of the most significant, yet elusive features, of Jewish culture to many outsiders, is in understanding why many religious Jews are adamant about not eating pork. While the Torah does say that the pig is unclean, both Leviticus 11 and Deuteronomy 14 also list other animals that are unclean. The only reason why the pig is considered unclean is "because it divides the hoof but *does* not *chew* the cud." Also to be noted is "You shall not eat any of their flesh nor touch their carcasses" (Deuteronomy 14:8, NASU; cf. Leviticus 11:7). But other than these regulations, what makes the pig so detestable to religious Jews? It all goes back to the Maccabean period, and how the Seleucid Greeks sacrificed pigs in the sacred precincts of the Temple (1 Maccabees 1:47).

But sacrificing swine and other unfit animals on the altar in the Temple is only a part of the problem. The Epitomist of 2 Maccabees records two examples of people who were murdered by the authorities because they refused to eat pork. The first, a scribe named Eleazar, was an old man willing to give up his life rather than eat pork:

"Eleazar, one of the scribes in high position, a man now advanced in age and of noble presence, was being forced to open his mouth to eat swine's flesh. But he, welcoming death with honor rather than life with pollution, went up to the rack of his own accord, spitting out the flesh, as men ought to go who have the courage to refuse things that it is not right to taste, even for the natural love of life" (2 Maccabees 6:18-20, RSV).

Eleazar's colleagues actually urged him to just pretend to eat pork, so that he might save his life in the process, but he refused (2 Maccabees 6:21-23). He responded to them, "Such pretense is not worthy of our time of life...lest many of the young should suppose that Eleazar in his ninetieth year has gone over to an alien religion" (2 Maccabees 6:24, RSV). He further said, "For even if for the present I should avoid the punishment of men, yet whether I live or die I shall not escape the hands of the Almighty" (2 Maccabees 6:26, RSV). And so for not eating pork, Eleazar went to the rack and was martyred (2 Maccabees 6:28-31).

The second, and by far most serious scene of not eating pork, is witnessed in 2 Maccabees 7. Seven brothers are taken before their mother, and with Antiochus Epiphanes present, each one of them is tested as to whether he will "partake of unlawful swine's flesh" (2 Maccabees 7:1, RSV). 2 Maccabees 7 summarizes how each one of the brothers defiantly refuses to give in, facing a painful death. They appeal to the God of Israel as their final Vindicator, and how they will each be resurrected into the new world He will one day inaugurate. The mother who has had to watch all of this too dies, and all the Epitomist can say afterward is, "Let this be enough, then, about the eating of sacrifices and the extreme tortures" (2 Maccabees 7:42, RSV).

The horror of thinking about Torah-faithful Jews being tortured, and dying, for not eating pork, is not something that goes away easily. (And recall here how we are dealing with the broad Biblical period, not Jews during the Middle Ages being forced to convert to Christianity by Roman Catholicism, and then forced to eat pork as a sign of loyalty.) Later in 2 Maccabees, following the death of Antiochus Epiphanes, and as his son Antiochus V becomes king, attempts are made (albeit temporarily) to patch up relations with the Jewish nation. A letter is sent from the new King Antiochus to the Jewish leaders, and permission is extended "for the Jews to enjoy their own food and laws, just as formerly" (2 Maccabees 11:31, RSV). For a very brief moment, the Seleucid Greek leaders recognized that forcing the Jews to give up the Torah was a foolish errand. They also recognized how important it was for the Jews to follow their kosher dietary laws, and that by forcing people to eat pork—it only made the Jews hate them even more.

The Impact of the Maccabees on First Century Judaism

New Theology from the Greeks, or Old Theology for Inspiration?

Today's New Testament theologians recognize that understanding the period of the Maccabees is extremely important for understanding Judaism in the First Century C.E. It is quite easy to see how the Maccabean crisis, where the Jewish people faced religious and cultural extermination, would leave a significant mark on succeeding generations, and with it a general suspicion of anyone outside of the Jewish community (discussed further). Yet we also cannot overlook the fact that some of today's interpreters argue that the time period of the Maccabees reflects a significant change in Jewish theology—in particular when it comes to beliefs and convictions that you and I probably hold quite dear to us. Consider the words of George Robinson's *Essential Judaism*:

> "Belief in the resurrection of the dead, a key element in traditionally observant Judaism's vision of the Messianic age, dates from the period of the Pharisees, and may be an outgrowth of Greek or Persian influence. . .According to at least one Jewish historian. . .the idea of resurrection of the dead gained its first currency at the time of the Maccabees, around the second century B.C.E., a period of great suffering for the Jews. In the face of such trauma. . .the notion of another life after death promised a final, cosmic release."[8]

It is correct that in the Apostolic Scriptures, the Pharisees are known for their staunch belief in the resurrection of the dead (i.e., Acts 23:6), but did this view originate entirely from the period of the Maccabees?

Liberal theologians commonly argue that the doctrine of resurrection was not fully developed until the time period of the Maccabees, and it is thus a rather late import to Judaism, not really being witnessed to in the Tanach (Old Testament). It is absolutely undeniable that for the martyrs of 2 Maccabees 7, the resurrection played an important reason in why they willingly gave up their lives. In the future, they would be resurrected and would enter into a new world that their tormenters would not be permitted to enter:

> **the second brother:** "And when he was at his last breath, he said, 'You accursed wretch, you dismiss us from this present life, but the King of the universe will raise us up to an everlasting renewal of life, because we have died for his laws'" (2 Maccabees 7:9, RSV).

---

[8] George Robinson, *Essential Judaism: A Complete Guide to Beliefs, Customs, and Rituals* (New York: Pocket Books, 2000), 192.

the fourth brother: "And when he was near death, he said, 'One cannot but choose to die at the hands of men and to cherish the hope that God gives of being raised again by him. But for you there will be no resurrection to life!'" (2 Maccabees 7:14, RSV).

the mother: "Therefore the Creator of the world, who shaped the beginning of man and devised the origin of all things, will in his mercy give life and breath back to you again, since you now forget yourselves for the sake of his laws" (2 Maccabees 7:23, RSV).

It would seem rather difficult to argue that the concept of resurrection was imported from Hellenistic philosophy, because even though there were diverse Greek views about the afterlife (including no afterlife and just oblivion), classic Platonic philosophy argued that death involved the permanent separation of the soul from the body.[9] No future recomposition of a disembodied human consciousness, with a resurrected and restored body, was to take place according to these Hellenists. Many Greeks, and likewise Romans, looked forward to death, and rather than their bodies being buried with respect in anticipation of a future resurrection, they were often cremated and thrown away as though they were garbage.

Was the concept of resurrection a late import to Judaism, popularized during the Maccabean period? No. The Tanach itself does speak of the resurrection. Isaiah 26:19 declares, "Your dead will live; their corpses will rise. you who lie in the dust, awake and shout for joy, for your dew *is as* the dew of the dawn, and the earth will give birth to the departed spirits" (NASU). In the dry bones prophecy of Ezekiel 37:6, the Lord declares to a restored Israel "I will put sinews on you, make flesh grow back on you, cover you with skin and put breath in you that you may come alive" (NASU). And the famed Daniel 12:2 says, "Many of those who sleep in the dust of the ground will awake, these to everlasting life, but the others to disgrace *and* everlasting contempt" (NASU).

If one holds to Isaiah, Ezekiel, and Daniel all including genuine prophecies of authentic prophets who bore these names, it should not be difficult to see how belief in the resurrection was *not* a late import into Judaism from the Maccabean period. **From the Tanach, the Maccabean martyrs would have known that their deaths were not in vain.** They would one day be resurrected into a new world, where God's peace and justice reigned supreme,

---

[9] In the words of Socrates, Plato's predecessor from the Fifth Century B.C.E.,

"Death, as it seems to me, happens to be nothing other than the separation of two things, the soul and the body, from each other. When, therefore, they are separated from each other, each of them is in a condition not much worse than when the human being was alive, and the body has its own nature" (*Gorgias* 524b; Plato: *Gorgias*, trans., James H. Nichols, Jr. [Ithaca and London: Cornell University, 1998], 125).

something that their captors would not experience. Yet liberal theologians, in varying degrees, have all dated Isaiah, Ezekiel, and most especially Daniel, rather late. Furthermore, rather than speaking of a future resurrection of righteous individuals, the above prophecies are frequently allegorized, believed to only be speaking of the corporate restoration of Israel.

A much longer account of the seven brothers being martyred is seen in 4 Maccabees chs. 8-12. Interjected into the narrative is a great deal of philosophizing about their faithfulness. Nothing is stated that would contradict the emphasis in 2 Maccabees about the resurrection, but what is added to what they say concerns what happens immediately after death. The seven brothers are portrayed as eagerly waiting to die, taunting Antiochus Epiphanes with these words:

"For we, through this severe suffering and endurance, shall have the prize of virtue and shall be with God, for whom we suffer; but you, because of your bloodthirstiness toward us, will deservedly undergo from the divine justice eternal torment by fire" (4 Maccabees 9:8-9, RSV).

When the seventh brother prepares to die, he tells King Antiochus, "on you he will take vengeance both in this present life and when you are dead" (4 Maccabees 12:18, RSV). When observations are made of the seven brothers' death, it is simply asserted, "For if we so die, Abraham and Isaac and Jacob will welcome us, and all the fathers will praise us" (4 Maccabees 13:17, RSV). These sentiments all point to a belief in some kind of conscious, disembodied state immediately after death. The righteous will experience some kind of time in a Paradise (cf. Luke 23:43), and the unrighteous will experience some kind of punishment, culminating in an eternal torment. The seven brothers who were martyred knew that after death, they would be welcomed into something wonderful, something that King Antiochus would never be able to experience.

Similar to how liberal theologians will argue that belief in the resurrection was late and is not found in the Tanach, so do they conclude that a belief in an intermediate afterlife prior to the resurrection is also a late import from the Maccabean period. Quite contrary to this, though, the Tanach does allude to an existence for the deceased in *Sheol*, the location of which is often contrasted to be as low in the cosmic spectrum, as Heaven being the realm of God, is high in the cosmic spectrum (Deuteronomy 32:22; Isaiah 7:11).[10] The Torah forbids the Ancient Israelites from consulting spiritists and mediums (Leviticus 19:31; 20:6; cf. Isaiah 8:19-20), which very much presupposes that the consciousness of a human person can exist separate from the body. The

---

[10] *Sheol* is not the same as the grave, as a burial place or tomb in Hebrew is a *qever*. The Greek LXX and NT equivalent of *Sheol* is *Hadēs*, whereas in contrast the word for a burial place or tomb would be *mnēma*.

spirit of Samuel came to taunt King Saul, prior to his defeat (1 Samuel 28:13-15). And, the King of Babylon is actually greeted by other fallen kings, as he enters into Sheol after his death (Isaiah 14:9-11, 18-20).

Without getting into the much larger debate over what takes place between death and resurrection, suffice it to say the Tanach gives ample clues that some kind of temporary, disembodied, post-mortem state, is to be expected for people. The belief in an intermediate afterlife, affirmed by the Jewish Pharisees of the First Century C.E. (Josephus *Antiquities of the Jews* 18.14), by no means had to come as a late import during the Maccabean era—even if ultimately resurrection into a restored Kingdom of God on Earth is to be expected.

The Holy Scriptures teach that a redeemed person's salvation will not be fully consummated until the resurrection, when the human consciousness and human body will be entirely restored (Romans 8:22-23). This is an affirmation that the human being is different from the animal creation, being made in God's image (Genesis 1:26-27), and being partially made of another dimension. An intermediate, disembodied afterlife attended by a future resurrection runs completely contrary to Platonic Greek philosophy, because a Biblical worldview sees the physical Creation as ultimately good. Even if a Believer is to enter into the presence of the Lord at time of death (2 Corinthians 5:8; Philippians 1:23), such a disembodied condition is only a temporary time until the resurrection (Philippians 3:21).

If one is tempted to think that the doctrine of an intermediate afterlife prior to resurrection, originated exclusively from Jewish interactions with the Greeks—he or she really needs to consider the source from which such sentiments originate. Do the teachings of Holy Scripture, something which we believe to be inspired by God's Spirit via the hands of human beings, not ultimately come from God? Or is Holy Scripture *entirely* the product of human beings interacting with other human beings—including copying off mythology—adopting it for the sake of the Supreme Being? I say this only to warn you that as important as it is to understand the period of the Maccabees, many liberal theologians and interpreters will consider this to be a time of significant change for ancient Judaism—**and you need not be caught thinking that ultimately, Yeshua the Messiah resurrected from the dead, is some kind of "Greek" concept.**

The Torah and Establishing God's True Israel
—and the Maccabean Priesthood

When reviewing the complicated events that transpired in the Maccabean crisis, we need to seriously consider putting ourselves in the place of the Maccabees. If we had seen it mandated by law that it was illegal for us to

The Impact of the Maccabees on First Century Judaism

worship God, how would we respond? Many, if not most of us, would "head for the hills" and escape. But in the case of the Maccabees, they stood their ground and fought against it.

The rallying cry for battle by Mattathias was, "Let every one who is zealous for the law and supports the covenant come out with me!" (1 Maccabees 1:27, RSV). The Torah became every bit as much a **national symbol** as it did a religious symbol for the Maccabees. Those who were loyal to the Torah, were loyal to God *and* they were loyal to Israel.

Several of the usages of "Israel" or "Israelites," appearing in 1 Maccabees, have an undeniable nationalistic tenor to them. The Seleucids "drove Israel into hiding in every place of refuge they had" (1 Maccabees 1:53, RSV) and "They kept using violence against Israel" (1 Maccabees 1:58, RSV). The resolve was that "many in Israel stood firm" (1 Maccabees 1:62, RSV), and of those who were loyal that "Many from Israel came to" the Maccabees (1 Maccabees 2:16, RSV), assembling "mighty warriors of Israel" (1 Maccabees 2:42, RSV), and how they all "gladly fought for Israel" (1 Maccabees 3:2, RSV). We see that "the Gentiles in Gilead gathered together against the Israelites who lived in their territory" (1 Maccabees 5:9, RSV), but then after being defeated "Judas gathered together all the Israelites in Gilead" (1 Maccabees 5:45, RSV), leading them to safety. Other usages of "Israel, from a cursory reading of 1 Maccabees, are likely reflective of how t"he Jews in the Maccabean period were fighting as the covenant people of God, formed at Mount Sinai. There is a definite rhetorical effect of being "Israel" in various places, and of who is loyal to God—something that goes beyond ethnicity.

2 Maccabees too reflects on how the Torah became a symbol of national identity for the Jewish people during this period of crisis. The Epitomist writes how when defeated, Nicanor had to recognize, "that the Jews had a Defender, and that therefore the Jews were invulnerable, because they followed the laws ordained by him" (2 Maccabees 8:36, RSV).

As the Torah took on a very nationalistic role during this period, it is also difficult to avoid how the Maccabees themselves took on a very prominent political role. The Maccabean movement started out initially to oppose the persecution and intended Hellenization of the Jews, so that the Torah—and most especially worship of the One True God—would be preserved. Yet after the rededication of the Temple, the Maccabean movement shifted to wanting to impose a political order, an Israel independent from the neighboring powers. Some people, reviewing the historical record of 1 Maccabees, are very uncomfortable with seeing how the Maccabees took over direct oversight of the office of high priest. Furthermore, some of those same people believe that it is inappropriate for us to honor *Chanukah*, because they think that a non-Levitical priesthood is totally contrary to the intent of the Torah. They overlook some important things.

Prior to the desecration of the Temple ordered by Antiochus, the office of high priest was already something that had to be approved by the Seleucid monarch. The opening chapters of 2 Maccabees show how different people vied for the position of high priest—some being loyal to the Torah, and others being opportunists. Inevitably in this environment, men of non-Levitical descent would become high priest. And the larger issue of—Can we even have a high priest and Temple?—cannot be overlooked. This is where a simplistic interpretation of the events will not suffice for us.

Because of the corruption that had been allowed to fester, which included the high priest Menelaus *helping* Antiochus Epiphanes loot the Temple (2 Maccabees 5:15), it is very easy to see why the Maccabees thought it significant to impose a kind of military government, and see that the old Jewish leadership be replaced with a new Jewish leadership and priesthood. The Maccabees themselves (Jonathan, Simon, and John) becoming "priests" actually did have a basis in prior history, because their father Mattathias, is recorded as being "the son of John, son of Simeon, a priest of the sons of Joarib" (1 Maccabees 2:1, RSV; cf. 14:29). "Mattathias' family might have been a prominent one, since it is so described in 1 Macc 2:17 and because it belonged to the order of Jehoiarib, which is the first in the priestly orders' list in 1 Chr 24:7" (*ABD*).[11] Assuming that Mattathias was indeed a legitimate descendant of a recognized priestly line, it would not be inappropriate for his two sons and grandson—in some capacity—to serve as either priests or caretaker priests.

Looking at the two sons and grandson of Mattathias, who serve as priests, what do they actually do? Alexander, one of the men vying for control of the Seleucid throne, writes a letter to Jonathan, brother of the late Judah Maccabee. He says, "'We have heard about you, that you are a mighty warrior and worthy to be our friend. And so we have appointed you today to be the high priest of your nation; you are to be called the king's friend' (and he sent him a purple robe and a golden crown) 'and you are to take our side and keep friendship with us'" (1 Maccabees 10:19-20, RSV). While Jonathan being high priest certainly had political ramifications, as it is said that in attaining this office, "he recruited troops and equipped them with arms in abundance" (1 Maccabees 10:21b, RSV), it also had spiritual ramifications: "Jonathan put on the holy garments in the seventh month of the one hundred and sixtieth year, at the feast of tabernacles" (1 Maccabees 10:21a, RSV).

---

[11] Uriel Rappaport, "Mattathias," in David Noel Freedman, ed., *Anchor Bible Dictionary*, 6 vols. (New York: Doubleday, 1992), 4:615.
  This entry, from a largely liberal encyclopedia, does go on to say: "Yet we may suspect some effort on the part of our sources to promote the status of the Hasmoneans" (Ibid.).

The Impact of the Maccabees on First Century Judaism

The focus of the author of 1 Maccabees, though, is more on the political, rather than spiritual function, of Jonathan as high priest. Later in his record, Jewish diplomats go to the Roman Senate, telling them, "Jonathan the high priest and the Jewish nation have sent us to renew the former friendship and alliance with them" (1 Maccabees 12:3, RSV). Likewise, in a letter Jonathan writes to the Spartans, he says, "Jonathan the high priest, the senate of the nation, the priests, and the rest of the Jewish people..." (1 Maccabees 12:6, RSV).

After Jonathan is killed, his brother Simon takes over in the role of high priest. When the people know that a successor is to be chosen, they declare "You are our leader in place of Judas and Jonathan your brother" (1 Maccabees 13:8, RSV), indicating that the role of high priest has become more political than spiritual. Later in the record, King Demetrius writes to Simon, with the opening greeting, "King Demetrius to Simon, the high priest and friend of kings, and to the elders and nation of the Jews, greeting" (1 Maccabees 13:36, RSV). Simon's role as a political leader can be seen later when "the yoke of the Gentiles was removed from Israel...the people began to write in their documents and contracts, 'In the first year of Simon the great high priest and commander and leader[12] of the Jews'" (1 Maccabees 13:41-42, RSV). The role of Simon as a political high priest is also seen in the narrative of what occurs when the Romans and Spartans hear of Jonathan's death: "they heard that Simon his brother had become high priest in his place, and that he was ruling over the country and the cities in it" (1 Maccabees 14:17, RSV).

There is no significant record in 1 Maccabees of either Jonathan or Simon really performing priestly duties, as much as them exercising political power and diplomacy. We could wonder if these two men really did take on the daily religious tasks of high priest, or instead served more as overseers and caretakers of the office of "high priest"—not too dissimilar to how today the British monarch is considered to be head of the Church of England, and "defender of the faith," even though the current Queen plays no role in the determination of religious policy. When King David took over Jerusalem, "Benaiah the son of Jehoiada was over the Cherethites and the Pelethites; and David's sons were chief ministers" (2 Samuel 8:18, NASU) or "priests" (RSV).[13] This indicates, at least in a titular capacity, that King David probably inherited the role originally possessed by the figure Melchizedek, king of Salem (Genesis 14:18-20). So with this in mind, Jonathan and Simon serving as high priest may have had a more titular role. And such a titular role would

---

[12] Grk. *archiereōs megalou kai stratēgou kai hēgoumenou*; "eminent high priest, commander-in-chief and ethnarch" (New Jerusalem Bible).

[13] Heb. *kohanim hayu*.

have been very important—because of all the corruption that had preceded them, **and how what the Maccabees fought for need not have been lost.**

The last major figure to occupy the office of high priest is John, the son of Simon, making him the grandson of Mattathias. We do not see that much of him in 1 Maccabees, as he enters in at the close of the book. What we do see is fairly positive, as the author says, "The rest of the acts of John and his wars and the brave deeds which he did, and the building of the walls which he built, and his achievements, behold, they are written in the chronicles of his high priesthood, from the time that he became high priest after his father" (1 Maccabees 16:23-24, RSV). This John, while attested to have been supported by the people "because of the benefits they had received from his father" (Josephus *Antiquities of the Jews* 13.229),[14] was not altogether popular with the people, particularly in actions that he took when Jerusalem was later attacked and had to submit again to the Seleucid Empire. Yet later in history, John Hyrcanus did achieve full independence for the Jewish nation, and saw its influence increase.[15]

Prejudices to Overcome

The Jewish people have always had enemies who have wanted to destroy them. Simply read the Book of Esther, and see how there have been people who have wanted to wipe the Jews from off the face of the Earth. But the Maccabean crisis was a rather unique one, insomuch that a tyrannical king actually wanted to see the Jewish people wiped out via cultural and religious assimilation, a far more insidious form of destruction than just exterminating them by killing. He saw that the Jerusalem Temple was defiled, and that those who followed God's Torah—circumcising their sons, keeping the Sabbath, and even eating kosher—be put to death. While things later returned to some level of normalcy for your average Jew, with the Temple cleansed and with people permitted once again to keep God's Law, **memories of these events are not at all to be forgotten.** So serious is the period of the Maccabees for the Jewish people, that one cannot blame the later Jews of the First Century for not only being suspicious, *but even a bit paranoid*, when it came to interacting with other people. This was especially true of any outsider who expressed some kind of belief in the God of Israel, connecting themselves to the Jewish community.

How significant an impact did the Maccabees leave on First Century Judaism? Because the Books of the Maccabees are a part of the historical record, and not a part of the Protestant canon, too many of today's

---

[14] *The Works of Josephus: Complete and Unabridged*, 350.
[15] "John Hyrcanus," in Jacob Neusner and William Scott Green, eds., *Dictionary of Judaism in the Biblical Period* (Peabody, MA: Hendrickson, 2002), 337.

The Impact of the Maccabees on First Century Judaism

evangelical Christian Bible readers fail to even know about what the Jewish people had undergone prior to the arrival of Yeshua and the missionary endeavors of the Apostles. Not enough of today's Believers understand the nationalistic role that Torah had taken, precisely because of the injustices decreed by Antiochus Epiphanes, and how many Jews fought and died for God's Law. The crisis of the Maccabean period would very much be remembered by First Century Jews, and then compounded with more recent history as the Roman Empire had expanded, engulfing Judea in the process.

One of the most significant Rabbinical sentiments seen in the Mishnah, which would have guided a great deal of Jewish identity in the First Century C.E., is "All Israelites have a share in the world to come" (m.*Sanhedrin* 10:1).[16] With some exceptions, what this would equate to is that all ethnic Jews were believed to be granted an inheritance in the future age simply because they were born Jewish. If an outsider wanted to participate in the future resurrection age, then that person had to become a part of the covenant people. And for many of the Jewish leaders of the First Century, that process began with circumcision—but not so much circumcision as a medical procedure—as much as *ritual proselyte circumcision.*

In too many cases, this kind of circumcision took precedence to people entering into covenant with God first on the basis of *faith in Him*. The Biblical pattern seen in the Torah is that the Patriarch Abraham first believed in God, and was then circumcised at a later point in time (Romans 4:9-11; cf. Genesis 15:6). Even though God-fearers were allowed on the outside of the Synagogue, as they expressed some belief in the God of Israel and accepted a basic Torah morality, I. Howard Marshall notes that "such people were regarded as still pagans by the Jews in Palestine, [although] there appears to have been a more liberal attitude in the Dispersion."[17] Only proselytes who had undergone ritual circumcision would not be considered fully "pagan," or at least not treated with a high degree of suspicion.

Was not the need to be circumcised based on Torah passages such as Genesis 17:9, 14, which insisted "Now as for you, you shall keep My covenant, you and your descendants after you throughout their generations...But an uncircumcised male who is not circumcised in the flesh of his foreskin, that person shall be cut off from his people; he has broken My covenant" (NASU)? To Jews of the First Century C.E. the need to be circumcised in order to stand in covenant with God was absolute. Yet this was an unbalanced reading of the Torah, because earlier in Genesis 15:6, because of Abraham's trust in the

---

[16] Jacob Neusner, trans., *The Mishnah: A New Translation* (New Haven and London: Yale University Press, 1988), 604.

[17] I. Howard Marshall, *Tyndale New Testament Commentaries: Acts* (Grand Rapids: Eerdmans, 1980), pp 183-184.

Almighty, "He reckoned it to him as righteousness" (NASU)—a covenant status noted *before* Abraham was circumcised. **Belief in God always precedes the sign of the covenant,** something that many Jews in the First Century C.E. had overlooked.

It is not at all difficult, though, to see why many First Century Jews would have had an unbalanced reading of the Torah. In lieu of the Maccabean crisis and the illegalization of circumcision by the Greek Seleucids on threat of death, the Jewish religious establishment deemed that circumcision for proselytes was *the only* viable way for an outsider attracted to the God of Israel to be considered a full member of the Jewish community. Josephus expresses the opinion that the reason God gave Abraham circumcision was "in order to keep his posterity unmixed with others" (*Antiquities of the Jews* 1.192).[18] To the Jewish person of the First Century, a non-Jew undergoing circumcision was going to do more than lose his foreskin—he was going to become one with an ethnic people in a very significant, physical, and visible way. James D.G. Dunn further describes,

"The Maccabean crisis simply reinforced the teaching of Genesis that circumcision was a 'make or break' issue for Jews; insistence on circumcision was integral to the emergence of 'Judaism'...The position, then, was simple for most Jews: only the circumcised were Jews; only the circumcised were members of the covenant; only the circumcised belonged to the people chosen by God to be his own."[19]

Having once faced religious and cultural assimilation by the decrees of Antiochus Epiphanes, any outsider wishing to become a member of the Jewish community, would be subject to some extreme scrutiny. Ritual proselyte circumcision would only reckon one a full member of God's covenant people, requiring a convert to take a significant step in recognizing the God of Israel as one's single Deity to worship.[20]

Was ritual proselyte circumcision as *the main* process for one being considered a member of God's covenant—often over and against faith in God—a direct result of Jewish paranoia stemming from the Maccabean period? What we can detect is that the Maccabean period stirred an entire array of important social and political changes among the Jewish people, that

---

[18] *The Works of Josephus: Complete and Unabridged*, 40.

[19] James D.G. Dunn, *Black's New Testament Commentary: The Epistle to the Galatians* (Peabody, MA: Hendrickson, 1993), 96.

[20] Also not to be overlooked is the erection of a barrier wall in the Second Temple complex (cf. Ephesians 2:14-15), separating the inner sanctuary from the so-called Court of the Gentiles. Those who passed unauthorized were threatened with death (Josephus *Antiquities of the Jews* 15.417; *Jewish War* 5.194). This ran entirely contrary to the House of God being a place for all nations to stream toward (1 Kings 8:41-43; Isaiah 56:6-7.

would later affect the mission of the Apostles and the early controversies the First Century *ekklēsia* would face.

Some theologians today conclude that the Jewish people felt threatened by external forces, beginning with the Seleucid Greek invasion of the 160s B.C.E. all the way to the Roman occupation of Judea. In the 40s C.E.—when the gospel started significantly going out to the nations—an entire series of events helped fuel Jewish xenophobia toward Greeks and Romans, including (but by no means limited to): Caligula insisting that a statue of himself be set up in the Jerusalem Temple (40 C.E.), a series of poor Roman governors and administrators (44-46 C.E.), and the demand that the vestments of the high priest be held for safekeeping by the Romans (Josephus *Antiquities of the Jews* 20.1-9). When we add to this the challenges caused by the Zealot movement, and increasingly disparate relations with Rome—at the very least we see that Jews would often want to remain constrained to themselves and limited in their contact with others.

The xenophobia that many First Century Jews had toward outsiders was also compounded with some of the common views that those same outsiders had toward Judaism. While written near the end of the First Century C.E., the Roman historian Tacitus makes some very anti-Semitic remarks, which could have easily been shared by many of the Greeks and Romans in the Apostles' era. The following is a fair summary of the social anti-Semitism present:

> "Whatever their origin, these observances are sanctioned by their antiquity. The other practices of the Jews are sinister and revolting, and have entrenched themselves by their very wickedness. Wretches of the most abandoned kind who had no use for the religion of their fathers took to contributing dues and free-will offerings to swell the Jewish exchequer; and other reasons for their increasing wealth may be found in their stubborn loyalty and ready benevolence towards brother Jews. But the rest of the world they confront with the hatred reserved for enemies...Proselytes to Jewry adopt the same practices, and the very first lesson they learn is to despise the gods, shed all feelings of patriotism, and consider parents, children and brothers as readily expendable" (*The Histories* 5.5).[21]

Simply considering the rise of ritual proselyte circumcision, required in order for an outsider to be reckoned among the redeemed, and common Greco-Roman attitudes toward the Jews—**how did this all affect the Apostles' mission in the First Century?**

---

[21] Cornelius Tacitus: *The Histories*, trans. Kenneth Wellesley (London: Penguin Books, 1992), pp 273-274. See also Juvenal *Satires* 14.95-104.

When we take these things into consideration, we should more easily understand some of the negative attitudes that the early Jewish Believers displayed toward the non-Jewish Believers, which were very difficult for many to overcome. Many of them thought that short of proselyte conversion, that non-Jews should not be allowed into the assembly as members, even if they did acknowledge Yeshua. They would have been very hostile to the Apostle Paul—who taught that the entryway for inclusion among God's people *was faith in Israel's Messiah*, as opposed to more national and/or sectarian identity markers like ritual proselyte circumcision. In his rather emotional letter to the Galatians, addressing the early issue of how non-Jewish Believers were to be considered a part of God's covenant community, he has to remind his audience that faith in God is what first reckoned Abraham as righteous:

"Therefore, be sure that it is those who are of faith who are sons of Abraham. The Scripture, foreseeing that God would justify the Gentiles by faith, preached the gospel beforehand to Abraham, *saying*, 'ALL THE NATIONS WILL BE BLESSED IN YOU' [Genesis 12:3]. So then those who are of faith are blessed with Abraham, the believer" (Galatians 3:7-8, NASU).

The issue of faith in God, and by extension the Messiah He has sent—coming first—**is considered by Paul to be a gospel issue.** His quotation of Genesis 12:3, "in you all the families of the earth will be blessed" (NASU), is that very early promise of God to bless all via Abraham. Immediately requiring ritual proselyte circumcision of new, non-Jewish Believers, would skew such a serious mandate. Paul is clear in later writing that circumcision does have value (Romans 3:1-2), but in no small part due to the Maccabean crisis, many people in the Jewish community *overvalued* circumcision and *undervalued* faith in God. This was an unacceptable understanding for people placing their trust in the Messiah who died for their sins, was resurrected, and then who ascended into Heaven.

The early Jewish Believers would need to quickly get over any prejudices they had toward the non-Jewish Believers. They needed to recognize that all were reckoned as a part of God's covenant community not via any "works of law" or sectarian *halachah* (4QMMT) requiring ritual proselyte circumcision,[22] but instead *dia pisteōs Iēsou Christou*, "through the faithfulness of Yeshua the Messiah" (Galatians 2:16, my translation). People were recognized as a part of God's covenant community **by the faithful obedience of Yeshua to His Father unto death, to atone for humanity's sin.**[23]

---

[22] Consult the article "What Are 'Works of the Law'?" by J.K. McKee (appearing in *The New Testament Validates Torah*).

[23] Consult the article "The Faithfulness of Yeshua the Messiah" by J.K. McKee (appearing in *The New Testament Validtes Torah*).

The Impact of the Maccabees on First Century Judaism

For many Jews of the First Century C.E., the Torah, and most especially circumcision, became symbols of national pride and identity. Was circumcision not something that the Maccabees fought and died for? It is certainly understandable that many of the first Jewish Believers, upon hearing that significant numbers of non-Jews were recognizing Yeshua as *Israel's* Messiah, would require them to become Jewish proselytes before moving any further. But Biblically given the example of Abraham, this was no different than putting the cart before the horse. Acknowledging Israel's Messiah as Savior takes precedence over anything else.

After the problems addressed in Galatians, the Jerusalem Council of Acts 15 would meet to rule on the claim that some Jewish Believers were making: "Unless you are circumcised according to the custom of Moses, you cannot be saved" (Acts 15:1, NASU). According to these early Jewish Believers, to not be circumcised was tantamount to not being a member of God's people. The Jerusalem Council ruled against this, concluding that instead the early non-Jewish Believers did not have to undergo ritual proselyte circumcision, because as the Apostle Peter testified, "He made no distinction between us and them, cleansing their hearts by faith" (Acts 15:9, NASU). James the Just ruled that the new, non-Jewish Believers had to follow four, definite guidelines in order to enter into the faith community (Acts 15:19-21), effectively severing their religious and social ties with paganism. The salvation of the nations was something to be anticipated in Tanach prophecy (Acts 15:15-18). So, the New Covenant promise of God writing His Law onto the hearts of all His people would come steadily at the right pace (Jeremiah 31:31-34) by His Spirit—and the non-Jewish Believers would start not with circumcision, but with faith in God and in His Messiah, who Himself taught that love for God and neighbor was the essence of the Torah (Matthew 19:16-19; 22:35-40; Mark 12:28-34; Luke 10:25-28).

While the Maccabees rightfully fought and died for the right of the Jewish people to not only practice the Torah, including circumcision—**but also to survive**—subsequent Jewish generations would forget the Divine mandate that Israel had to be a light to the nations and a kingdom of priests (Exodus 19:6; Isaiah 49:6). The Apostolic Scriptures give witness to how many of the early Jewish Believers in the Messiah had prejudices to overcome when scores of non-Jews came to faith in the same Messiah. The Pauline Epistles are spent addressing how these non-Jewish Believers are to be reckoned as equal members of the *ekklēsia* on the basis of their faith, and not whether they had undergone ritual proselyte circumcision (Romans 3:29-30). The most important issue that many early Jewish Believers had to overcome, is seen in Paul's words:

"But now apart from the Law *the* righteousness of God has been manifested, being witnessed by the Law and the Prophets, even *the* righteousness of God through faith in Yeshua the Messiah [or, the faithfulness of Yeshua the Messiah][24] for all those who believe; for there is no distinction; for all have sinned and fall short of the glory of God" (Romans 3:21-23, NASU).

Up until this point in history, the main event that would have defined God's people would have been the Exodus from Egypt. As important as the Exodus is for Paul (1 Corinthians 10:1-4), the same righteousness of God[25]—"God's saving justice" (Romans 3:21, New Jerusalem Bible) that delivered Ancient Israel—has now been manifested in an event separate from the Torah. This event is the Messiah's faithfulness to His Father unto death for humanity's sin. But the thought that this is somehow contrary to God's Torah is the last suggestion in Paul's mind. He is clear to say that "the Law and the Prophets bear witness to it" (Romans 3:20, ESV), preceded earlier with his attestation that the gospel was "promised beforehand through His prophets in the holy Scriptures" (Romans 1:2, NASU).

The ultimate challenge is that if the Torah is viewed too much from the perspective of being a nationalistic possession, one can overlook the fact that it points to something much greater, **the Messiah Yeshua,** who is "the culmination of the law" (Romans 10:4, TNIV). A main purpose of the Torah is that it condemns all people (Romans 3:10-18)—including Jews (Romans 2:17-29)—as sinners, requiring all people to fall on the Father's grace via Yeshua for redemption. It was difficult for many of the early Jewish Believers to fully see this, as nationalistic possession of the Torah was sometimes believed to be enough for final redemption, a thought stemming from the long-term effects of the Maccabean crisis.

Appreciating the Maccabees, but Recognizing the Effect on Later Generations

As men and women of faith, we all need to be very appreciative for what the Maccabees struggled and died for. Without the sacrifice of the Maccabees, the Jewish people could have been wiped out, and with them the hope that there would be a chosen people from whom the Messiah would come forth and save the world. **I fully believe that every year the Messianic community should remember the Festival of Dedication, *Chanukah*, and honor what they endured.** But we need not remember *Chanukah* in ignorance of how this period affected later generations of Jews. The message and themes contained in the Books of Maccabees highly influenced the Jews of the First Century, who first heard the good news of Messiah Yeshua. It also

---

[24] Grk. *dia pisteōs Iēsou Christou*.
[25] Grk. *dikaiosunē Theou*.

gives us a witness to how negative, inappropriate Jewish attitudes toward outsiders in the First Century arose.

These negative Jewish attitudes toward outsiders complicated the spread of the gospel among the nations, in the early decades of the Messianic movement, as many Jewish Believers (but certainly not all) still had ungodly prejudices and paranoia to overcome. For many Jews, even Believers in Yeshua, God's Torah had become a nationalistic document, rather than a testament to His plan of salvation history and how "the scripture, foreseeing that God would justify the Gentiles by faith, declared the gospel beforehand to Abraham" (Galatians 3:8, NRSV; cf. Genesis 12:2-3). Circumcision was a matter of who was "His," rather than faith in the Messiah designating who was "His."

How we learn to appreciate what the Maccabees fought and died for, being sensitive to the legitimate Jewish needs of the First Century, but also how many Jewish Believers found it difficult to embrace non-Jewish Believers as their fellow brothers and sisters—**will doubtlessly be a feature of our Biblical Studies in the future.** Knowing about the Maccabees, and those who came after them, will assist us greatly in understanding some of the early controversies faced in the Book of Acts, as well as in Paul's letters to the Galatians and the Romans, which affirm how the non-Jewish Believers did not at all have to become proselytes. Knowing about the long-term impact of the Maccabees on the First Century Jewish psyche, can aid us to adequately piece together the complex circumstances of the early Believers.

Most intriguing of all will be examining what the First Century Believers experienced—including all of the prejudices they had to overcome—and how much of it is being paralleled parts of today's Messianic movement. There may very well be more going on than we realize, *and we may need to learn the lessons of history a bit closer.* We need to learn to be a people who will fight for the sanctity of God's Torah (1 Maccabees 2:27, 42), but also be a people who should desire their righteousness to be a Divine righteousness based in trusting Yeshua (Philippians 3:9). In so doing, **may we learn to overcome any prejudices that may keep Yeshua from being recognized as the Savior of all.**

Messianic Winter Holiday Helper

-11-

The Forgotten Past

J.K. McKee

2014 is an important year for many across the world, as many people—principally in Europe, the United Kingdom, and British Commonwealth countries—are remembering the centennial or centenary of The Great War or World War I.[1] Earlier this year, 888, 246 ceramic poppies, to commemorate the British and Empire war dead, were placed around the Tower of London. The Great War totally changed our world, not just in terms of the technology and tactics of warfare—but because when it started, four of the five empires who were belligerents were gone (Russian Empire, German Empire, Austro-Hungarian Empire, Ottoman Empire), dominions in the British Empire like Canada, Australia, or New Zealand began to assert a wider degree of independence, and an emerging world power in the United States began to wield its influence. When the war was over, and Britain and France demanded that Germany pay heavy reparations, inflation hit the German mark at unfathomable proportions, and extremist groups like the National Socialist or Nazi party were able to feed on the resentment of the people. The Russian Empire had become the new Soviet Union. At the same time, with the liberation of the Holy Land from the Ottoman Empire, the Balfour Declaration gave an impetus to the growing Zionist movement and world attention was focused to some degree on the need for a Jewish homeland and state.

It is not difficult to deduce how understanding World War I, and its aftermath, is important for the succeeding conflict of World War II, the rise of the United States as the principal Western power, as well as the Holocaust and birth of the State of Israel, and even the Cold War to follow. **But many of you who are reading this are Americans who do not know that much about World War I, because it was mainly a European conflict.**

---

[1] This article originally appeared in the December 2014 issue of Outreach Israel News.

Messianic Winter Holiday Helper

As a student of history, as well as a Bible teacher, not understanding World War I and how it radically changed Planet Earth—is very much like not understanding the Maccabean crisis of the Second Century B.C.E. I do not have direct experience as to what it might be like when Jewish people either in Israel or in the Diaspora gather to remember *Chanukah* or the Feast of Dedication. But, I suspect that not a huge amount of attention is given to the historical record, and more attention is given to the traditional lighting of the *menorah*, eating fried foods, and giving presents to children. *This is what most of the Messianic community does. . .* A group called the Maccabees cleansed the Temple from a defilement, it was believed that the *menorah* stayed lit for eight days via a miracle, and without the Temple having been rededicated there would have quickly been no Jewish people and hence no Messiah.

Why do we not understand the circumstances surrounding the Feast of Dedication a little better? Part of this is due to how the main record of the Maccabean crisis is not contained in canonical Scripture, but rather in reliable ancient writings from the Biblical period. The main record is present in the Books of 1&2 Maccabees in the Apocrypha, texts widely preserved in Greek, that make up what some Christian traditions label as the deutero-canon, in a second tier of religious writing, perhaps semi-inspired, which would sit just under the inspired Tanach and Apostolic Scriptures (Old and New Testaments). Other related texts are the Books of 3&4 Maccabees, as well as a record contained in the works of the First Century Jewish historian Josephus. There are various ecumenical study Bibles (from the RSV, NEB, REB, and NRSV), which will have English translations of the Apocryphal books, and perhaps some running commentary as well.

I have written extensively on the Maccabean crisis in the **Messianic Winter Holiday Helper**, but it is important that each of us not forget some of the major components of what took place. Even though there was a large Jewish Diaspora, the Babylonian exile was over, and Jewish people were living in the Land of Israel, with an operating priesthood and Temple, widely serving as a vassal state of the Seleucid-Greek faction that had arisen from the dividing up of Alexander the Great's empire. The dangers of Jewish people assimilating into the more dominant Hellenistic culture and religion, had widely been present (1 Maccabees 1:11-15), but with the reign of Antiochus Epiphanes (175-164 B.C.E.) and his mad thirst for power, Judea found itself caught in the middle of larger kingdoms vying for control of the region. When Antiochus left a less-than-successful campaign against the Ptolemaic-Greeks of Egypt, he came to Jerusalem and ransacked the Temple of its treasures (1 Maccabees 1:20-24; 2 Maccabees 5:16-17). While Antiochus was responsible for killing many at this time, what receives more attention is how several years later he wanted all in his realm to be the same, religiously and culturally.

The Forgotten Past

And what this meant for the Jews living in Israel, is that keeping the Torah and its instructions would become illegal on threat of death:

> "And the king wrote to all his kingdom for all to be as one people and for each to abandon his own precepts; all the nations complied with the dictum of the king. And many also from Israel approved of his service and sacrificed to idols and profaned the sabbath. And the king sent documents carried by the hand of messengers to Ierousalem and the cities of Iouda for them to follow precepts foreign to the land and to withhold whole burnt offerings and sacrifice and libation from the holy precinct and to profane sabbaths and feasts and to defile holy precinct and holy ones, to build altars and sacred precincts and houses to idols and to sacrifice swine and common animals and to leave their sons uncircumcised, to make their souls abominable in every unclean and profane thing, so as to forget the law and change all the statutes. And whoever would not abide by the command of the king would die. According to all these words he wrote to all his kingdom and appointed supervisors over all the people and commanded all the cities of Iouda to sacrifice city by city. And many of the people joined them, everyone who abandoned the law, and they did evil in the land. And they forced Israel into hiding places, into every one of their places of refuge. And on the fifteen day of Chaseleu in the one hundred and forty-fifth year, he constructed an abomination of desolation on the altar, and in the cities around Iouda they built altars and burned incense at the doors of the houses and in the city squares. And the books of the law which they found they tore up and burned with fire. And wherever there was found in someone's possession a book of the covenant, of if someone was conforming to the law, the judgment of the king put them to death" (1 Maccabees 1:41-57, NETS).

The scene of what took place on the Temple Mount is what tends to really garner our attention, as the appointed place where Israel met with the One True God, got quickly turned over into a pagan temple, with the record here even making some connection with the Daniel 9:27 Abomination of Desolation (cf. Matthew 24:15). What should also not go unnoticed, is how while Yeshua had said, "It is written, 'MY HOUSE SHALL BE CALLED A HOUSE OF PRAYER'; but you are making it a ROBBERS' DEN" (Matthew 21:13, NASU; also Mark 11:17; Luke 19:46), appealing to Tanach Scripture (Isaiah 56:7; Jeremiah 7:11) and how many were being shortchanged—the author of 2 Maccabees presents a scene of what took place as being far worse, as the House of God literally became a whorehouse:

> "Not long after this, the king sent an Athenian senator to compel the Judeans to forsake their ancestral laws and no longer to live by the laws of God—also to pollute the shrine in Hierosolyma and to call it the shrine of Olympian Zeus and to call the one on Garizim the shrine of Zeus-the-

Friend-of-Strangers, as the people who lived in that place had petitioned. Harsh and utterly grievous was the onslaught of evil. For the temple was filled with debauchery and reveling by the nations, who dallied with prostitutes and had intercourse with women within the sacred precincts, and besides brought in things for sacrifice that were unfit. The altar was covered with abominable offerings that were forbidden by the laws. People could neither keep the sabbath nor observe their ancestral feasts nor so much as confess themselves to be Judeans" (2 Maccabees 6:1-6, NETS).

Much of the record contained in 1&2 Maccabees records the guerilla war and resistance of those Jews in the Land of Israel, who remained faithful to God and their ancestral heritage, and who fought against the Seleucid-Greeks. The ones who gain the most attention are the family of Mattathias (a derivative of Matthew), who died of old age during the conflict (1 Maccabees 2:49), but who passed on the mantle of leadership to his son Judah, being nicknamed *Makkabbi* or "hammer." The record of 1&2 Maccabees details some of the events which involved the rise of Antiochus Epiphanes, his limited success in seeing many Jews assimilate to Greek religion and culture, his defiling of the Temple, but then his defeat and the Maccabees' victory. The immediate aftermath in seeing the Maccabees consolidate themselves as leaders of an independent Jewish realm—although still in a shifting Mediterranean world, given the rise of Rome as an up and coming power (1 Maccabees 8:1)—is also detailed. What is important for the Bible student, is while understanding and appreciating the history and sacrifice of those Torah-faithful Jews during this period is doubtlessly needed—**is evaluating the social impact of what took place among many Jewish people of the Second Temple era.**

It is not as though the decrees of Antiochus Epiphanes were just general prohibitions, forbidding the Jews in Israel to worship their own God at their own Temple, and from neither reading nor following the Torah or Law of Moses. *Specific* Torah practices were targeted as being illegal, and hence we see in the record of what took place, that these practices were not only "illegally observed" as a matter of resistance—but even fought and died for.

The most striking of all the Torah practices that was prohibited on the threat of death, had to be **circumcision.** An ancient process, known as epispasm, did see that circumcised male Jews could effectively remove their physical circumcision, what the NETS renders as "they fashioned foreskins for themselves" (1 Maccabees 1:15), and never totally went away, as it is noted later in 1 Corinthians 7:18. It is described how many mothers who circumcised their sons during this time, did suffer the consequence of being executed:

"And the women who had circumcised their children they put to death according to the ordinance, and they hung the babies from their necks and put

The Forgotten Past

to death their families and those who circumcised them" (1 Maccabees 1:60-61, NETS; also 2 Maccabees 6:10).

During his campaign in fighting the Seleucid-Greek occupiers, it is actually witnessed that the Jew Mattathias saw that many Jewish boys were circumcised:

"And Mattathias and his friends went around and tore down the altars and circumcised by force all the uncircumcised boys they found within the borders of Israel" (1 Maccabees 2:45-46, NETS).

A defiling or dismissal, of the **Sabbath,** is also seen in the record of the Maccabean crisis. One of the main reasons why God gave His people the weekly Sabbath rest, was for them to remember the Israelite slaves in Egypt, who had no rest (Deuteronomy 5:15). During the time of Seleucid dominance, there was a total loss of such a Sabbath rest. It is indeed witnessed, though, how there were groups of Jews, keeping the Sabbath, and were slaughtered for not defending themselves (1 Maccabees 2:31-38). While these people were mourned, Judah Maccabee and his party all agreed that if they did not fight on the Sabbath, that they would all be completely slaughtered:

"And they said, a man to his neighbor, 'If we all do as our brothers did and do not fight against the nations for our lives and for our statutes, now quickly they will annihilate us from the land.' And they decided on that day saying, 'Every person who comes against us in battle on the day of the sabbaths, let us fight against them, and we will not all die as our brothers died in the hiding places'" (1 Maccabees 2:40-41, NETS).

The third major feature of the Maccabean crisis, which has actually repeated itself in multiple ways throughout history since, was **forced consumption of pork** upon Jews, as a matter of demonstrating their dismissal of God's ways. Pigs were not the only animals sacrificed on the Temple Mount by the Seleucids, as traditional Greek religion did employ sheep, goats, or cattle, which would be technically considered "clean." Pigs, however, were not clean (cf. Leviticus 11; Deuteronomy 14), and Ancient Israelite avoidance of pork is often thought to have been rooted in a need for them to stay away from Ancient Near Eastern paganism, among other reasons. The author of 2 Maccabees records two significant examples of those who died because they refused to eat pork. The first, a scribe named Eleazar, was an old man willing to give up his life rather than eat pork:

"Eleazaros, one of the scribes in high position, a man now advanced in age and of noble presence, was being forced to open his mouth to eat swine's flesh. But he, welcoming death with honor rather than life with pollution, went up to the rack of his own accord, spitting out the flesh, as all ought to do who have the courage to refuse things that it is not right to taste, even for the natural love of life" (2 Maccabees 6:18-20, NETS).

Eleazar's colleagues actually urged him to just pretend to eat pork, so that he might save his life in the process, but he refused (2 Maccabees 6:21-23). He responded to them, "To pretend is not worthy of our time of life...for many of the young might suppose that Eleazaros in his ninetieth year had gone over the allophylism [alien religion, RSV]" (2 Maccabees 6:24, NETS). He further said, "Even if for the present I would avoid the punishment of mortals, yet whether I live or die I shall not escape the hands of the Almighty" (2 Maccabees 6:26, NETS). And so for not eating pork, Eleazar went to the rack and was martyred (2 Maccabees 6:28-31).

The second, and by far most serious scene of not eating pork, is witnessed in 2 Maccabees 7. Seven brothers are taken before their mother, and with Antiochus Epiphanes present, each one of them is tested as to whether he will "partake of unlawful swine's flesh" (2 Maccabees 7:1, RSV). 2 Maccabees 7 summarizes how each one of the brothers defiantly refuses to give in, facing a painful death. They appeal to the God of Israel as their final Vindicator, and how they will each be resurrected into the new world He will one day inaugurate. The mother who has had to watch all of this too dies, and all the author can say afterward is, "Let this be enough, then, about the eating of sacrifices and the extreme tortures" (2 Maccabees 7:42, RSV). Biblical examiners and commentators are in general agreement that the brothers tortured to death here, are actually those referenced in Hebrews 11:35: "and others were tortured, not accepting their release, so that they might obtain a better resurrection" (NASU).

By the time the military campaign turns in the Maccabees' favor, with the Seleucids being driven out, and the Temple cleansed and rededicated—it is hardly a surprise that a national commemoration would be declared so that what took place would never be forgotten (1 Maccabees 4:52-59), a commemoration which was present during the time of Yeshua (John 10:22-23). While the story and traditions surrounding *Chanukah* effectively end at 1 Maccabees ch. 4, the continuing record describes how the military conflict was not over, and did involve additional threats to the Jewish people, as well as internal strife among the Seleucid-Greeks themselves.

How did many Jewish people during the time of Yeshua perceive themselves, being the descendants of those who fought and died to preserve a Torah way of life? How did Jews contemporary to the Apostles think of the rite of circumcision, or of their Greek and Roman neighbors who were uncircumcised? How much did the events of the Second Century B.C.E. Maccabean crisis affect the spread of the good news among Jewish people *and* pagans out in the Mediterranean basin? Did the Maccabees, while rightly having fought against the defilement committed—also leave **a legacy of xenophobia and extreme suspicion against outsiders to the Jewish community?** When the gospel message of Israel's Messiah was received by

Greeks and Romans, many Jewish Believers did not act too positively—because they thought their introduction into the faith community would be the end of the Jewish people, and a reintroduction of paganism.

Not forgetting the Maccabean crisis is important for us as Messianic students of Scripture. When we recognize its significance, much of the complex sociology of God cleansing all people via Peter's vision (Acts 10), the Galatian problem, the Acts 15 Jerusalem Council, and even the challenges in Romans, become clear!

Messianic Winter Holiday Helper

-12-

A Restoration of Israel—Without the Jews?

J.K. McKee

This month of December 2016, the Jewish and Messianic Jewish communities will be commemorating *Chanukah* or the Festival of Dedication.[1] *Chanukah* is a very warm time for Jewish and Messianic Jewish families, mainly as they reflect back on different family memories, special times of fellowship, gift giving, and of course eating many specialty foods. In many Messianic congregations the world over, there will be dedicated times of reading from the Books of Maccabees, focusing on the ancient history of the Seleucid invasion of the Land of Israel, the resistance that opposed Hellenism and upheld God's Torah, and which assured not just a Jewish victory over evil but the very survival of the Jewish people. For those of us in Biblical Studies, the Maccabean crisis of the Second Century B.C.E. significantly impacted the Second Temple Jewish world of Yeshua of Nazareth, and in particular the attitudes of many within the Jewish community to their Greek and Roman neighbors. Many of the conflicts in the First Century *ekklēsia* that took place, as Greeks and Romans began receiving the Messiah of Israel into their lives—and whether these people had to be circumcised as Jewish proselytes in order to truly be reckoned as God's own—can trace their way back to the effects of what we review during the season of *Chanukah*.

In 2005-2006, in my family's Messianic quest, we fully embraced the remembrance of *Chanukah*. Up until this point, we had moved beyond Christmas on December 25, but were unsure of the Festival of Dedication. We certainly had no problem with joining in to various congregational activities that remembered *Chanukah*, which mainly included various readings from 1&2

---

[1] This article originally appeared in the December 2016 issue of Outreach Israel News.

Messianic Winter Holiday Helper

Maccabees and lighting the *chanukia*. The significance of the Maccabean crisis really began to come into focus for us, as I started writing Messianic commentaries on various books of the New Testament, and found myself referencing not just the Maccabean revolt—but its psychological impact on later Jewish generations. **Without the victory of the Maccabees over the Seleucid Greeks, there would be no Jewish people into which the Messiah of Israel would be born.** *Chanukah* should be remembered by today's Messianic community, no different than how Americans celebrate the Fourth of July.

Today, if you are a part of a Messianic Jewish congregation, some significant remembrance of *Chanukah* is going to take place, likely including various teachings which compare the Maccabees' cleansing of the Temple to how we as Yeshua's followers need to be cleansed by Him. If you are part of some informal Messianic home group or Torah study, you may also have some kind of *Chanukah* remembrance. But, if you are part of the widely independent Hebrew/Hebraic Roots movement—something mainly, if not exclusively, composed of non-Jews—then you will see variances in approach to *Chanukah*. Many people who identify as being a part of the Hebrew/Hebraic Roots movement, think that the Festival of Dedication is something spiritually edifying and worthwhile for God's people to remember (cf. Philippians 4:8). Many others, however, would consider *Chanukah* to be a hollow Jewish custom that the Messiah's followers should not be observing, and they think that when the Festival of Dedication is mentioned in John 10:22-23 that Yeshua was not commemorating it along with the rest of the Jewish community, but stood off to the side in disapproval.

As a Messianic Bible teacher, and not only as someone who has been a part of this movement since 1995—but who actively uses social media—I interact with people all across the spectrum, who identify with any number of different labels. While I am not always successful, I do try my best to be a consensus builder, being a firm believer that **what the Messiah of Israel has accomplished for us, in being sacrificed for our sins, is the most important thing.** If you are going to divide with someone, make sure that it is over something directly related to the Messiah's work. In my many years of being involved in Messianic things, I have certainly witnessed my share of controversies, and I am astutely aware of the competing spiritual forces which can manifest across our faith community.

What we call "the Messianic movement" today is something that has its origins deeply rooted within Protestant evangelistic outreaches to the Jewish community, first in Europe and Britain, and later in North America, starting in the early Nineteenth Century. The Hebrew Christian movement, of the late Nineteenth and Twentieth Centuries, was an association of Jewish Believers in Jesus, usually as a sub-sector of Protestantism, where various aspects of

A Restoration of Israel—Without the Jews?

Torah could be observed as a part of Jewish culture, in parallel to conventional Protestant observances. The Messianic Jewish movement, which really entered onto the scene in the 1960s and 1970s, emphasized Jewish outreach and evangelism via congregations established on a synagogue model, and where various aspects of Torah—such as keeping *Shabbat*, the appointed times, or a kosher diet—were no longer just aspects of Jewish culture to be remembered, but were aspects of Jewish obedience to God via the expectations of the New Covenant (Jeremiah 31:31-34; Ezekiel 36:25-27). **The primary mission of the Messianic movement has always had a basis in Jewish outreach, Jewish evangelism, and Israel solidarity.** And this is the way it should be, as is declared so affluently in Romans 1:16: "For I am not ashamed of the Good News, for it is the power of God for salvation to everyone who trusts—to the Jew first and also to the Greek" (TLV).

Within the 1980s and 1990s, as the Messianic Jewish outreach widened, and new Messianic Jewish congregations and synagogues began being established—it is safe to say that something did take place, which was widely not anticipated by some of the early Messianic Jewish leaders. During this time, many evangelical Christians were being directed by the Lord to Messianic congregations, for a variety of reasons. **The primary reason that non-Jewish Believers are drawn to Messianic congregations, is to remember the significance of Yeshua the Messiah in the appointed times.** My own family was among those steadily drawn into their Jewish Roots throughout the 1980s, via studying "Jesus in the feasts." Concurrent with this, many non-Jewish Believers drawn into Messianic congregations get quickly acclimated to the weekly study of the Torah portion, and in reconnecting with the Tanach or Old Testament in a very tangible way not witnessed in contemporary evangelicalism.

Today in 2016, if you asked many individual Messianic people, they would have to agree that there is a dual mission being achieved within the Messianic movement. First and foremost, the Messianic movement is here to see Jewish people come to saving faith in Israel's Messiah, in fulfillment of prophecy (cf. Romans 11:12, 26-27), and plugged-in to assemblies where Jewish Believers can remain in fidelity to their Jewish heritage—not finding themselves assimilated away into a Gentile Christianity, which might see that their grandchildren and great-grandchildren have no comprehension or knowledge of their Jewish ancestry. Secondly, the Messianic movement has witnessed many non-Jewish Believers take a tangible hold of their Hebraic Roots in the Tanach and Jewish Roots in Second Temple Judaism and the Synagogue, in fulfillment of the nations coming to Zion in the end-times to be taught God's Torah (Micah 4:1-3; Isaiah 2:2-4), recognizing that God is with His Jewish people (Zechariah 8:23).

Messianic Winter Holiday Helper

All of us, as God's children, should be willing and eager to learn from each other—particularly as there are many godly and edifying virtues from both Judaism and Protestantism, which can definitely be employed as we contemplate the final stages of history before the return of the Messiah. While Jewish and non-Jewish Believers are not exactly the same, and there are natural differences among God's people—namely that only Jewish Believers can expect to be given a tribal inheritance in the Promised Land, and that the Torah and Tanach composes not just their spiritual but also ethnic and cultural heritage—**we have far more in common than not.** If we focus on what we have in common, *first*, then our differences can be used to enrich and aid us in encountering the challenges of life—not encourage suspicion, division, and rivalry.

This December is a season when I get to join with my fellow Jewish brothers and sisters in Messiah Yeshua, and I get to celebrate *with them* in the triumph of their ancestors over the forces of Antiochus Epiphanes. I consider my commemoration of *Chanukah* to be no different than when we remember the birth of the State of Israel in 1948, or the retaking of the Old City of Jerusalem in 1967. **Chanukah is a celebration of victory.** And, in no uncertain terms do I hide the fact that I think that everyone in the Messianic movement—if they are genuinely committed to the original mission of Jewish outreach, evangelism, and Israel solidarity—should remember the eight days of the Festival of Dedication as well. The Maccabees' resistance against pagan assimilation, as important as it was for past Jewish history, has much to teach each of us about the future end-times. For, just as Antiochus Epiphanes had demanded that people worship his image, so the coming antimessiah/antichrist will demand that people worship him, and reject the God of Israel and His ways (cf. Revelation 13:4-7).

Our family returned to the Dallas-Ft. Worth Metroplex in 2012, where we got our original start in the Messianic movement back in 1995-1996. We not only reconnected with our old Messianic Jewish friends, and made some new Messianic Jewish friends, becoming part of a vibrant Messianic Jewish congregation—but we have even been welcomed into positions of leadership and teaching. The biggest "controversy" I have witnessed regarding *Chanukah* is over who is going to set up, and take down, the decorations in the sanctuary. While improvements can always be made regarding what lessons there are to learn from the Maccabean revolt, **I am thankful to report that there are no controversies whatsoever about whether or not we even need to learn from the Maccabean revolt.**

Things get much more interesting, however, in my ministry service through Outreach Israel and Messianic Apologetics—because most of what we do actively involves online social media. In open forums, you encounter people from all sorts of religious persuasions, in particular as it involves the

A Restoration of Israel—Without the Jews?

many, who in some form or another, associate themselves with the label "Messianic." To be sure, the significant number of people with whom I interact are Jewish and non-Jewish Believers, who want unity and stability within the Messianic movement, and who want us all to get along, learning from one another. At the same time, when one moves into the more independent Hebrew/Hebraic Roots persuasions, things can get very, very interesting. While I think many of us can understand—especially after the election cycle of 2016—much of the frustration that people have with "the establishment," some people are so anti-establishment that they are of the mindset that neither Christianity nor Judaism have ever made any significant, positive contribution, of any kind, to human civilization.

The kind of person who has become particularly odious to me, over the past few years, **is the non-Jewish "Believer" who claims to be a part of the polity of Israel, but wants little or nothing to do with the Jewish people or with mainline Jewish traditions and customs.** Almost all of the non-Jewish Believers I interact with are of the conviction that, along with their fellow Jewish Believers, they are a part of the polity of Israel. They believe that they are a part of what Ephesians 2:11-13 calls the "Commonwealth of Israel," the Galatians 6:16 "Israel of God," the Romans 11:16-17 phenomenon of being wild olive branches "grafted-in" to Israel's olive tree (cf. Jeremiah 11:16-17; Hosea 14:1-7), participants in Israel's Kingdom restoration along with their fellow Jewish Believers, witnessing David's Tabernacle being restored (Acts 15:15-18; Amos 9:11-12)—a part of an enlarged Kingdom realm of Israel, with a restored Twelve Tribes at its center, and its dominion welcoming in the righteous from the nations. Many of these people know the horrors resultant of Christian anti-Semitism and replacement theology, and so if they are claiming to be "fellow heirs and fellow members of the body, and fellow partakers of the promise" (Ephesians 3:6, NASU), this better be joined with the thrust of Romans 12:10 in mind: "love one another with mutual affection; outdo one another in showing honor" (NRSV).

Certainly, if someone like me has a Biblical responsibility to outdo my fellow brothers and sisters in showing honor to them, then what it means is that I have to show an appropriate amount of respect to the spiritual and theological heritage that I have in the Jewish Synagogue. *That is, if I really do regard myself as a part of the Commonwealth of Israel.* There are things that I have to legitimately learn and appreciate from the Jewish experience with God. My writings to date bear witness to the fact that I have been spiritually and intellectually enriched by not just many of the Jewish writings of the Second Temple period and immediately thereafter, but I have learned immense things from the Jewish struggle the past two centuries, particularly as they involve the rise of Zionism, the Holocaust, and the creation of the

Messianic Winter Holiday Helper

State of Israel. I am learning new things all the time from the Jewish experience in history, that everybody needs to especially learn and integrate into their psyche, as we get closer and closer to the Messiah's return.

As it involves living out a lifestyle of Torah obedience unto God, my writings to date also bear adequate witness that I am very philo-traditional when it comes to mainline Jewish traditions and customs. While I am hardly what one would consider to be "Orthodox," I do not haphazardly dismiss some of the major traditions and customs practiced in Conservative and Reform Jewish settings. I do not eschew, for example, men wearing a *yarmulke* or *kippah* in worship services. I do not have any problem with the Hebrew liturgy at my Messianic congregation's *Shabbat* service. I adhere to the longstanding convention since Second Temple times of not speaking the Divine Name YHWH/YHVH in public arenas. Whenever I encounter a Jewish tradition or custom that I do not understand, I expel some effort of investigating it first, before commenting on it, much less dismissing it. For certain, I will encounter Jewish perspectives or practices that I consider non-Biblical and in error—just as I have encountered Protestant perspectives or practices that are non-Biblical and in error. At the same time, the wide majority of Jewish perspectives and conventions I find to be genuinely edifying. Certainly for this December, remembering *Chanukah* or the Festival of Dedication would be an edifying Jewish practice.

Unfortunately, not everyone with whom I interact throughout the week, shares my commitment to fairness and equity. While I do believe, as someone from an evangelical Protestant background, that there are edifying virtues and perspectives from which today's Messianic movement can benefit that originate from my Reformed and Wesleyan heritage—the fact is that as a non-Jewish Believer in Israel's Messiah, I have cast my lot with the Jewish people and the restoration of Israel's Kingdom. I do not just look to the return of the Messiah and His eventual reign from Jerusalem, but I pay attention to what is happening in modern Israel, and I oppose anti-Semitism when I encounter it. I cannot be arrogant or haughty in regard to the widespread Jewish dismissal of Yeshua, but I have to instead act as a vessel of grace and mercy, and be facilitating a widespread Jewish acceptance of Yeshua (Romans 11:30-31). I have to be very conscientious of the Apostle Paul's warning, "for if God did not spare the natural branches, He will not spare you, either" (Romans 11:21, NASU).

What do you do with a non-Jewish Believer, who legitimately partakes of his or her spiritual heritage in the Scriptures of Israel, considering himself or herself a part of Israel's Commonwealth or polity, and is looking for the return of the Messiah to Jerusalem—but then wants little or nothing to do with mainline Jewish traditions or customs? Perhaps more education in Second Temple Judaism and Jewish history would be in order. But what about those non-Jewish people who want to claim that they are a part of the community of Israel via their faith in Israel's Messiah—but then take no interest in the original Messianic mission of Jewish outreach, evangelism, and Israel solidarity? Be aware that these people have made commitments to a live a life of Torah obedience, in emulation of Yeshua and His early followers. They keep *Shabbat*, the appointed times, and eat a kosher style of diet, among other things. They may even read the weekly Torah portions. *No one is saying that being a part of the Messianic movement is only a one-way street for them, as though they are only here to provide various forms of support for Jewish ministry;* such people should have their spiritual needs met and questions answered, just as Jewish Believers have their own spiritual needs and unique questions. Yet, while it is to be properly acknowledged and recognized that God has sovereignly drawn many non-Jewish Believers into the Messianic movement, **we have a serious problem on our hands if a number of them want little or nothing to do with their fellow Messianic Jewish Believers.**

While the Messianic movement is broad and diverse, and there are certainly instances of various Messianic Jewish congregations being unwelcome toward non-Jewish Believers—today in 2016 many Messianic Jewish congregations welcome non-Jewish Believers, provided they are respectful and understanding of various Jewish sensibilities. I have Messianic Jewish friends who have no problem with my family living a life of Torah obedience in emulation of Yeshua the Messiah. Part of it, they understand, is being involved with the Messianic community. Another part of it, they understand, involves the prophecies of the nations coming to Zion to be taught God's Instruction (Micah 4:1-3; Isaiah 2:2-4). *They just want to make sure that we are doing this as a part of the Messianic Jewish experience, and not off on our own.* How are we helping see the Romans 11:25-26 trajectory of salvation history come to pass—"until the fullness of the nations has come in; and in this way all Israel will be saved" (PME)? Certainly, if such a mission is to be achieved, it will involve expelling the proper efforts to understand Judaism, accept Messianic Jewish Believers as one's fellow brothers and sisters, and help declare the Messiah to Jewish people who do not know Him!

How much concern does the widely non-Jewish, Hebrew/Hebraic Roots movement really have for the Messianic Jewish movement which preceded it? While I do not want to be found broad-brushing any group of religious people, in the past several years—especially since our family relocated back to North Texas—legitimate concerns as they involve the original mission of the Messianic movement are not too important for Hebrew Roots aficionados. Recently this past Summer, a video documentary called The Way started circulating around social media, and by this time at the end of 2016, it has probably had hundreds of thousands of views. I have seen The Way several times, as its producers visited a number of Hebrew Roots related conferences, independent home fellowships, and interviewed a wide number of popular teachers, as well as individual people. As I have watched The Way: A Documentary, I have tried to practice a method I learned a long time ago as a political science undergraduate: *separate data from noise.*

There are many non-Jewish Believers whom the Lord is sincerely stirring to look into parts of the Bible which have remained closed to them. Many are partaking of the Sabbath and appointed times. Many are studying the Torah. Many have a genuine desire to want to live like their Savior, and they are willing to make the sacrifice to do it—which at times can include being spurned by their family, ostracized from their friends, and accused of being cultic from their former pastors and Sunday school teachers. Many non-Jewish Believers, who have been directed by the Holy Spirit to be Torah pursuant in their obedience to our Heavenly Father, have experienced some of the same rejection as Jewish Believers who have been ostracized from their families, considered crazy, and maybe even regarded as dead, for placing their trust in Yeshua of Nazareth. I am blessed to say that in my own family's experience of being a part of Messianic things, we have come together with our Jewish brothers and sisters in Yeshua, and in getting to know one another—and join in common cause—we have been able to have a reciprocal recognition of the sacrifices we have made to walk this path.

Among the many individuals and couples interviewed in The Way: A Documentary, the common thread was that the Lord was moving on people to dig into the Bible like never before. Many of them were indeed cut off from their faith origins in the Old Testament. Many of them had a sincere desire to want to live like Yeshua. Even though many of these people were rough around the edges, particularly in the newness of their experiences, you could tell that these people were ready and willing—not unlike some of the people who in the early days of the Protestant Reformation, first encountered a Bible. One can tell from The Way: A Documentary, that the numbers of non-Jewish Believers awakening to their faith heritage in Israel's Scriptures, cannot be ignored or dismissed.

But the producers of The Way: A Documentary made one, very critical mistake. They may have traveled across the United States, to Canada, to Costa Rica, and to the United Kingdom. (I was not expecting them to travel to Israel.) They interviewed many Hebrew Roots teachers, and individuals, couples, and families. They may have attended various Hebrew Roots conferences. But not only did the producers of The Way: A Documentary not bother to attend a single *Shabbat* service at a local Messianic Jewish congregation, and interview the rabbi—**they did not even mention the existence of the Messianic Jewish movement.** Even though no religious movement is without its challenges and growing pains and errors at times:

A Restoration of Israel—Without the Jews?

there would be no move of non-Jewish Believers embracing their faith heritage in Israel, **without first** a modern Messianic Jewish movement with origins going back to at least the same time as the emergence of Zionism.

What does some of this say? Was this just an oversight of the producers of The Way: A Documentary? Or, is it reflective of the fact that many non-Jewish Believers who have embraced their Hebrew Roots in the Tanach Scriptures, are not too interested in embracing their Jewish Roots in the Second Temple religion of Yeshua the Messiah and His Jewish Apostles? Even more so, are there non-Jewish Believers—believing themselves to be a part of the Commonwealth of Israel, grafted into the olive tree by faith in Israel's Messiah—who think that Judaism and the Jewish experience have nothing to teach them about their relationship with the God of Israel, or even just the human experience of encountering and overcoming trials on Earth?

That there is more going on in the Messianic movement than just Jewish evangelism is clear enough. But, to forget and/or dismiss the original vision of Messianic Jewish outreach to Jewish people who need Yeshua the Messiah is a grave sin. The agony of Paul over the salvation of his countrymen needs to be heard: "I could wish myself actually under God's curse and separated from the Messiah, if it would help my brothers, my own flesh and blood" (Romans 9:3, CJB/CJSB).

It might take a little more work, but one can be a part of a Messianic movement with a dual mission of Jewish outreach and evangelism *and* in equipping the non-Jewish Believers God has sovereignly drawn in to be a part of the restoration He is performing. Yet as obvious as it may be to some: **you cannot have an authentic restoration of Israel's Kingdom without the Jews.** I am afraid that many presently run the severe risk of being cut off (Romans 11:21).

Messianic Winter Holiday Helper

-13-

Handling the Holidays

Mark Huey

Every year as we approach the Winter holiday season, many in the Messianic community tend to suffer through a form of spiritual apoplexy.[1] For a variety of real, and/or perceived, reasons, some Messianics lose control of their ability to comfortably walk in the life-changing message that they have received. Whether many want to admit it or not, most are still influenced by the milieu of a "post-Christian" America, that in and of itself, is struggling to redefine the politically correct way to celebrate religious occasions. Consequently, an environment charged by "unspeakable subjects," such as politics and religion, has family, friends, and neighbors adding pressure that simply exacerbates the problem. In many cases, the added emotional and relational stress that many have during the Winter holiday season takes away the joy traditionally associated with this time of the year, giving impetus to the thoughtful question, "Is there any way we can skip December this year?"

Unless you act like an ostrich, ignoring life around you by hiding your head in the sand, or are a modern-day Ebenezer Scrooge, you will not be able to avoid noticing that the world around you is recognizing an event celebrated on December 25, that in the English-speaking world has been labeled "Christmas." At about the same time, if you are paying attention, you will also see that Jewish people around the world are taking eight days to celebrate the tradition known as *Chanukah* or the Feast of Dedication. And by the way, it will be impossible to avoid detecting the "spirit of mammon" serenading you with a variety of methods to get your attention to spend your money!

But putting the commercial interests aside, the emerging Messianic community is in desperate need of some talking points that will allow the inevitable seasonal conversations to be a pleasant experience, rather than full

---

[1] This article originally appeared in the December 2003 issue of Outreach Israel News.

of angst and controversy. After all, are not Believers to be in the world, but not be of the world (John 17:14-16)? How are we going to let the light of God's truth shine from within, if we avoid the subjects at hand and hibernate in thought? Should we not be witnessing some basic truths to those around us, that just might provoke some correct thinking about what really did and did not happen in centuries past?

When you really think about it, celebrating historical events like the birth of the Messiah of Israel or the rededication of the Temple in Jerusalem are not necessarily bad things for people to be doing. This is especially true when you consider that it is recorded that the Messiah Himself actually came to the Temple during *Chanukah* almost two millennia ago:

"At that time the Feast of the Dedication took place at Jerusalem; it was winter, and Yeshua was walking in the temple in the portico of Solomon" (John 10:22-23, NASU).

An unfortunate problem is that the basic truths about the birth of the Messiah and the Feast of Dedication have been obscured during the Winter season. Many, from a variety of perspectives, often unmercifully attack one or both celebrations, or in some cases, simply ignore the facts that the Messiah was born and that God's Temple was rededicated.

Rather than spend time going through all of the minutiae that others have written about the inaccuracies of Yeshua's purported birth date, and whether the miracle of the properly prepared oil for the *menorah* really manifested itself, we need to consider a different perspective. This is not to say that the conclusions derived from analyzing the text of Luke 2, and comparing it with the Rabbinic records concerning the duties of the different Levitical priestly families, are not important. Some speculative analysis has proposed that Yeshua could have been conceived around the Winter Solstice (December 21-22), and that His actual birth occurred around the time of the Feast of Tabernacles in the Fall. It is also clear from a reading of 1-4 Maccabees, and other historical sources, that the sons of Mattathias, and in particular, Judah Maccabee, indeed liberated Jerusalem and the Temple Mount in the 160s B.C.E. Most importantly, they rededicated the Temple complex, and reconstituted the sacrificial system that had been suspended by Antiochus Epiphanes.

A Messianic Perspective

Over the years, as our family has considered many of the arguments, theories, and debates about the challenges presented to Messianics concerning Christmas and the celebration of *Chanukah*, we have come to some important conclusions. But before sharing our perspective, let me first state that we, like most Messianic families, have been on a progressive path, learning more and more about what is pleasing to the Holy One of Israel on a yearly basis, if not a daily basis. As a ministry, we are frequently asked questions about how Messianic Believers should navigate through the often uncharted December waters, truly seeking to glorify the Dispenser of "Living Waters."

Without getting into the pros and cons of celebrating the birth of the Messiah, we are simply thankful that our Heavenly Father, in His infinite mercy toward us, concluded that it was necessary for Yeshua to be our blameless sacrifice. As the Psalmist has put it, "No man can by any means redeem *his* brother or give to God a ransom for him—for the redemption of his soul is costly, and he should cease *trying* forever—that he should live on eternally, that he should not undergo decay" (Psalm 49:7-9, NASU).

We see that God requires Himself to be a ransom or payment for the separating transgressions of a human being. No mere man can atone for the sins of another man. You must have an unblemished or perfect sacrifice that will be acceptable before a holy and righteous God as a substitution for your sin. At the time preceding the Passover, Moses designated the sacrifice to be an unblemished lamb:

"Your lamb shall be an unblemished male a year old; you may take it from the sheep or from the goats" (Exodus 12:5, NASU).

This pattern was repeated in the atoning work of the Messiah of Israel, who was also called "a lamb unblemished and spotless" (1 Peter 1:19, NASU).

In order to receive the permanence of eternal life, rather than temporary relief from sin accomplished by animal sacrifices, God Himself must be the sacrifice. The Apostle Paul clarifies it for the Philippians, regarding what many theologians today label the "hypostatic union" of Yeshua being fully God and fully human, thus being the perfect sacrifice for our sins:

"Let the same mind be in you that was in Christ Jesus, who, though he was in the form of God, did not regard equality with God as something to be exploited [to be used to his own advantage, TNIV], but emptied himself, taking the form of a slave, being born in human likeness. And being found in human form, he humbled himself and became obedient to the point of death—even death on a cross. Therefore God also highly exalted him and gave him the name that is above every name, so that at the name of Jesus every knee should bend, in heaven and on earth and under the earth, and every tongue should confess that Jesus Christ is Lord, to the glory of God the Father" (Philippians 2:5-11, NRSV; cf. Isaiah 45:23).

This understanding is amplified when Paul explains the concept of reconciliation to the Believers in Rome:

"For while we were still helpless, at the right time Messiah died for the ungodly. For one will hardly die for a righteous man; though perhaps for the good man someone would dare even to die. But God demonstrates His own love toward us, in that while we were yet sinners, Messiah died for us. Much more then, having now been justified by His blood, we shall be saved from the wrath *of God* through Him. For if while we were enemies we were reconciled to God through the death of His Son, much more, having been reconciled, we shall be saved by His life. And not only this, but we also exult in God through our Lord Yeshua the Messiah, through whom we have now received the reconciliation" (Romans 5:6-11, NASU).

During the Winter holiday season many of our Christian brothers and sisters, who celebrate Christmas, focus on the One who was born, only to die for our sins. The Messianic community should not forget Yeshua's atoning work for us, and His miraculous birth into the world!

Timing is Everything

Every Believer in Yeshua must recognize that it was absolutely critical for two things to happen in order for us to be redeemed: (1) God had to come in human form as One who would live a perfect life, and offer Himself up as an unblemished sacrifice for our sins. (2) The procedures of following in the succession of an operating Levitical system, established in the Torah, had to take place. The perfect sacrifice must be made in order to secure eternal life for redeemed man.

When you go back and look at the historical record by reading through 1-4 Maccabees in the Apocrypha, you discover that Antiochus Epiphanes was on an assignment from the enemy to destroy the Levitical priesthood and God's Temple, so that the Redeemer could not comply with any of the Torah while coming to Earth. Here is a brief statement from 1 Maccabees that indicates just what Satan, through Antiochus and others, tried to accomplish:

"And the king sent letters by messengers to Jerusalem and the cities of Judah; he directed them to follow customs strange to the land, to forbid burnt offerings and sacrifices and drink offerings in the sanctuary, to profane sabbaths and feasts, to defile the sanctuary and the priests, to build altars and sacred precincts and shrines for idols, to sacrifice swine and unclean animals, and to leave their sons uncircumcised. They were to make themselves abominable by everything unclean and profane, so that they should forget the law and change all the ordinances. 'And whoever does not obey the command of the king shall die'" (1 Maccabees 1:44-50, RSV).

As you read this account, you realize that the primary goal of Antiochus was to destroy the Levitical priesthood that existed among the inhabitants of Judea and Jerusalem. If God had allowed this to take place, then it is probable that the Temple, and all that pertained to the Jewish people which was being maintained during this time—roughly 160 years before the birth of the Messiah—could have been terminated. And of course, if the Levitical system had been eliminated, then when Yeshua was born, it would have been impossible for Him to fulfill the various statutes that were required for Him to be the unblemished sacrifice for our sins.

Instead, our Almighty God put the zeal of Phinehas in the heart of Mattathias (1 Maccabees 2:26-27; cf. Numbers 26:7-8), the father of the five sons who followed the leadership of Judah, who was called Maccabee. Reading the historical record, you discern that God definitely used these zealots to overcome incredible odds to reclaim Jerusalem, the Temple complex, and reestablish the Levitical priesthood. If you take the time to really consider what has been testified of the events, you will discover that even Antiochus Epiphanes himself had what could be called his own epiphany, or revelation of the Divine:

"Then the abominable fellow made a vow to the Lord, who would no longer have mercy on him, stating that the holy city, which he was hastening to level to the ground and to make a cemetery, he was now declaring to be free; and the Jews, whom he had not considered worth burying but had planned to throw out with their children to the beasts, for the birds to pick, he would make, all of them, equal to citizens of Athens; **and the holy sanctuary, which he had formerly plundered, he would adorn with the finest offerings; and the holy vessels** he would give back, all of them, many times over; and the expenses incurred for the sacrifices he would provide from his own revenues; and in addition to all this he also would become a Jew and would visit every inhabited place to proclaim the power of God" (2 Maccabees 9:13-17, RSV).

The turn around from the destruction of all that was Jewish, particularly the Temple complex, was a tremendous testimony of how God used a very dramatic set of circumstances to reconstitute the Levitical priesthood in Jerusalem. Approximately 160 years later, the Temple was still functioning in proper order, and the Jewish people had retained their national identity, not being assimilated into the nations as Antiochus originally wanted. Just imagine if Mary and Joseph had not fulfilled the ordinances required for circumcision or purification as required by Leviticus 12:3 and 12:6-8, attested to us in the account of our Lord's birth:

"And when eight days had passed, before His circumcision, His name was *then* called Yeshua, the name given by the angel before He was conceived in the womb. And when the days for their purification according to the law of Moses were completed, they brought Him up to Jerusalem to present Him to the Lord" (Luke 2:21-22, RSV).

If the Temple had remained defiled, and the Maccabees had not taken a stand against the forces of Antiochus, then humanity's redemption could have been in jeopardy. If the Temple had not been rededicated, the Son of God may not have qualified to be the unblemished Lamb of God that was required.

Furthermore, and most significantly, there would have likely been no Jewish people for the Messiah to have been born into.

December Discussions

As you become more knowledgeable about some of the historical events that occurred during the time of the Maccabees and around the time of Yeshua's birth, the actual date becomes less and less of a problem. As you begin to understand some of the requirements necessary for Him to be the sacrificial Lamb, and see how the Father used religious Jewish zealots to accomplish His will to thwart the plans of the enemy, you begin to have a greater appreciation for all of the events associated with December.

Instead of hibernating for a month, perhaps you can be used to enlighten your family, friends, and neighbors about some of the things you have been learning about—how the Father of Lights does indeed bestow every good gift from above (James 1:17)! Maybe, as you listen to the prompting of the Spirit of God, it is just possible that He will allow you to share your knowledge of the greatest gift that He has given to humanity. **This gift is the salvation of His Son, Yeshua, who in His sacrifice paid the price required to atone for all of our sins.**

But let me remind you of this one thing. If you are given that precious opportunity to share some of your newfound knowledge at this "holiday season," be aware that knowledge has a tendency to make one arrogant and full of pride (1 Corinthians 8:1). And pride, as you know, has its failings: "When pride comes, then comes dishonor, but with the humble is wisdom" (Proverbs 11:2, NASU).

I would encourage you to model your approach after the Messiah, who demonstrated the epitome of humility, emptying Himself of His glory in Heaven, coming to Earth as a human man, and finally bearing our sins upon the tree. Consider the fact that He actually took upon Himself the ultimate curse of the Torah, that apart from Him, was destined for all of us:

"Messiah redeemed us from the curse of the Law, having become a curse for us—for it is written, 'CURSED IS EVERYONE WHO HANGS ON A TREE' [Deuteronomy 21:23]" (Galatians 3:13, NASU).

We have much to talk about during the Winter holiday season. Whether or not this is the actual timeframe of His birth is not worth debating when you consider what is most important. He was born into this world, He fulfilled the requirements of the Torah, and He bore our sins as the sacrifice that only He could be. May we as the redeemed be forever grateful that we can proclaim these truths, no matter what time of the year it is!

-14-

Being Messianic in a Post-Christian World

Mark Huey

Despite the uniqueness of walking out a Messianic lifestyle since 1995 in my pursuit of the Holy One, it has been my experience that the Winter holiday season still generates some personal and familial challenges—especially in what appears to be a steadily devolving post-Christian world.[1] This is particularly true when you subject yourself to spending quality time with family and friends, who do not necessarily understand or embrace your steadfast belief that Yeshua (Jesus) is the Savior of the world. The great irony is that during this time of year—almost universally chosen to celebrate the birth of our Lord—family and friends dealing with their nominal *or nonexistent* beliefs about God, His Son, or the need for atonement are challenged and increasingly more confused. This reality all came into focus for me as I spent the week of Christmas (2007) in Boulder, Colorado visiting my octogenarian parents, my sister and brother-in-law, nephews, and my daughter accompanied by her boyfriend.

First, I need to tell you that back in 1978 when I was born again and changed by the power of the gospel, the transformation in my life was, in and of itself, **very confusing for my immediate family.** Like many Americans, we had attended various Protestant churches from Methodist to Presbyterian to Congregational to Episcopal during the 1950s to 1970s, and thus my family (parents and siblings) have always considered themselves to be "Christians." When I explained the need to have a personal salvation experience with the Risen Savior, they thought I had gone overboard. They simply did not understand. Over time, as my pleas fell on deaf ears, I came to understand the

---

[1] This article originally appeared in the January 2008 issue of Outreach Israel News.

fuller meaning of Paul's words to the Corinthians about the difference between the natural man and the spiritual man:

"But a natural man does not accept the things of the Spirit of God, for they are foolishness to him; and he cannot understand them, because they are spiritually appraised" (1 Corinthians 2:14, NASU).

After years of frustrating attempts to share the gospel with my family, I purposed in my heart to fervently pray for their salvation. I would attempt to live out my life in such a way as to be a testimony to them, of a life dedicated to my relationship with God. To this very day, I continue to believe that my prayers will bear fruit, recognizing that the timing is in the Lord's capable hands.

Yet in spite of my prayers, things have gotten complicated since 1995. To further confuse the natural minds of my family, the Lord led Margaret and me into a Messianic walk that year. For the next several years, my family's reaction from a respectable distance was basically, "Are you all trying to become Jewish?" Please understand that they naturally considered themselves "Christian" because they were not Buddhist, Muslim, or Jewish. *They thought we had gone off the deep end.* While we did not impose our perspectives on *Shabbat* and the appointed times, or put them down for celebrating Christmas as they always had—the most pronounced difference actually came when we had the occasion to share a meal with them. This was somewhat perplexing, because we were not eating things that we had eaten during our upbringing. Having grown up eating various shellfish delicacies, and bacon and ham, this radical departure from our typical diet made them somewhat uncomfortable. However, despite some of the heated debates that went on for a number of years, with a growing understanding about the health issues related to eating certain foods, my family has finally accepted our "peculiar" eating habits with a certain degree of respect.

With all of this in mind, perhaps you can personally relate to ongoing issues between your own family or friends when you subject yourself to their environment and mores, especially around the time of the year when the world at large recognizes and celebrates the birth of Jesus. During the month of December 2007, more so than others because of my visit with my parents around Christmas, coupled with our ongoing ministry discussions and emphasis on "Messianics and modernity," I was specifically tuned into how being Messianic I could relate to those family and friends who do not necessarily understand spiritual matters the way we view them.

During the course of the week with my family, certain questions and thoughts percolated in my mind, as I dealt with the juxtaposition of memories from my childhood and my more mature Messianic understanding of life. How am I going to relate to those who do not have a relationship with Yeshua? How am I going to extend the love of Messiah to those who I have been praying for over the past thirty years, without any significant visible change? What am I going to say to my family when questions about religion inevitably arise? How can I point them to the Lord when the crass commercialization associated with Christmas is discussed? What about trees, decorations, presents, food choices, etc.? Am I going to unconditionally love my family, in spite of obvious differences of opinion on many aspects of the season? What would Yeshua do in these circumstances? Or better yet—how is *Yeshua in me* going to handle each and every opportunity to extend His love to my family?

The more time I spent analyzing these questions, and dealing with additional thoughts as they arose in my mind and heart, the more I received a peace about simply letting things come together—without trying to make anything happen in my own strength. Needless to say, my family generally knows where I am coming from, and if they want some clarification or greater understanding, then they will initiate a discussion that will give me the opportunity to share. I have learned from experience that trying to force my knowledge upon them has been somewhat fruitless. With this experiential wisdom, I had to conclude that I was simply going to enjoy their presence and continue to pray for them throughout the course of my visit.

As Christmas Eve approached in 2007, I could remember the last time at Christmas 2001 when I was in Colorado with my parents, my daughter (as an undergraduate at the University of Colorado), and my sister's family, and how I was absolutely surprised when my unbelieving sister insisted that we all go to a Christmas Eve service at a Presbyterian church. Back then, despite my knowledge about some of the inaccuracies associated with Christmas, I was delighted that everyone was going to have to at least hear some Christmas hymns, and perhaps a sermon on the birth of the Messiah. I had the wisdom to keep my mouth shut, and to simply pray that something sung or said would spark something in the hearts of my loved ones.

In an answer to my prayers, and to my surprise that year, my sister and brother-in-law decided that we would all go to a high church Episcopal service for Christmas Eve that was geared for the children of the church. Here once again in what is obviously an annual family tradition, my parents, my sister's family, and my daughter and her boyfriend had to contend with Christmas chorals, Scripture readings appropriate for the Lord's birth, and even a homily about the blessing of serving rather than being served. As I sat through the service with tears welling up in my eyes, I prayed that something said or read or heard would pierce the hearts of my relatives. Whether it was Isaiah 9 or Psalm 96 or Titus 2 or Luke 2 (the Scriptures read), or the words of *O, Come All Ye Faithful* or *Joy to the World* (the hymns sung), or the reading of the Lord's Prayer, really did not matter. I was just thankful that at least once a year, each of these people had to deal with these truths as they were being articulated. I never once thought about how I could improve their understanding of Christmas with all of my "Messianic knowledge," because for largely non-religious people I knew it would confuse them more than anything else. **I thought about faith the size of a mustard seed,** especially regarding my aging parents. I just prayed that at some point in time, they will have enough faith to be saved from the ravages of an eternity outside the presence of God. As Yeshua summarizes it,

"Because of the littleness of your faith; for truly I say to you, if you have faith the size of a mustard seed, you will say to this mountain, 'Move from here to there,' and it will move; and nothing will be impossible to you" (Matthew 17:20, NASU).

I recognize that it is not my responsibility to save my family; I am leaving this up to God through the agency of His Holy Spirit. I am simply required to pray for them and to have a witness for the hope that is within me:

"But sanctify Messiah as Lord in your hearts, always *being* ready to make a defense to everyone who asks you to give an account for the hope that is in you, yet with gentleness and reverence." (1 Peter 3:15, NASU).

Acknowledging the mystery of the Messiah in me **is the hope of glory**:

"The mystery which has been hidden from the *past* ages and generations, but has now been manifested to His saints, to whom God willed to make known what is the riches of the glory of this mystery among the Gentiles, which is Messiah in you, the hope of glory" (Colossians 1:26-27, NASU).

When you read Scriptures like these above, unless you are a spiritual person with at least a modicum of faith, perhaps the size of a mustard seed, you will not as a natural person be able to comprehend what is being stated by God's servants. As Messianic Believers in an increasingly post-Christian world, should we not be wise with whom we share our understanding about our particular (or even particularized) walk with Messiah Yeshua? Are my relatives ready for a discussion on the timing of the birth of the Messiah? If the concept of a virgin conception is too much for someone to fathom, let alone believe—as my sister related to me—why would I even bring up the origins of the Christmas tree? She cannot even see the forest of faith, let alone the trees. *And my view of Christmas concerns the "tree bark"!*

Do you remember Yeshua's admonition about casting pearls before swine? In the greater context, Yeshua actually admonished His followers about the traps of judging others:

"Do not judge so that you will not be judged. For in the way you judge, you will be judged; and by your standard of measure, it will be measured to you. Why do you look at the speck that is in your brother's eye, but do not notice the log that is in your own eye? Or how can you say to your brother, 'Let me take the speck out of your eye,' and behold, the log is in your own eye? You hypocrite, first take the log out of your own eye, and then you will see clearly to take the speck out of your brother's eye. **Do not give what is**

Being Messianic in a Post-Christian World

holy to dogs, and do not throw your pearls before swine, or they will trample them under their feet, and turn and tear you to pieces. Ask, and it will be given to you; seek, and you will find; knock, and it will be opened to you. For everyone who asks receives, and he who seeks finds, and to him who knocks it will be opened" (Matthew 7:1-8, NASU).

Now I am certainly not considering my family to be dogs or swine, but rather in their ignorance of the truths of Scripture, I might actually be doing them *more harm* if I place before them spiritual truths that they are not ready to hear—let alone accept. If I share some of my distinct Messianic knowledge with my family, it could actually create greater barriers for future, profitable spiritual discussions. The admonition from Yeshua is not to judge those who may not yet have some kind of spiritual understanding *that we might already have*. There comes a point when each of us has to be very discerning, and to just get others to talk about "God" may be as far as we can go.

By extension, if today's Messianics really do have some truth about living a life in a way that is reminiscent of the First Century Apostles, are we to force-feed our beliefs onto others? Are we to chastise those who may not yet understand the blessings of a Messianic lifestyle? I myself do not believe that this would be profitable, recognizing that in the concluding remarks by Yeshua, He reminds us that those seeking truth will ask, seek, and knock. As they do so in their curiosity and pursuit of the Holy One, they will be given the understanding they desire.

Lamentably, every year since 1995 that we have walked out the Messianic lifestyle, we have encountered teachings from various voices that do their utmost to condemn those who are still stuck in their Christmas traditions. There appears to be a total disregard for where people presently are in their individual quests for God. For the record, we as a ministry **do not believe** that such a mean-spirited approach is from the Holy One of Israel, but rather has been cleverly disguised by the Adversary and old flesh patterns to do *irreparable harm* to those seeking Him. Our prayer is that you would disassociate yourselves from any who promote these tactics, and seek more constructive and edifying solutions among *all Believers* this time of year.

On the other hand, speaking of those seeking God, it is interesting to note that on my visit to Colorado, I was given the opportunity to meet with a Christian ministry leader who is actually moving his ministry in a direction that is slowly embracing a Messianic perspective. For the past twenty years, it is obvious from this man's writings that he is pursuing a relationship with the God of Israel that desires dynamic change. This led him to write a book in 1992 that dealt with aspects of the "ancient paths" of the Patriarchs. Over the years, this has morphed his outreach into an "Ancient Paths seminar" that deals specifically with the blessings of following many aspects of the Torah. In our lengthy conversation, it was interesting to note that the Holy Spirit has

Messianic Winter Holiday Helper

been slowly moving him, and those he influences through his ministry, to the point of finally understanding the blessings associated with a Messianic lifestyle. He acknowledged that his ministry disciples are finally to the point where they are struggling with some of the aspects of the Christmas season, as opposed to the appointed times of the Lord. He further told me that they are getting a proper handle on the significance of *Shabbat* and how to follow the basic dietary laws of the Scriptures.

As we shared back and forth, I admitted that in our family's relatively rapid progression to embrace a Messianic lifestyle, I was always convinced in my mind that once seekers of God saw the significance of greater obedience to Him, they would immediately adopt Messianic ways. Little did I realize that the Father is going about His business to draw people into a Messianic perspective *from a wider variety of ways* than I could have originally understood. I was humbly reminded of some distinct words declared by the Prophet Isaiah several millennia ago:

"For My thoughts are not your thoughts, nor are your ways My ways, declares the LORD. For *as* the heavens are higher than the earth, so are My ways higher than your ways and My thoughts than your thoughts" (Isaiah 55:8-9, NASU).

In retrospect, during the course of my week in Colorado, the Lord actually allowed me the privilege of casting some pearls of wisdom before someone who did not trample them underground. I was allowed to be used by Him to confirm many of the things someone else had been led to do over the previous two decades. *Thank you, Father!*

I do have some gratifying news to report, especially as we consider God's mysteries and His thoughts and ways being higher than our thoughts and ways. As a result of going to the Christmas Eve service with my parents, the next morning at breakfast, it was quite easy to follow up many of the previous evening's conversations on a variety of family related topics. One point of family concern regards one of my nephews. Without any hesitation, I was able to discuss what the Bible says about blessings and curses as articulated in Deuteronomy chs. 28-29. All of a sudden, I found a Bible I had given my father years earlier, and turning to this passage of Scripture I read it aloud so that *both of my parents* could hear what God had to say about the consequences of certain actions. It was not long before we were all agreeing that what God said He would bless, and what He would curse, all made perfect sense. There was no animosity toward the Bible, but rather common agreement that it was accurately depicting some things that were manifesting themselves in my nephew's life. Additionally, as I started to get concerned over the bacon and eggs that my father was beginning to serve me, I simply gently moved the bacon to the side of my plate. My father, an adamant defender of "pig's meat," looked at me like I was doing something wrong.

When I humbly mentioned that I was not a fan of bacon, he smiled and said, "It's turkey bacon. Have you got a problem with turkey bacon?" To my surprise I said, "Of course not!" His reserved explanation was that you just have to know how to *cook it*.

In some small, relatively insignificant way, I felt like being a Messianic in a post-Christian world was actually having an impact on my family—albeit somewhat limited. But you never know, because His thoughts and ways—especially as they concern matters of the human heart—are certainly above ours. I do know this above all: I will continue to pray for my family members so that they can at least gain a mustard-seed-size faith to spend eternity with those who already know God. I also know that what God is doing in this world, with those of us walking out a Messianic lifestyle, is *way beyond* my ability to comprehend. His timing on bringing about the restoration of all things is simply that: **His timing**. How He is going to achieve what He has promised is His problem, *not mine*.

In the interim, I believe it is incumbent on every one of us who claim to be Messianic to not only grow in our faith, but also exemplify a condemnation-free love toward all who we come into contact within our respective walks. This particularly applies to our close family and friends, who, whether we admit it or not, are observing our every word and deed. **Have you ever thought about how you are measuring up to the standards established by Yeshua?**

It is my sincere prayer that you will no longer identify with the sentiments of some in the Messianic community who make statements echoing this thought: *"From Thanksgiving to the first of the year, I simply want to hold my breath or hide my head under the covers!"*

My friends, this is not how we are going to impact our world for the Lord. We cannot hibernate during certain times of the year because we might not have answers to not only our Christian brethren celebrating Christmas, but also people without God. There are scores of examples in the Bible where God's people have carefully, yet directly, tackled the issues of their day. **May we each grow in His wisdom and guidance, so that He might use us to draw others to Himself!** Truly, a great mission lies before us, and we have to be up to the challenge.

Messianic Winter Holiday Helper

-15-

Chanukah and Encountering Worldly Philosophies

J.K. McKee

reproduced from the McHuey Blog

One of the responsibilities of any Bible teacher is to bridge the gulf that exists between Scripture passages given in an ancient historical context, and providing practical application for those living in the Twenty-First Century. Human nature often remains the same between an ancient period and modern society: people still commit sin, people still need redemption, people still desire to be loved. Certainly as Messianic Believers, we learn and encounter many things that teach us about ourselves from the weekly Torah portions, from the Tanach, and from looking at the Apostolic Scriptures in their ancient Jewish and Mediterranean setting.

Making a connection between the *Chanukah* story and society today is actually quite easy, but it is also very complicated. I will not disagree with anyone who says that a main feature of the *Chanukah* story is resistance to Hellenism or errant Greek philosophy. But what we define as Hellenism or errant Greek philosophy is very much contingent on a teacher **actually knowing a few things about classical Greek philosophy**, and being able to provide documentation from primary and secondary sources when one defines a concept or idea as specifically being "Greek." Again, it is easy for me to talk about this, because in our Wednesday Night Bible Study (2005-2016), when we encounter classical concepts that the Apostles are directly confronting—engagement with the relevant Greek or Roman philosophers, historians, or politicians is offered.[1] Yet for many who promote the concept of a so-called Hebrew mind versus a Greek mind, such engagement is often not provided. It should make one wonder if this soundbyte is often used to just be a smokescreen to promote some ear-tickling teaching (2 Timothy 4:3).

Whether you are aware of it or not, 1 Maccabees 1:44-50 actually gives us specific examples of the kind of Hellenism directly imposed upon the Jews by Antiochus Epiphanes, and rightly opposed by the Maccabees:

"And the king sent letters by messengers to Jerusalem and the cities of Judah; he directed them to follow customs strange to the land, to forbid burnt offerings and sacrifices and drink offerings in the sanctuary, to profane sabbaths and feasts, to defile the sanctuary and the priests, to build altars and sacred precincts and shrines for idols, to sacrifice swine and unclean animals, and to leave their sons uncircumcised. They were to make themselves abominable by everything unclean and profane, so that they should forget the law and change all the ordinances. And whoever does not obey the command of the king shall die" (1 Maccabees 1:44-50, RSV).

The Hellenism that the Maccabees fought against included:

- following the Greek religion, which included the worship of multiple gods and images, and making sacrifices to them with unclean and unfit animals
- a prohibition on animal sacrifices and prescribed offerings according to the Torah
- a prohibition on keeping the seventh-day Sabbath
- a prohibition on circumcision
- a prohibition on studying the Torah and its ordinances, so the people would forget their covenant status with the God of Israel

The "Hellenism" that was **not** fought against was learning, speaking, or using the language in which the Apostolic Scriptures or New Testament were inspired by the Holy Spirit.[2] The Hellenism that was fought against was a way of life that would lead people away from the God of Israel and His Teaching.

Chanukah is to be a time of rededicating ourselves to the Lord, and to one another as fellow brothers and sisters. Yet there is one concept that I would like us to consider, one that is very Hebraic as seen in the Torah, and one that

---

[1] For a strident example, note the comments under the subheading "The Greek View(s) of Immortality" in the publication *To Be Absent From the Body* by J.K. McKee, which actually addresses the diverse views of the afterlife as held by the Ancient Greeks and Romans.

[2] I am fully aware of the fact that many of today's Messianic Believers think that the whole of the Apostolic Scriptures were written in Hebrew. This is more of an opinion, though, rather than a fact. Such a view would need to be substantiated by specific book-by-book analysis, and also engagement with relevant scholastic research. No one I have ever encountered advocating a so-called "Hebrew New Testament" has ever really done this.

seldom receives any attention from Messianic leaders or teachers: **the corporate identity of God's people.**

In Deuteronomy 6:25, the Ancient Israelites declare, "It will be righteousness for us if we are careful to observe all this commandment before the LORD our God, just as He commanded us" (NASU). Many people read this verse and assume that if an individual keeps all of God's commandments then that individual will be considered righteous. Of course, there are no examples that individual Ancient Israelites ever did this, as human actions are considered "filthy rags" (Isaiah 64:6, NIV) before God, and as soon as the Ancient Israelites entered into the Promised Land—idolatry largely prevailed (Book of Judges). The problem with this interpretation of Deuteronomy 6:25 is that it just assumes that individuals are in view. Whether you are aware of this or not, *tzedaqah* has a corporate context that relates to one being a part of God's people.[3] What is likely being said in Deuteronomy 6:25 is that if one keeps God's commandments he or she can be identified as being in covenant status before Him as a part of His people.

This kind of corporate identity is significantly foreign to a post-Enlightenment Western mind. How many of you have ever heard that there are places in the Bible when "righteousness" or "justification" is being talked about, where anything but individuals are probably in view? Various Christian theologians within the New Perspective of Paul (like James D.G. Dunn or N.T. Wright) have pointed out some possible places in Galatians and Romans where *dikaiosunē*, the Greek equivalent of *tzedaqah* via the Septuagint, has corporate connotations.[4] The reaction to their proposals have been met with a great deal of resistance among some evangelicals, as though they somehow deny the Biblical concept of justification by faith. All they have proposed, however, is that perhaps in a place like Romans 3:28, "For we maintain that a man is justified by faith apart from works of the Law" (NASU), inclusion among God's covenant people is the likely issue. Does this covenant inclusion come about via faith in God, or by "works of law" (whatever these "works of law" actually are)? This is a worthy topic of exploration for your Biblical studies.[5]

The problem is not that God is concerned with individuals; He surely is. Individual salvation is more important than any other concept we can emphasize! The problem comes when we over-emphasize the individual at the

---

[3] Cf. Harold G. Stigers, "*tz-d-q* (root)," in R. Laird Harris, Gleason L. Archer, Jr., and Bruce K. Waltke, eds., *Theological Wordbook of the Old Testament* (Chicago: Moody Press, 1980), 2:752-755.

[4] Consult the commentaries *Galatians for the Practical Messianic* and *Romans for the Practical Messianic* by J.K. McKee, for more information on this.

[5] For a further examination on how "works of law" likely related to ancient Jewish sectarian observances, consult the article "What Are 'Works of the Law'?" by J.K. McKee (appearing in *The New Testament Validates Torah*).

expense of the whole corporate Body of Messiah. Many of the divisions we have seen in Judaism, Christianity, and even the Messianic movement have largely come about because of an emphasis on hyper-individuality—**a direct result of our Western culture.** It is as simple as people not demonstrating enough concern for others, because when others' needs are considered as being more important than your own (Philippians 2:3), then the Body of Messiah can truly flourish. Consider how most interpret Romans 12:1, versus what the issue really is within the larger scope of Paul's letter:

"Therefore I urge you, brethren, by the mercies of God, to present your bodies a living and holy sacrifice, acceptable to God, *which is* your spiritual service of worship" (NASU).

The NIV actually renders this as "offer your bodies as living sacrifices," even though *thusian* appears in the singular, **not the plural.** While we are each to surely live our individual lives as a living sacrifice to God, in his teaching to the Romans Paul is more concerned about stopping the divisions present among them. He wants them to understand, "we, who are many, are one body in Messiah, and individually members one of another" (Romans 12:5, NASU). The living sacrifice that Paul has in mind here is not exclusively one of individuals being living sacrifices—but of the corporate Body of Messiah, *which is made up of individuals*, functioning as a singular living sacrifice. Lives of self-sacrifice and mutual submission to one another within the corporate Body of Messiah are able to accomplish the mission of God much better than individuals off on their own.

Similar to this is how Paul instructed the Corinthians, "Do you not know that you are a temple of God and *that* the Spirit of God dwells in you?" (1 Corinthians 3:16, NASU). And also, "Or do you not know that your body is a temple of the Holy Spirit who is in you, whom you have from God, and that you are not your own? (1 Corinthians 6:19, NASU). As important as it may be for us to individually think of ourselves as being a receptacle of the Holy Spirit, it is undeniable that *oidate*, "know," and *en humin*, "in you," appearing in 1 Corinthians 3:16, are in the **plural.** Likewise, 1 Corinthians 6:19 has references to *to sōma humōn...en humin...echete apo Theou, kai ouk este heautōn*—"your body...in you...you have from God, and that you are not your own" (NASU)—also with you in the **plural.** What does this all mean? It means that once again the corporate Body of Messiah is principally what is in view. Only by functioning together can we fully be a Temple of God's presence that will attract others to Him.

I believe that if there is anything distinctly Western that our faith community suffers from, it is our inability to function with corporate unity. It will not be impossible for us to function with corporate unity in the future, but in order for this to be achieved we must have a more refined understanding of what God's mission is for His people, what we need to be

Chanukah and Encountering Worldly Philosophies

doing in order to achieve that mission, and how we can be men and women empowered by the Holy Spirit who live in mutual submission to one another. **And the biggest challenge of all is to actually have hearts and minds transformed by the Holy Spirit!** If we have hearts and minds transformed by the Holy Spirit, then every single one of us will have a burden for the lost, and we will be able to "be subject to one another in the fear of Messiah" (Ephesians 5:21, NASU).

As you confront worldly philosophies at this *Chanukah*, consider your relationship to other Believers and how you can contribute to us all being a pleasing *corporate* living sacrifice before Him! How are we to *all* function as His Temple, and not necessarily individual "temples"? Rededicate yourselves not only to the Father, but to your fellow brothers and sisters, and we will definitely go far!

Messianic Winter Holiday Helper

-16-

Celebrating Chanukah Today

Margaret McKee Huey

Since 1996, our family has been in a state of transition concerning the Winter holiday celebrations. As evangelical Believers, we were originally raised to celebrate and observe Christmas, thinking that it was indeed a Biblical holy day. Was not the account of the birth of the Messiah recorded for us in Luke 2? Was not the event so exciting that a multitude of angels appeared to the shepherds in Bethlehem, to announce to them that the Messiah of Israel had been born? However, how many of our past Christmas celebrations have *only* had the simplicity of that wonderful message of, "Do not be afraid; for behold, I bring you good news of great joy which will be for all the people; for today in the city of David there has been born for you a Savior, who is Christ the Lord" (Luke 2:10-11, NASU)? Most of us who celebrated Christmas did not hold to this simplicity of observance. Instead, the Christmas we remember is full of traditional practices that often have nothing to do with the event that the angels proclaimed happened in Bethlehem in the ancient province of Judea. And, it is safe to say, that it is *these traditional practices* that so many of us have been challenged to stop.

Are the events recorded in Luke 2 Biblical? Absolutely! Is it appropriate to remember the birth of the Messiah and its proclamation by the angelic host? Most certainly! But we are not to continue to embrace the non-Biblical practices that have been handed down to us in ignorance by our forbearers. Why were they handed down to us in the first place, we must ask? Simply put, the answer for those of us who are not Jewish, is that many of our ancestors were not entirely grounded in the ways of God's Torah. Many of them simply did not know any better. They did not know that we were not to mix the holy with the profane, and were largely ignorant surrounding the Jewish background of the Apostolic Scriptures or New Testament. But for those of us who have been awakened and have embraced a Messianic walk with the Lord, we can no longer have this excuse.

Personal Family Testimony

For our family, the walk of faith that has led us to become Messianic has caused us to actively change three areas in our faith observance, which are different from our Church upbringing. First, we now observe a *Shabbat* rest every week, instead of participating in Sunday Church. Second, we now eat Biblically kosher, instead of anything that our palate desires. And third, we now observe the Biblical appointed times that are listed in Leviticus 23, instead of the Church holidays that were passed down from Catholicism to Protestantism. Has this transition been an easy one? No, because family traditions are hard to change. But I am happy to say that within our own small family, we have been able to adopt the Biblical practices and drop the non-Biblical ones "fairly" easily.

The main reasons that the changes have not been too hard are two-fold. First, we earnestly desire to be as Biblical as possible, and to continue down the path that the Protestant Reformers did before us. Not all of them, unfortunately, know what we know today about the Torah, the appointed times, *Shabbat*, the dietary laws, and the common heritage we share with Judaism. And second, we desire as a family to be like our Messiah Yeshua in all things, as much as possible.

I can say that in the continual transformation that our family has been through to become as Biblical as possible, we have been able to put away our Christmas observance. Instead, we celebrate *Chanukah*. Of course, as stated in the preceding articles in this publication, we are aware that *Chanukah* is not listed in Leviticus 23 (which it obviously could not be as it commemorates events over 1,000 years after the Exodus and Mount Sinai). It is considered to be an "extra-Biblical" observance.

With that in mind, some we have encountered think they do not have to observe it. But our family has come to the conclusion that to observe *Chanukah* is to do another thing that Yeshua did. That alone is reason enough to observe the feast! In John 10:22-23, the following is recorded:

"Then came *Hanukkah* in Yerushalayim. It was winter, and Yeshua was walking around inside the Temple area, in Shlomo's Colonnade" (CJB).

How did I never see that Yeshua was in Jerusalem for *Chanukah* all those years that I was in the Church? The answer is so simple, and one that we as Messianics see over and over again. The English translation for *Chanukah* is "Feast of Dedication." It never even occurred to me to go find out what that was. Remember, in the Church I had been taught that the "Jewish holidays" were not for us. Even if I had seen the word "*Chanukah*," it still would not have caused me to want to observe it.

Celebrating Chanukah Today

Some people downplay Yeshua's celebration of *Chanukah* by saying that "Just because Yeshua was there at this feast, it doesn't mean He was observing it since He was only on the portico." Others put down the idea of our remembering the miracle of the oil for eight days, because it appears in the Talmud (b.*Shabbat* 21b). But consider the words of the First Century historian Josephus, who records the law and practice that Judah Maccabee instituted for *Chanukah* that was in place during the lifetime of Yeshua:

"Now Judas celebrated the festival of the restoration of the sacrifices of the temple for eight days, and omitted no sort of pleasures thereon; but he feasted them upon very rich and splendid sacrifices; and he honoured God, and delighted them by hymns and psalms. Nay, they were so very glad at the revival of their customs, when, after a long time of intermission, they unexpectedly had regained the freedom of their worship, **that they made it a law for their posterity, that they should keep a festival, on account of the restoration of their temple worship, for eight days. And from that time to this we celebrate this festival, and call it Lights**" (*Antiquities of the Jews* 12.324-325).[1]

Family Observance

Our family has come to that place in our lives where memories of Christmas are just that—memories. We have extended family and friends who do not understand why we no longer have a Christmas tree, mistletoe, Santa Claus, reindeer, holiday wreathes, tinsel, or Christmas stockings. In fact, they never understood **why we did not have Santa Claus when we still celebrated Christmas!** As much as I love my extended family and friends, I love my Savior more. It is He whom I wish to please! So, with that in mind, I want to share with you just a bit of our family celebration of *Chanukah*.

The wonderful thing about the Biblical holidays is that our Heavenly Father wants us to remember the great events of Ancient Israel by celebrating them! *Chanukah* has so many wonderful truths that we can remember and consider. When Yeshua observed *Chanukah*, He did so in the very Temple that had been cleansed and rededicated by the Maccabees. As Josephus states, it was a time of great merriment and delight for the Jewish people. We, like they, can remember with great joy that God's Temple had been restored, so that our Messiah could obey the commandments that He needed to perform there, as the Redeemer of Israel. We can rejoice in the rededication of God's Temple, and to then remember to rededicate the "Temple" (1 Corinthians 6:18-20) that is our (corporate) body. We can light the candles of a *chanukia*, a nine-branched *menorah*, starting on the 25th of

---

[1] Flavius Josephus: *The Works of Josephus: Complete and Unabridged*, trans. William Whiston (Peabody, MA: Hendrickson, 1987), 328.

Messianic Winter Holiday Helper

Kislev, for eight days to remember the miracle of the oil. We can say the blessings over our meals and we can delight in being part of the household of faith. We can delight in joining our Jewish brethren by celebrating *Chanukah* with them.

Our family keeps a very simple holiday observance in mind. First, to our extended family and friends, we still send out holiday greetings as we approach the calendar New Year, letting them know how our previous year has been and how our family has been doing, but these are not Christmas cards. Second, we still send holiday gifts, often wrapped in generic blue and white (*Chanukah*) paper, but not Christmas presents. And third, we can still invite them to a holiday meal, but not Christmas dinner. When our family and friends send us Christmas cards, we receive them as holiday greetings. When they send us Christmas presents, we receive them as holiday gifts and open them as a part of our *Chanukah* festivities. When they invite us to eat with them during Christmas, we go and enjoy the fellowship and love. They believe that they are reaching out to us at this time of year, because this is how they celebrate the birth of the Messiah. We receive their holiday tokens to us with the same love for the Messiah that they have. **We do not make ourselves odious to our extended family during this time.**

As to our own observance in our home, that too is kept simple. We have always loved to center celebrations around the dinner table. Each night of *Chanukah*, we will have a special dinner, and say the prayers and light the appropriate candles on the *chanukia*. (See **Liturgical Resources** section) A member of our family might read part of the account from the Books of the Maccabees, or we may at least discuss a theme seen about the Maccabees and relate it to contemporary events. Traditional foods that have been cooked in oil are served to remind us of the miracle of the oil. (See **Kosher Your Plate for Chanukah** section) When one of the nights is on *Shabbat*, we will celebrate it with our congregational body. All in all, we use the special days to delight in the Lord and in His goodness to us. Gifts can be given and exchanged during the holiday season, either one each night, or all at once if some family members are visiting. Songs can be sung at the table. A general feeling of family and fellowship should permeate each night. The love of the Messiah should be strongly felt in each home.

As to decorating one's house, there are many things that can be done. We like to display all of our *menorahs* as decorations. We use small white lights in different areas of our house. The traditional colors for *Chanukah* are blue and white. These colors can be introduced around your home. In our home, this is very easy, because it is already my basic color scheme!

Lights, candles, and festive color that now go with the wonderful meals are planned for eight different nights! These are the basic ingredients for a wonderful time with your family, when you can all reflect on the Messiah, who is the Light of the World. What could be easier? It is so simple, and yet so rich in history and meaning. Our family can truly say that it is not missing out on anything during the holiday season!

Loving Each Other

If our extended family or friends question why we do not celebrate Christmas anymore, we make sure to let them know that even though we have stopped practicing various non-Biblical traditions that Christmas represents today—we still very much believe in the Biblical account of the birth of Yeshua as it is recorded in Luke 2. We believe that He may have been conceived by the Holy Spirit during the *Chanukah* season and born nine months later during the Feast of Tabernacles (*Sukkot*). Although they usually do not understand what we are sharing, our Christian family and friends will certainly still see that we have not stopped believing in the Messiah. Consider the fact that, for many people, if you announce that you "Don't believe in Christmas because of all the pagan practices that have been added to the event," they often do not understand what you mean. They think you do not believe in the miraculous birth of the Messiah anymore!

How do we deal with our extended family and friends who still do not understand why we are not celebrating Christmas like they are? Our family believes that this is a very special time of year! It is a time when people generally and genuinely want to reach out to others in the love of the Messiah. As Messianics, how can we act like such behavior is wrong or evil? We cannot! We, who are to walk as Messiah Yeshua walked, must reach out to others in love at this time of year more than ever. Yeshua told us that people would know that we are His disciples by the love that we have for one another (John 13:35).

During the Winter season, we need to love our family and friends in such a way so that they will be drawn to us, and not be repelled. It is only through our unconditional love for them that one day they will want to know what we know about walking like the Messiah. One day they will want to know why we have put aside the celebration of Christmas and are observing *Chanukah*. One day they will want to know why we love to walk as Yeshua walked. One day they will want to know why we have become thoroughly Messianic. So, let us reach out in love and show them a better way.

And, just as I also stated in the Introduction, only by demonstrating Yeshua's love, will any one of us be able to demonstrate who the Messiah is to a Jewish person, who is celebrating *Chanukah* without the knowledge of the Light of the world who delivers us from darkness. When you go to purchase any of your *Chanukah* celebration resources: your *menorah*, candles, traditional foods for the season, etc., a non-believing Jewish person might see you in the store. You will have the opportunity to wish him or her a Happy

Chanukah! If you yourself are non-Jewish, you will certainly have the ability to fulfill the Apostle Paul's mandate of the nations provoking his brethren to salvation (Romans 11:11). While Jewish people are often perplexed at why a non-Jew would want to celebrate *Chanukah*, seeds that can later germinate in them coming to salvation in the Jewish Messiah can certainly be planted!

Let us enjoy this Winter holiday time within our homes, and rejoice in the history and drama of *Chanukah!* And in all things let us reflect on Yeshua our Messiah, who is the Light of the World.

Have a blessed holiday season!

FAQs on the Winter Holiday Season

adapted from the Messianic Apologetics website

Christmas and the Nativity

Do you celebrate Christmas?

Christmas is, without question, a very sensitive subject for many Believers—and we would emphasize understanding between those who do not celebrate it, and those who celebrate it in ignorance. We cannot find in Scripture where God mandates that we observe a holiday with decorated trees, mistletoe, holly, Santa Claus, and presents. On the contrary, the Prophet Jeremiah tells us that we are to not be as the heathen who adorn trees:

"Thus says the LORD, 'Do not learn the way of the nations, and do not be terrified by the signs of the heavens although the nations are terrified by them; for the customs of the peoples are delusion; because it is wood cut from the forest, the work of the hands of a craftsman with a cutting tool. They decorate *it* with silver and with gold; they fasten it with nails and with hammers so that it will not totter'" (Jeremiah 10:2-4, NASU).

This same concept is reemphasized for us in Deuteronomy 16:21: "You shall not plant for yourself an Asherah of any kind of tree beside the altar of the LORD your God, which you shall make for yourself" (NASU).

We do not celebrate Christmas, nor do we endorse a "substitute" for it, either. We do not believe that the celebration of Christmas was God's original intention. Christmas today is highly commercialized and is often more about self-indulgence than anything else. Of course, we are not against "giving gifts," but the purpose of Christmas today for many people, including purported Believers, is about *self* rather than about seeing the Messiah lifted up.

We do not celebrate Christmas. But, we are not against people remembering the birth of Yeshua, either, although it probably did not occur during the Winter. The birth of Messiah Yeshua is a part of the Bible that is to be remembered and taught upon, something appropriate for *any* time of year. So with this in mind, it is important to remember that at "Christmas time," people are relatively free to talk about Yeshua and the gospel, and many are presented to Him who would normally not be during the rest of the year. Obviously, in spite of the questionable origins of December 25, God is going to work through those who sincerely believe that they are honoring Him.

Messianic Winter Holiday Helper

Without question, this issue will continue to baffle many Messianic Believers in years to come, as we learn to properly deal with those who celebrate Christmas in ignorance, not knowing where it comes from. As a faith community we will need to change all the "Christmas is pagan!" rhetoric to something less sensationalistic, yet still be able to properly communicate that we do not celebrate it. We also must emphasize understanding and fairness for others in this area. Christmas as it is known today is not a Biblically mandated holiday, and on this basis we do not celebrate it. But there is also the Biblical reality of the Child born at Bethlehem who is our Savior, so with this issue, let us truly not "throw out the Baby."

Consult the article "**The Christmas Challenge**," appearing in this publication, for a further discussion of this issue.

I have heard it said that your ministry does not believe that Christmas and Easter are pagan holidays. Could you please explain?

Messianic Apologetics is a solution-driven Messianic ministry. In dealing with Messianic theology, spirituality, and controversial subject matters—we try to deal in fair-minded and scholarly terms, demonstrating the testimony of people who have changed for the better spiritually, and not worse. As it relates to the holidays, for example, all too often during *Chanukah* in the Winter, and Passover in the Spring, we as Messianic Believers can spend too much time focusing on what our Christian brothers and sisters are doing in ignorance, and not focusing enough on the holidays that we are celebrating, and uplifting Messiah Yeshua in them.

It has been our observation that "pagan" is a buzzword that is used far too frequently by those in the Messianic community today. "Pagan" can be used by anyone to lambast any Christian doctrine or belief—and often not in any clear Biblical, historical, or even rational context. Much of the usage of the word "pagan" is done emotionally, on the part of self-disenfranchised Messianics who errantly believe that mainstream Christianity has nothing, and/or has had nothing, to offer the Body of Messiah for centuries. Their pursuit is often to expose anything perceived as "pagan," rather than becoming Scripturally compliant with the Word of God, and demonstrate to our Christian brothers and sisters the example of people who have changed for the better by becoming Messianic and Torah obedient. If, however, Christians see that all we do is condemn them because they "do this" or "don't do that," they may want nothing to do with us, and perhaps rightfully so. We have to have the appropriate attitude in approaching them and be constructive and spiritually edifying, which sadly is not evident in some sectors of our faith community today.

As it relates to the Christian holidays of Christmas and Easter, we have addressed them in the articles **"The Christmas Challenge"** and **"What is the Problem With Easter?"**[1] Let us state on the record that we do not encourage the celebration of these holidays, and are fully aware of their questionable origins. These are replacements for the *moedim* or appointed times of the Lord in Leviticus 23, that were officially established by the Roman Catholic Church, and many Protestants today thus celebrate them (albeit in ignorance). There are traditions associated with these two holidays that originate from paganism and not the Bible.

Nevertheless, we know that as a Messianic family when we were still Church-going Christians that when we celebrated Christmas and Easter, **we did not** worship Christmas trees and the Easter bunny. We celebrated these two holidays with the understanding that we were commemorating the birth of the Messiah and the resurrection of the Messiah. We did not know of their questionable origins. But the questionable origins we are talking about are *the traditions* of the Christmas tree, evergreen, mistletoe, the Easter bunny, and Easter eggs. All too often, when Christians see many Messianics' attitudes related to these two holidays, they believe that what is in actuality being criticized and branded as "pagan" are the events of the birth of our Savior and His resurrection—as opposed to the traditions that have been commonly associated with them, whose origins are certainly not in the Bible.

Many Christians in ignorance celebrate Christmas and Easter without knowing how these two holidays came into being. We know as a family that God honored us in our ignorance for what we did, because in our minds we were celebrating the birth and the resurrection of Yeshua. But we also know that when we were shown the truth about the origins of these two holidays, that we were given a choice by Him and we had to change. We have changed, and now celebrate the Biblical holidays of Leviticus 23, emphasizing the Messianic richness that is in these festivals and what they teach us about God's ongoing plan of salvation history. We have no intention of celebrating Christmas or Easter again. It is our choice, however, that in dealing with Christian friends and family, we show them what we should be doing from the Scriptures, and what they have missed out on by not celebrating the Biblical holidays. Once you commit yourself to celebrating the Lord's appointed times, we have discovered that you will not want to go back to the human substitutions that are often made.

We believe that Christmas and Easter are holidays of a different variety than holidays such as Halloween. Halloween is a holiday that is obviously

---

[1] This article is reproduced in our *Messianic Spring Holiday Helper*.

totally committed to the glorification of witches, goblins, ghouls, demons, and Satan. It can, in no uncertain terms, be called a pagan holiday. There are no Biblical overtones or undertones to it. Christians who celebrate Halloween need to be reprimanded for it, and there are a host of Christian apologetic ministries that speak against it.[2]

Christmas and Easter are of a different variety because they do have Biblical overtones to them. We have to remember that when we speak about the origins of these two holidays, we must put ourselves in the position of those sincere Believers who are celebrating them, thinking that they are religious holidays founded in Scripture, and are celebrating them *not* for the sake of the Christmas tree or Easter bunny—but to remember the birth of Yeshua and His resurrection. These are Biblical events worthy of our remembrance. However, the way that Christianity has chosen to remember them is improper, because we are not to follow the fallen ways of the nations (Deuteronomy 18:9).

In our dealings with Christians, it is our opinion that it is inappropriate to call Christmas and Easter "pagan" because such comments are easy to be misinterpreted as criticizing the events of Messiah's birth and resurrection, as opposed to the participation of traditions that originate in anything but the Bible. We call these holidays non-Biblical because it will force our Christian brothers and sisters into God's Word to see if their celebration is truly justified and based in the Bible. The Messianic community uses the word "pagan" far too frequently, and it is often because we do not feel spiritually and Scripturally sound to defend ourselves. Sadly, the word "pagan" is used as a crutch and a self-defense mechanism because some feel unsure of themselves, and are unable to adequately defend their beliefs from the Bible and history.

We believe that a much better way to answer the question, "Do you celebrate Christmas and Easter?" is to respond with a question: "Are Christmas and Easter listed among the appointed times of Leviticus 23?" This will hopefully force fellow Believers back into the Word of God, as opposed to getting them unnecessarily offended. And if there is anything that the Messianic community desperately needs right now, it is a return to the Scriptures, and letting the Bible answer people—rather than insulting them *ad naseum* with the term "pagan," as is the case far too frequently.

---

[2] Consult the article "A Messianic Perspective on Halloween" by J.K. McKee (appearing in the *Messianic Fall Holiday Helper*).

Should I attend Christmas dinner with my extended family?

Many of today's Messianic Believers, who once celebrated Christmas, still have to interact with their Christian family during the Winter holiday season. The Spring holiday season is admittedly much easier, because Easter does not have the same kind of commercialism associated with it as Christmas, and many churches today hold some kind of Passover *seder* meal. It is much easier to tell Christian family, who are familiar with the Passover *seder* to some degree, that you remember Yeshua's resurrection in conjunction with your Messianic congregation's Passover remembrance.

How you answer your family's request as to what Messianics do to remember Yeshua's birth is not as easy, not only because there is no agreement in today's Messianic community as to what is to be done, but even more so because of the significant commercialism during this time of year. Christmas parties are held throughout the month of December, and traditionally extended family does get together for some kind of Christmas dinner. It is easy for Messianics who do not live close to extended Christian family to say that it will be difficult to attend Christmas dinner, but this is not everyone.

Too frequently, our ministry has heard stories of those who will write mean-spirited letters to Christian family, telling them not to send them any Christmas presents or invite them to Christmas dinner as they "are not pagans anymore." This implies to extended family, who are God-fearing Christians who love Jesus, that they really do not know the Lord. The damage that this has done, and the bad reputation this has given our faith community, **is immense.** A person can always choose his or her friends, but a person can never choose his or her family. When you face the most difficult seasons in your life such as when a member of your immediate family dies, or when you are facing severe financial problems, your extended family will often be there to help, whereas your friends may not. You have the responsibility to always have good relations with your extended family, beyond the Fifth Commandment's requirement to honor father and mother (Exodus 20:12; Deuteronomy 5:16).

So when the month of December comes, should you turn down an invitation to Christmas dinner? *Only you can decide this for yourself.* Some will answer "No!" But some will attend. They will recognize that this might be the only time of year to see all of their extended family, especially those who are aging and who may not live long. Many of us just recognize Christmas dinner as yet another meal, and will keep our comments regarding "Christmas" to "Did you have a good holiday?" **Some of us desire good** relations with our extended family. And, in demonstrating a degree of good will to them, we actually find it appropriate to invite them into our homes during one of the nights of *Chanukah*—even if it might be via the "guise" that we will be eating some rather tasty fried foods!

When should Messianic Believers remember Yeshua's birth?

Almost all authorities are agreed that Yeshua the Messiah was not born on December 25, and that the choice of December 25 for Christmas was an arbitrary date in ancient history, giving former pagans an opportunity to remember something different than what they had previously observed.[3] Today's Messianics, recognizing the questionable origins and traditions associated with Christmas on December 25, will still often recognize that the birth of Yeshua, as principally recorded in Luke 2, is still an event worthy of remembering. But when should it be done? What would be a date or season that is much more appropriate for us considering the entry of the Messiah into the world at Bethlehem?

Many of today's Messianic Believers are of the conviction that Yeshua the Messiah was born in conjunction with the Feast of Tabernacles. This is primarily based on passages such as John 1:14, which speak of how "the Word became flesh, and dwelt among us" (NASU). The Greek verb *skēnoō* is employed in this verse, with its noun form *skēnē* frequently used in the Torah (i.e., Leviticus 23:34, 42-43) to render the Hebrew *sukkah*. YLT actually renders John 1:14 with "the Word became flesh, and did tabernacle among us." It is not at all inappropriate to connect the typology of *Sukkot* to the Incarnation of Yeshua. Yet, just like with those ancient Christian leaders who arbitrarily chose December 25 to remember Yeshua's birth, so might concluding that Yeshua was born during the Feast of Tabernacles also be a bit arbitrary. There is simply no way for us to know for certain.

It is sad, though, that those who are of the opinion that Yeshua might have been born during Tabernacles, have usually been met with varying degrees of resistance when they have tried to integrate this into their *Sukkot* festivities. Attacks along the lines of "We should not be remembering anyone's birth!" are usually issued. The actual, Biblical record of Yeshua's birth can be literally ripped to shreds. A few contentious people who will

---

[3] J. Theodore Mueller, "Christmas," in Everett F. Harrison, ed., *Baker's Dictionary of Theology* (Grand Rapids: Baker Book House, 1960), 117; Ronald V. Huggins, "Christmas," in David Noel Freedman, ed., *Eerdmans Dictionary of the Bible* (Grand Rapids: Eerdmans, 2000), 240; Brett Scott Provance, *Pocket Dictionary of Liturgy & Worship* (Downers Grove, IL: InterVarsity, 2009), pp 37-38.

without hesitation claim that "Christmas is pagan!" now want nothing to do with what the Gospels tell us about the birth of the King of Kings, and prefer to excise it from their Bibles. So to avoid controversy and encourage unity during the *Sukkot* season, those who believe that Yeshua was born during this time often never bring it up, and keep their thoughts to themselves.

Certainly, it is justified to question the spiritual maturity (and even salvation) of those who will not even read passages like Luke 2 or Matthew 1-2 that detail the nativity, and what took place during the early years of Yeshua's life, yet claim Him as their Savior. **Anyone who has placed his or her trust in Yeshua still has to deal with the Biblical text.** Disregarding it completely, as though it does not exist or that it is too "Churchy" for us to consider—even when not celebrating Christmas—is sad evidence of how a number of people in our faith community are utter neophytes when it comes to reading Scriptures about Yeshua's life and ministry.

Not all are convinced that Yeshua was born during the season of *Sukkot*, or are at least skeptical of this proposal and think it needs more research. Yet, it is clear that because the birth of Yeshua is a part not only of Scripture—but also our faith—that we should find *a time* to consider what its message means for us. Aside from celebrating Christmas, or trying to remember the nativity during the Feast of Tabernacles, **it might be that the "safest" time to address the birth of Yeshua is when *Shemot*** (Exodus 1:1-6:1) **appears in the yearly Torah cycle.** What makes this an appropriate time to consider the message of Yeshua's birth, is that parallels between the birth of Moses and the birth of the Messiah—who came as a "second Moses"—can be considered.

Of course, even if we choose to examine the birth of Yeshua when *Shemot* appears in the Torah cycle, there will still be those few who will oppose it, because they have adopted a very immature and ungodly attitude toward Christmas and their Christian brothers and sisters. Unfortunately, there is nothing that can really be done with this kind of people, other than to ask them whether they think the Biblical account of Yeshua's birth should be removed from the Holy Scriptures. And if they actually say yes—then we should wonder whether or not 2 John 7 applies concerning such people:

"For many deceivers have gone out into the world, those who do not acknowledge Yeshua the Messiah *as* coming in the flesh. This is the deceiver and the antimessiah" (NASU).

Chanukah

Where can I find information about the *menorah* being lit for eight days, on one cruse of oil, following the Maccabees' rededication of the Temple?

The Maccabees drove the Seleucids out of the Land of Israel in the month of Kislev 165 B.C.E., which is in about the month of December. They had the task of cleaning up the mess that the Seleucids had left, notably in the city of Jerusalem and in the Temple complex. Antiochus' forces had completely ransacked the Temple and made it into a haven of idolatry. The Temple needed to be cleansed of its defilement and restored to its previous position so proper sacrifices could once again be performed. Of all of the items of Temple furniture that had to be cleansed and rededicated, one of the most important was the great lampstand or *menorah*. The *menorah* required special consecrated oil in order to be lit. Some historical traditions actually indicate that the Maccabees had to setup a "makeshift *menorah*" out of iron bars covered with zinc (Scholium to *Megillat Ta'anit*),[4] while a new gold *menorah* was being crafted.

The Festival of Dedication or *Chanukah*, as attested in the historical record, was mandated as a national celebration so that the community could remember the sacrifice of the Maccabees, and the rededication of the Temple in Jerusalem:

"Then Judas and his brothers and all the assembly of Israel determined that every year at that season the days of dedication of the altar should be observed with gladness and joy for eight days, beginning with the twenty-fifth day of the month of Chislev" (1 Maccabees 4:59, RSV).

The historian Josephus wrote about the establishment of *Chanukah* as a new, national celebration for the Jewish people in his work *Antiquities of the Jews*:

"Now Judas celebrated the festival of the restoration of the sacrifices of the temple for eight days; and omitted no sort of pleasures thereon: but he feasted them upon very rich and splendid sacrifices; and he honored God, and delighted them, by hymns and psalms. Nay, they were so very glad at the revival of their customs, when after a long time of intermission, they unexpectedly had regained the freedom of their worship, for eight days. And from that time to this we celebrate this festival, and call it Lights. I suppose

---

[4] Moshe David Herr, "Hanukkah," in Encyclopaedia Judaica. MS Windows 9x. Brooklyn: Judaica Multimedia (Israel) Ltd, 1997.

the reason was, because this liberty beyond our hopes appeared to us; and that thence was the name given to that festival" (12.323-325).[5]

The Greek name for this holiday as recorded by Josephus was *phōta*, meaning "Lights." The connection of *Chanukah* to the lighting of the *menorah* goes all the way back to the First Century B.C.E. Talmud tractates b.*Shabbat* 21b and 23a detail various *halachic* rulings from this period regarding the lighting of the *chanukia*, and debates between the Rabbinical Schools of Hillel and Shammai. These rulings date anywhere from 50-100 years before Messiah Yeshua.

The wonderful story that enlivens our *Chanukah* celebration concerns the fact that when the Maccabees were cleansing the Temple, only one cruse of consecrated oil was found to light the *menorah*. The Torah says that the oil used in the Tabernacle/Temple service was to be "clear oil of beaten olives for the light, to make a lamp burn continually" (Exodus 27:20, NASU; cf. Leviticus 24:2), and the prevailing *halachah* of the day required eight days for this oil to be produced. While there was plenty of olive oil present to use in the Land of Israel, only special consecrated oil could be used for burning in the *menorah*. The miracle of the eight days of oil is spoken of in the Talmud, in the midst of the arguments about how the *chanukia* was to be lit:

> "What's the point of Hanukkah? It is in line with what our rabbis have taught on Tannaite authority: On the twenty-fifth of Kislev the days of Hanukkah, which are eight, begin. On these days it is forbidden to lament the dead and to fast.
>
> "For when the Greeks entered the sanctuary, they made all of the oil that was in the sanctuary unclean. But when the rule of the Hasmonean house took hold and they conquered them, they searched but found only a single jar of oil, lying with the seal of the high priest. But that jar had enough oil only for a single day. But there was a miracle done with it, and they lit the lamp with it for eight days. The next year they assigned these days and made them festival days for the recitation of Hallel psalms [Psa. 113-118] and for thanksgiving" (b.*Shabbat* 21b).[6]

This story can be certainly deduced from the historical events recorded for us in 1-4 Maccabees, the writings of Josephus, and others. While some people today brand the miracle of the oil remaining lit for eight days as only a "legend," the fact of the matter remains that Orthodox Jews, most Conservative Jews, and the vast majority of the Messianic Jewish community today, believe with great faith that it actually happened. The challenge for

---

[5] Flavius Josephus: *The Works of Josephus: Complete and Unabridged*, trans. William Whiston (Peabody, MA: Hendrickson, 1987), 328.

[6] *The Babylonian Talmud: A Translation and Commentary*. MS Windows XP. Peabody, MA: Hendrickson, 2005. CD-ROM.

Messianic Winter Holiday Helper

some, particularly in the independent Hebrew/Hebraic Roots movement, is the fact that many are unwilling to accept Jewish works like the Mishnah or Talmud as having any valid history (or for that same matter, the writings of the Church Fathers). Many are disrespectful to Jewish custom and tradition, and assert that it has no place in their interpretation and application of God's Word.

What can you tell me about the Feast of Dedication being celebrated in place of *Sukkot* by the Maccabees when they rededicated the Temple?

When the Seleucid Greek invaders occupied the Land of Israel, it was forbidden for any of the Biblical holidays to be celebrated, possibly on the threat of death. Obviously, this would have included *Sukkot* or the Feast of Tabernacles. Many Jews continued to celebrate the appointed times in secret, or in some limited way without being caught.

Some in the independent Hebrew/Hebraic Roots movement, who largely frown on observing *Chanukah*, say that when the Maccabees rededicated the Second Temple that the eight-day festival they celebrated was Tabernacles, which they were unable to celebrate prior to this time. They base it on statements made in 2 Maccabees 10:5-6:

"It happened that on the same day on which the sanctuary had been profaned by the foreigners, the purification of the sanctuary took place, that is, on the twenty-fifth day of the same month, which was Chislev. And they celebrated it for eight days with rejoicing, in the manner of the feast of booths, remembering how not long before, during the feast of booths, they had been wandering in the mountains and caves like wild animals" (RSV).

The REB actually says "they recalled how, only a short time before, they had kept that feast while living like wild animals in the mountains and caves." Did the Maccabees actually try to "keep *Sukkot*" while evading the Seleucid armies in the wilderness? We might never have an answer to this question. But what we do know is that while there were various elements and themes of *Sukkot* brought into the first Festival of Dedication, it was celebrated and mandated as its own unique holiday. The text continues, clarifying what the Jews assembled in Jerusalem were actually doing:

"Therefore bearing ivy-wreathed wands and beautiful branches and also fronds of palm, they offered hymns of thanksgiving to him who had given success to the purifying of his own holy place. They decreed by public ordinance and vote that the whole nation of the Jews should observe these days every year" (2 Maccabees 10:7-8, RSV).

We are told that this new holiday, commemorating the rededication of the Temple, was "decreed by public edict, ratified by vote, that the whole nation of the Jews should observe these days every year" (NRSV). This makes *Chanukah* something new and unique that was not intended to be a substitute for *Sukkot*, even though *Sukkot* may have served as a template for much of it to be based upon.

Why is there a nine-branched *menorah* used for *Chanukah*, when there was a seven-branched *menorah* used in the Temple?

By and large in Judaism, there is a prohibition on recreating objects used in Tabernacle/Temple worship to be used in the local synagogue. This tradition developed during the time when the Temple was still in operation, and the synagogue was largely a place of assembly for teaching. As *Chanukah* developed as a holiday, the *chanukia* was formulated as an emblem that looked substantially similar to the seven-branched *menorah*, but it was intended to be lit for eight days to memorialize the miracle of the oil, mimicking the *menorah*, but not to be exactly like it. Today, of course, there are many kinds of *chanukia*s, which range from traditional ones looking similar to the Temple *menorah*, to others that only allow eight candle spaces for lighting that are anything but traditional.

In what way did Antiochus Epiphanes commit the "Abomination of Desolation"? I thought this was a future event.

The event describing the desecration of the Temple by Antiochus, even though it actually was carried out by an Athenian senator (2 Maccabees 6:1), was in fulfillment of the Prophet Daniel's words in Daniel 11:31: "Forces from him will arise, desecrate the sanctuary fortress, and do away with the regular sacrifice. And they will set up the abomination of desolation" (NASU). It may seem confusing for us because the eschatological term that often describes "the Abomination of Desolation" in most pre-millennial prophecy circles is used to refer to another event, that of Daniel 9:27:

"And he will make a firm covenant with the many for one week, but in the middle of the week he will put a stop to sacrifice and grain offering; and on the wing of abominations *will come* one who makes desolate, even until a complete destruction, one that is decreed, is poured out on the one who makes desolate" (NASU).

Without a doubt, what happened in the period of the Maccabees was an abomination before the God of Israel. But it was not the final abomination spoken of by Daniel that occurs at the end of the seventy-weeks prophecy. A future leader, much like Antiochus, eager to unite the world as one people worshipping him, will make all of the previous abominations that have occurred on the Temple Mount seem like nothing. The text uses the plural *kenaf shiqutzim*, indicating that there have been *multiple abominations* committed,[7] but this one will be the *extreme abomination*, topping all the others. This is perhaps reflected in the NLT rendering, "And as a climax to all his terrible deeds, he will set up a sacrilegious object that causes desecration." The Apostle Paul describes this in greater detail in 2 Thessalonians 2:3-4:

"Let no one in any way deceive you, for *it will not come* unless the apostasy comes first, and the man of lawlessness is revealed, the son of destruction, who opposes and exalts himself above every so-called god or object of worship, so that he takes his seat in the temple of God, displaying himself as being God" (NASU).

From Paul's vantage point, the Abomination of Desolation has yet to occur; and from our view today, it likewise has yet to occur. Yeshua the Messiah makes this clear in His Olivet Discourse of Matthew 24:

"Therefore when you see the ABOMINATION OF DESOLATION [Daniel 9:27] which was spoken of through Daniel the prophet, standing in the holy place (let the reader understand), then those who are in Judea must flee to the mountains. Whoever is on the housetop must not go down to get the things out that are in his house. Whoever is in the field must not turn back to get his cloak. But woe to those who are pregnant and to those who are nursing babies in those days! But pray that your flight will not be in the winter, or on a Sabbath" (Matthew 24:15-20, NASU).

Some have claimed that the Abomination of Desolation occurred in ancient times when Jerusalem and the Temple were destroyed in 70 C.E. But that is contingent on several things. While Yeshua has Daniel's description of the Abomination in mind, His statement is preceded by the ever-critical, "This gospel of the kingdom shall be preached in the whole world as a testimony to all the nations, and then the end will come" (Matthew 24:14, NASU). Even

---

[7] While many interpreters connect *kanaf* or "wing" (NASU) to a part of the Temple, it can also relate to the extremity of a garment or the wing of a bird (Francis Brown, S.R. Driver, and Charles A. Briggs, *Hebrew and English Lexicon of the Old Testament* [Oxford: Clarendon Press, 1979], 489). Because of the ambiguity of prophecy, while *kenaf shiqutzim* has most often been interpreted as "a wing *of the temple*" (NIV), we should be inclined to remember how *kanaf* is used to speak of a cloak spread out or the extreme ends of the Earth (H.F.W. Gesenius: *Gesenius' Hebrew-Chaldee Lexicon to the Old Testament*, trans. Samuel Prideaux Tregelles [Grand Rapids: Baker, 1979], 406), connecting it to how this final Abomination of Desolation will stretch far over the other abominations previously committed on the Temple Mount.

today, almost 2,000 years later, this word has yet to be fulfilled. Furthermore, we see the statement "let the reader understand" inserted into the text, presumably by Matthew when he composed his Gospel. When Matthew wrote his Gospel also tells us quite a bit as to whether or not this has occurred. If Matthew's Gospel post-dates the destruction of the Temple in 70 C.E., as most conservative and liberal scholars believe, then it is indeed an indication that this Abomination of Desolation is to occur in the future.

There has been no leader like Antiochus, or even an emissary of his, who has entered into the Temple in Jerusalem to be worshipped as God. In fact, there is no Temple in Jerusalem today where this prophecy could even be fulfilled. The seventy-weeks prophecy of Daniel has yet to be completely fulfilled, as when it is all over we are to see the restoration of Israel and God's Kingdom on Earth, stated clearly in Daniel 9:24:

"Seventy weeks have been decreed for your people and your holy city, to finish the transgression, to make an end of sin, to make atonement for iniquity, to bring in everlasting righteousness, to seal up vision and prophecy and to anoint the most holy *place*" (NASU).

We are still awaiting to see everlasting righteousness established in the Earth. That has not happened, and any claim by theologians or teachers that it has is misguided.

The example of Antiochus Epiphanes is very, very important to understand. It lays the historical precedent as being one of the many abominations that has occurred on the Temple Mount in Jerusalem. This abomination in 167 B.C.E. was followed by the Roman destruction of Jerusalem in 70 C.E., and the subsequent erection of a temple to Jupiter. Likewise, when Islam expanded throughout the Middle East the Dome of the Rock was built on the Temple Mount. Today, we await the reconstruction of the Temple by many of the Temple Mount faithful groups in Israel, and then we can see the climax of all of these abominations. Unlike those who committed abominations in the past, though, the man of lawlessness will be able to broadcast himself to the world, so everyone, not just those in Jerusalem, will be able to see him declare himself as God. Do you think Antiochus Epiphanes would have liked to do this? Well, the same spirit of antimessiah that was in him will be in someone else in the future.

Messianic Winter Holiday Helper

KOSHER YOUR PLATE

MESSIANIC
WINTER HOLIDAY
HELPER

Kosher Your Plate for Chanukah

Each night of *Chanukah* is a wonderful time of fun and fellowship. While you light your *menorah* and open gifts for each of the eight nights of *Chanukah*, it is also customary to enjoy special and filling meals of fried foods. The following are a variety of recipes that our family enjoys for this season, which you can use to set a special table, or employ at various *Chanukah* parties. But do note that not every main dish is something that has been "deep fat fried" and is an "artery clogger." Some of the fried foods included are side dishes, intended to complement a more "conventional" main dish.

MAIN DISHES

Beef Sauerbraten

1 (4-5 lb) beef brisket
1 cup water
1 cup vinegar
1 sliced lemon
2 sliced onions
4 bay leaves
2 tsp. pickling spices
12 gingersnaps

Place meat in a crock-pot dish and add all the ingredients, except gingersnaps. Marinate meat for 2 days in your refrigerator, turning it several times. Next, cook the beef in a crock-pot on low for 6–8 hours. When cooked, place the meat on a serving dish and keep it warm. Take the marinade and strain it. Then cook the marinade with the added gingersnaps on high for 15 minutes. Serve the Beef Sauerbraten with the gingersnap sauce over potato latkes.

Beef Burgundy

2-3 pound beef brisket
1 can French onion soup
½ can Burgundy wine

Prepare the beef brisket for cooking by soaking it in saltwater so that all the blood is drained out. Cut off all the fat. Place the beef in a crock-pot and pour the soup and wine over the meat. Cover and cook on high for 1 hour, then turn the heat down to low for 6-8 hours. When it is finished, serve as your main dish.

Marinated Lamb
5 pound lamb roast
2 cloves garlic
¼ cup kosher salt
2 tablespoons peppercorns, cracked
1 tablespoon rosemary
3 cups dry red wine

Prepare the lamb roast for cooking by soaking it in salt water so that all the blood is drained out. Cut off all the fat. Cut the garlic into 6 slices and put in small slits in the meat. Salt and pepper all over. Place lamb in a large bowl with one cup of wine over it. Refrigerate overnight. Drain lamb and place in a crock-pot with the remaining wine. Cover and cook on high for 1 hour, then turn the heat down to low for 8-10 hours, turning at least once. When it is finished, cut into thin slices and serve as your main dish. Enjoy!

Kosher Turkey—Florida Style
12 pound or larger kosher turkey
6 or more oranges
Salt
Vegetable Oil

Soak your kosher turkey in water for several hours to remove all blood. Rub the cavities of the turkey with salt. Fill the cavities with oranges that have been cut in quarters with the peel still on. Fold the wings across back with tips touching. Tuck drumsticks under the band of skin or tie together. Place breast side up in roasting pan. Brush with oil. Roast at 325 degree oven according to cooking time on your turkey package. The oranges in the cavity will keep your turkey moist and give it a wonderful flavor! (Kosher turkey can be ordered online, if your grocery does not carry it.)

Duck L'Orange
1 5-6 pound duck
1 large onion, chopped
3 tablespoons butter
Juice of 2 sweet oranges
Salt & pepper taste

Soak your duck in water for several hours to remove all blood. Wipe dry and lightly salt. Fill the cavity with rice stuffing (see recipe under Side Dishes). Tie the drumsticks to the tail. Place the breast side of duck up on the roasting pan. Brush with melted mixture of onion, butter and orange juice frequently. Roast at 350 degrees for about 2 ½ hours, or until done.

Kosher Your Plate for Chanukah

Easy Cranberry Chicken

8 chicken breasts, skinless and boned
1 can whole cranberry sauce
1 envelop Lipton onion soup mix
1 small bottle French dressing

Put chicken in casserole dish. Stir cranberry sauce, soup mix, and French dressing together. Pour over the chicken. Bake at 350 degrees uncovered for one hour. Serve with rice.

Pan-fried Fish (or Chicken)

2 pounds of fish fillets (boned chicken breasts can be substituted)
1 teaspoon salt
1/8 teaspoon pepper
1 egg
1 tablespoon water
1 cup Parmesan cheese
butter

Sprinkle both sides of fish with salt and pepper. Beat the egg and water until blended. Dip the fish into the egg mixture and then coat with cheese. Heat vegetable oil, or butter, in frying pan until hot. Fry fish over medium heat, turning carefully, until brown on both sides. It usually takes about 10 minutes.

Vegetable Lasagna

For one large pan (about 9x13 or even a bit bigger)
3 layers of lasagna noodles (regular, do not precook)
2 bottles of marinara sauce
15 oz ricotta
¾ 12 oz bag of shredded mozzarella
½ cup parmesan
2 eggs
(mix the cheeses and eggs together, carefree spreading)
1 10-oz bag baby spinach
about ½ large can of large black olives, sliced

One cup of sauce on bottom of pan/layer of pasta, cheese, sauce, half of spinach/layer of pasta, cheese, sauce, half of spinach, olives/layer of pasta and sauce/top with parmesan.

Bake covered 35-45 minutes at 350, uncovered 10-15, let cool 10-minutes.

SIDE DISHES

Potato Latkes
5 large potatoes, peeled and cut up
1 onion
2 eggs, beaten
1 ½ teaspoons baking powder
3 tablespoons flour
Salt to taste

Chop potatoes in a food processor. Put in drainer and run cold water over them for 1 minute. Drain. Chop onion in processor and place in mixing bowl. Add all the other ingredients to onions and mix well. Heat ½ inch oil in a large frying pan over medium heat. Drop a tablespoon of batter into hot oil for each latke. Flatten and fry for 3 minutes on each side until they are brown and crisp.

Sweet Potato Latkes
Prepare sweet potato latkes the same as potato latkes, except substitute sweet potatoes for regular potatoes, omit the onion and add 1/4 cup brown sugar and 1/2 teaspoon ground cinnamon.

Chunky Applesauce
8 cooking apples, cut into fourths and peeled
1 cup water
1 cup brown sugar
¼ teaspoon ground cinnamon
¼ teaspoon ground nutmeg
¼ teaspoon ground cloves

Heat apples and water until boiling then reduce heat. Simmer uncovered until the apples are tender. Stir them so they will break up into smaller chunks. Stir in the rest of the ingredients and bring to a boil. Boil and stir apple mixture about 1 minute. Serve warm!

Rice Stuffing

2/3 cup uncooked rice
½ cup chopped celery
1 small onion, chopped
2 tablespoons butter
½ teaspoon salt
1/8-teaspoon pepper
½ cup chopped pecans
1/3 cup raisins

Cook rice according to package directions. Cook celery, onion, butter, salt and pepper in frying pan until celery is tender. Remove from heat. Stir in rice, pecans and raisins. Makes 4 cups of stuffing. Use with Duck L'Orange.

Broccoli Casserole

1 box chopped broccoli, uncooked
½ cup cream of chicken soup
½ cup mayonnaise
½ teaspoon salt
cracker crumbs
butter

Mix the first four ingredients together, pour into an 8" x 8" casserole dish and dot the top with the butter and cracker crumbs. Bake at 350 degrees for 35 minutes.

Spinach Casserole

1 package spinach, thawed
1/2 can cream of chicken soup
1 cup shredded cheddar cheese
1 egg
1/2 cup mayonnaise
Parmesan cheese to sprinkle on top

Mix all ingredients and pour into an 8" x 8" casserole dish. Sprinkle parmesan cheese on top. Bake at 350 degrees for 35 minutes.

DESERTS

Sufganiyot
1 ½ tablespoons dry yeast
2 cups of warm milk
1 cup plus 2 teaspoons of sugar
5 cups of all-purpose flour
salt
6 egg yolks
1 teaspoon vanilla extract
rind of small orange, grated
¾ cup soft butter
¾ cup jam of choice
Vegetable oil for frying
Powdered sugar for topping

Mix yeast with ½ cup milk and 2 teaspoons of sugar. Put to side for 10 minutes. Mix flour, salt and rest of sugar in a large bowl. Pour in the yeast mixture and flour. Cover the bowl with a towel and let it stand for 20 minutes. Add the egg yolks, vanilla, orange rind and butter. Knead into soft dough using the remaining milk. Cover and let stand in a warm place for 2 ½ hours. Roll out the dough ½ inch thick and cut into 3 inch circles. Let circles rise for 1 hour. Heat 3 inches of oil in a deep saucepan to 360 degrees using a candy thermometer. Deep fry in oil on both sides, 4 at a time until lightly brown. Remove from oil and drain on paper towels. When cool enough to handle, make a small cut on the side and spoon 1 teaspoon of jam in. Sift powered sugar over the Sufganiyot. Eat and enjoy! Makes 3 dozen.

Fried Doughnuts
3 1/3 cups all-purpose flour
1 cup sugar
¾ cup milk
2 tablespoons shortening
3 teaspoons baking powder
½ teaspoons salt
½ teaspoons ground cinnamon
¼ teaspoons ground nutmeg
2 eggs
Vegetable oil for frying

Heat 3 inches of oil in a deep saucepan to 375 degrees. Beat 1 ½ cups of flour and the rest of the ingredients in a large mixing bowl on low speed, scraping the bowl frequently for 30 seconds. Beat on medium speed for 2 minutes. Stir in remaining flour. Turn the dough onto a floured cutting board. Roll around lightly to cover with flour. Gently roll 3/8 inch thick. Cut with floured doughnut cutter. Slide doughnuts into the hot oil with a wide spatula. Turn the doughnuts as they rise to the surface. Fry until golden brown – about 1 – ½ minutes each side. Remove carefully from oil, drain on paper towels. Serve plain or shake powdered sugar on top. Make 2 dozen.

Crepes

1 ½ cups all-purpose flour
1 tablespoon sugar
½ teaspoon baking powder
½ teaspoon salt
2 cups milk
2 tablespoons melted butter
½ teaspoon vanilla extract
2 eggs

Put all ingredients into a mixing bowl. Beat with a hand beater until smooth. Lightly butter an 8 inch frying pan over medium heat until butter bubbles. For each crepe: pour ¼ cup of the batter into the frying pan and immediately rotate pan until a thin film covers the bottom. Cook until light brown. Run a wide spatula around the edge to loosen. Turn it over and cook until other side is light brown. Stack the crepes by placing wax paper between each one. Keep covered until ready to use. You can then spread jam, jelly, etc. on each on and then roll up. Powered sugar may be sprinkled on the top. Makes 12 crepes.

Cherry Blintzes

Use the Crepe recipe above plus the following for filler:

1 cup dry cottage cheese
1½ cup sour cream
2 tablespoons sugar
1 teaspoon vanilla extract
½ teaspoon grated lemon peel
¼ cup butter
1 can cherry pie filling (21 oz)

Prepare crepes, but only brown one side. Mix the cottage cheese, ½ cup sour cream, sugar, vanilla and lemon peel. Spoon 1½ tablespoons of the cheese mixture onto the browned side of each crepe. Fold sides of crepe up over the filling and overlap the edges, then roll them up. Heat butter in a frying pay over medium heat until it bubbles. Place blintzes in the pan, seam sides brown. Cook, turning once, until golden brown. Top each blintz with tablespoon of sour cream and 3 tablespoons of cherry pie filling. Serve! Makes 12 blintzes.

Molasses Cookies

¾ cup shortening
1 cup brown sugar – packed
1 egg
¼ cup molasses
2 ¼ cups flour
2 tsp. soda
¼ tsp. salt
½ tsp. cloves
1 tsp. cinnamon
1 tsp. ginger
granulated sugar

Mix the shortening, sugar, egg, and molasses thoroughly. Measure flour and blend all dry ingredients; stir in. Chill dough.

Heat oven to 375 degrees. Roll dough in 1 ¼" balls. Dip tops in sugar. Place balls, sugared side up, 3" apart on greased baking sheet. Sprinkle each with 2 or 3 drops of water. Bake 10 to 12 minutes, or just until set but not hard. Makes 4 dozen cookies.

Butterscotch Brownies

¼ cup melted butter
1 cup brown sugar
1 egg
¾ cup all-purpose flour
1 teaspoon baking powder
½ teaspoon salt
½ teaspoon vanilla

Sugar Cookies

Blend sugar with butter; add egg, and all dry ingredients. Pour into a greased 8" x 8" baking dish and back at 350 degrees for 25 minutes. Cut into 2" x 2" squares.

Sift together:
2 1/4 cups of all-purpose flour
1/2 teaspoon baking soda
1 teaspoon baking powder
1/8 teaspoon salt
Add:
1/2 cup shortening
1 cup sugar
2 eggs
1 teaspoon vanilla extract
1 tablespoon milk

Blend all well, wrap dough in waxed paper and chill for 2 hours. Roll out on a floured surface to 1/8 thickness and cut with cookie cutter. Sprinkle with sugar. We use Star of David cutters and sprinkle with blue sugar.

Bake at 425 degrees for 8 minutes or until done. Makes about 2 1/2 dozen large sugar cookies.

Fudge

3/4 stick of butter
2 squares Baker's Chocolate
1/4 teaspoon salt
5 -6 tablespoons milk
1 box confectioner's sugar
1 teaspoon vanilla extract
1 cup chopped nuts, if desired

Melt chocolate and butter in sauce pan and slowly add the rest of ingredients. Pour into 8" x 8" casserole dish and place in refrigerator to harden. Cut into squares and serve.

Oatmeal Spice Cake

1 cup oats
1 1/2 cups boiling water, pour over oats, let stand
1 cup brown sugar
1 cup white sugar
3/4 cup vegetable oil
2 eggs
1 1/2 cup all-purpose flour
1 1/2 teaspoons ground cinnamon
1/2 teaspoon ground cloves
1 teaspoon baking soda

Mix all ingredients together, then add oats. Bake at 350 degrees in preheated oven for 35-40 minutes in a rectangular pan. Ice with Lemon Icing. (A cream cheese icing may also be used.)

Lemon Icing

1/2 stick of butter
1/2 to 3/4 cup confectioner's sugar
juice for 1/2 to 1 lemon

Mix together to get the consistency for icing. Spread on Oatmeal Spice Cake.

BREADS

Wheat Germ Bread

1 cup whole wheat flour
1 1/2 - 2 cups all-purpose flour
2 tablespoons margarine
2 tablespoons molasses
1/2 cup wheat germ
2 teaspoons salt
2 packages yeast
1 1/2 cups hot tap water

Mix 1 cup whole wheat flour, wheat germ, and yeast. Add margarine, molasses, and hot water. Blend with electric mixer for 2 minutes at medium speed. Add 1/2 cup all-purpose flour. Mix 2 minutes at high speed. Add remainder of all-purpose flour to make dough stiff with mixer. Cover and rise in warm place for 1 hour until dough is double in bulk. Beat down by hand. Bake in a greased 1 1/2 quart casserole dish for 45 minutes at 350 degree preheated oven.

Biscuits

2 cups all-purpose flour
1/2 teaspoon salt
4 tablespoons shortening
2 teaspoons baking powder
2/3 cup cold milk

Mix all the ingredients, roll dough out on floured surface to ¼" and cut with biscuit cutter. Bake 10-15 minutes at 350 degree preheated oven.

Messianic Winter Holiday Helper

LITURGICAL RESOURCES

CHANUKAH

The Role of Liturgy

Many people who are not only new to the Messianic movement, but have been a part of it for a while, are somewhat skeptical regarding the role of liturgical worship. Reciting traditional prayers and hymns is sometimes thought to be dead religion, a throwback to Yeshua's warning, "when you pray, do not heap up empty phrases as the Gentiles do, for they think that they will be heard for their many words" (Matthew 6:7, ESV), or even, "for a pretense [the scribes] make long prayers. They will receive the greater condemnation" (Mark 12:40, ESV). Only if prayers are offered spontaneously, without the use of a special book or tradition, is it believed that God will find them acceptable.

A person who is skeptical of liturgical prayer cannot be entirely blamed for such opinions. There may be childhood memories of attending a Roman Catholic mass where endless liturgies in an unintelligible language, Latin, were repeated over and over. You might know some things about the Protestant Reformation, which fought against the highly formalized religion of Catholicism that had led to a corrupt clergy and deceived laity, and how you can go right to God with your prayers and not need anything else. Or, you might simply find all formal liturgy to be boring and that it takes away from the joy of worshipping the Lord.

Does all formal liturgy rob from the presence of the Holy Spirit? I hope not! The largest book of the Bible, and perhaps one of the most spiritually uplifting, is the Book of Psalms—a text full of liturgical prayers, songs, pleas, and laments. It is said of the early Believers, "they devoted themselves to the apostles' teaching and fellowship, to the breaking of bread and the prayers" (Acts 2:42, ESV). Theologians recognize how early hymns about Yeshua (Philippians 2:5-11; Colossians 1:15-20) from the ancient Messianic community, made their way into the Apostolic epistles. And at our Lord's Passover *seder* we are reminded, "when they had sung a hymn, they went out to the Mount of Olives" (Matthew 26:30, ESV). While we often associate liturgy with "High Church" worship, it is undeniably a part of the Biblical tradition that must be honored.

What is the role of liturgy? Liturgy can help provide structure and order to a worship service. It by no means has to be repetitive, endless, and *all* of it in a language that the people worshipping do not understand. It is, rather, to help create an environment of reverence and respect. It is to remind us that we are being invited into the presence of God, and that there are some things that we need to be considering. Even today's Protestant churches, which would be considered the least liturgical in comparison to both the Jewish Synagogue and Roman Catholic Church, still employ a fair amount of liturgy in the native tongues of the people, to create a sense of reverence.

Being raised at the United States Naval Academy in Annapolis, Maryland, my family frequently attended Protestant services at the Chapel, and we would hear and recite liturgy derived from Scriptures like Psalm 107:22-24:

Messianic Winter Holiday Helper

"And let them sacrifice the sacrifices of thanksgiving, and declare his works with rejoicing. They that go down to the sea in ships, that do business in great waters; these see the works of the Lord, and his wonders in the deep" (KJV).

When hearing this read, or declaring it with a congregation, you have to pause for a moment and remember that there are sailors and Marines who have sacrificed of themselves so that America might remain free. Tears might well up in your eyes as you recall a family member or friend presently serving in the armed forces, as you offer up a quiet prayer for their safety. You might remember a loved one who has died for the cause of freedom, and express thankfulness to God for how they gave their lives with honor.

This is the role of liturgy: **bringing us closer to a holy God in great awe and reverence.** We remember who we are as mortals in His sight, either hearing a compilation of important admonitions from His Word, or confessing them together in unison. We recall Moses' declaration to Ancient Israel, "Fear not, stand firm, and see the salvation of the Lord, which he will work for you today" (Exodus 14:13, ESV). We declare the goodness and infinite power of our Eternal King, and how grateful we are to receive His grace and mercy. Most liturgy employed in worship comes directly from the Holy Scriptures, so just as Bible readings should draw us into God's presence, so can special prayers and hymns draw us into His presence.

In the Jewish tradition, liturgy is a very important part of the worship service for *Shabbat* and the appointed times. It calls the people of God to attention, to remember who He is in their lives, where we as human beings have perhaps fallen short, and why we need His help. Messianic congregations, fellowships, and home groups, are experiencing a renaissance today as liturgical worship is being considered for the special power it possesses in helping us learn how to be reverent before Him. Far from being the product of dead religion, liturgical worship is being rightly recognized as an important part of not only the First Century *ekklēsia*, but something that has been used properly by many generations of Jews and Christians. Wanting to build upon this heritage, liturgy should play *a role* in the worship of Messianic Believers.

Each Messianic congregation or gathering, just like each person, is different—meaning that the liturgical needs and wants will vary from location to location. Some congregations focus their *Shabbat* services and observance of the appointed times almost entirely around liturgical worship, and others scarcely use it at all. Some want all of their liturgy to be delivered in Hebrew, others prefer a fair mix of Hebrew and English, and others prefer very little Hebrew and mostly English. Some have a designated cantor or *chazzan* deliver the prayers, and others have a variety of individuals involved. Whichever you choose, we wish the Lord's blessings on you!

We encourage you to incorporate liturgy as a vital component of your worship services, but not the only component. Likewise, if you have not considered how liturgy can give your worship structure, focus, and reverence, the appointed times can be an excellent season to experiment!

Kindling the Chanukah Lights

a template model for Messianic congregations, fellowships, and families

Candles are lit on each of the eight nights of Chanukah: One the first night, two the second, and an additional candle on each subsequent night. The candle for the first night is placed at the far right of the menorah (chanukia); on each subsequent night, another candle is added to the left. An extra candle, designated as the shamash *is lit first—then used to light the others as the blessings are recited. Each night, the candles are lit from left to right, starting with the new candle.*

On Shabbat Chanukah, the Chanukah lights are kindled before the Shabbat candles. On Erev Shabbat, it is customary to use special, extra-long Chanukah candles, since tradition requires that the Chanukah lights burn for at least one half hour after dark.

On Saturday night, the Chanukah candles are lit after Havdalah at home, but before Havdalah in the synagogue.

Traditional Blessing for Lighting the *Menorah*

Candle Lighter:

On the first night of Chanukah (only):

Barukh atah Adonai, Eloheinu melekh ha'olam, she'he'cheyanu v'ki'yemanu v'higi'anu la'zman ha'zeh.

Blessed are You O Lord our God, King of the universe, granting us life, sustaining us, and enabling us to reach this season.

For all nights of Chanukah:

Barukh atah Adonai, Eloheinu melekh ha'olam, asher kidshanu b'mitzvotav v'tzivanu l'hadlik ner shel Chanukah

Barukh atah Adonai, Eloheinu melekh ha'olam, she'asah nisim l'avoteinu b'yamim ha'hem u'v'zman ha'zeh

Blessed are You O Lord our God, King of the universe, instilling in us the holiness of commandments, and who commands (or, permits) us to light the lights of *Chanukah.*

Messianic Winter Holiday Helper

Blessed are You O Lord our God, King of the universe, accomplishing miracles for our ancestors from ancient days until our time.

Chanukiah is now lit with appropriate number of candles for day of Chanukah

All: These lights which we kindle recall the wondrous triumphs and the miraculous victories wrought through Your holy priests for our ancestors from ancient days until our time. These lights are sacred through all the eight days of *Chanukah*. We may not make use of their light, but are only to look upon them, and thus be reminded to thank and praise You for the wondrous miracle of our deliverance.

Assorted Blessings for Chanukah

Blessing After Meals for Chanukah

One of the major features of *Chanukah* is eating special meals with family and friends. Your dinner table should be a place for all to come, and not only enjoy special dishes, but also fellowship in the love and grace of the Lord, as we remember His deeds for us of old. A special blessing after eating a meal during *Chanukah* is offered, most especially in thanking God for various guests who may come to join you, perhaps having partaken of this special season for the first time.

Birkhat Ha'Mazon

Designated Reader:	When the LORD restored the fortunes of Zion, we were like those who dream. Then our mouth was filled with laughter, and our tongue with shouts of joy; then they said among the nations, "The LORD has done great things for them." The LORD has done great things for us; we are glad. Restore our fortunes, O LORD, like streams in the Negeb! Those who sow in tears shall reap with shouts of joy! He who goes out weeping, bearing the seed for sowing, shall come home with shouts of joy, bringing his sheaves with him (Psalm 126, ESV).
Leader:	Honored guests and friends, let us give thanks!
All:	*Y'hi shem Adonai mevorakh mei'atah v'ad olam.* **May the Lord be praised, now and forever.**
Leader:	*Y'hi shem Adonai mevorakh mei'atah v'ad olam, b'r'shut, rabotai/chaverai, n'varekh she'akhalnu mi'shelo.* May the Lord be praised, now and forever. With your consent, honored guests/friends, let us praise the One of whose food we have now partaken.
All:	*Barukh she'akhalnu mi'shelo u'v'tuvo chayiynu.* **Praised be the One of whose food we have partaken and by whose goodness we live.**
Leader:	*Barukh she'akhalnu mi'shelo u'v'tuvo chayiynu.* Praised be the One of whose food we have partaken and by whose goodness we live.

Messianic Winter Holiday Helper

All:	*Barukh hu u'varukh sh'mo*

Praised be God and praised be God's name.

Blessed are You O Lord our God, King of the universe, graciously sustaining the whole world with kindness and compassion, providing food for every creature, for God's love endures forever.

God, abounding in kindness, has never failed us; may our nourishment be assured forever. God sustains all life and is good to all, providing every creature with food and sustenance. Praised are You Lord, who sustains all life.

We thank you, Lord our God, for the pleasing, good, and spacious land which You have given us as a heritage, together with the Torah and covenant, life and sustenance.

Leader:	We thank You for the miraculous deliverance of our ancestors from ancient days until our time.

In the days of Mattathias son of John, the heroic Hasmonean priest, and in the days of his sons, a cruel power rose against Your people, demanding that they abandon the Torah. You, in great mercy, stood by Your people in the time of trouble, delivering the strong into the hands of the weak, the many into the hands of the few. Then Your children came into Your shrine and cleansed Your Temple. They set aside these eight days as a season for giving thanks and chanting praises to You.

For all this we thank You and praise You, Lord our God. You shall be forever praised by every living thing. Thus it is written in the Torah: "you shall eat and be full, and you shall bless the LORD your God for the good land he has given you" (Deuteronomy 8:10, ESV). Praised are You, Lord, for the land and for sustenance.

All:	Rebuild Jerusalem, the holy city, soon, in our day. Praised are You Lord, who in mercy rebuilds Jerusalem. *Amein*.

Praised are You Lord our God, who rules the universe, our Provider, our Sovereign, our Creator and Redeemer, our Holy One, the Holy One of Jacob, our Shepherd, the Shepherd of Israel, Sovereign who is good to all, whose goodness is constant throughout all time. May You continue to bestow upon us grace, kindness, and compassion.

Leader:	May the Merciful bless all who are gathered here.

May the Merciful grant us a day that is truly good.

Assorted Blessings for Chanukah

May the Merciful bless this land and preserve it.

May the Merciful bless the State of Israel, the promise of our redemption.

May the Merciful consider us worthy of the Messianic Era and life in the world to come.

God is a source of deliverance for His Kingdom, of lovingkindness for His anointed, for David and his descendants forever. May the One who brings peace to His universe bring peace to us and to all the people Israel. And let us say: *Amein.*

All: **May we be satisfied and nourished by all we have eaten and drunk. May whatever remains be a blessing to others in accordance with the wishes of God.**

Hallel for Chanukah

Hallel is recited on Chanukah, and when Shabbat Chanukah coincides with a Rosh Chodesh, the full Hallel is recited.

The Hallel Psalms recall for us the celebration of Festivals in the Temple. Through them we express our gratitude and joy for Divine providence. God's concern for us in reflected in our past redemption and deliverance, inspiring us to express our faith in the future.

Cantor: Blessed are You O Lord our God, King of the universe, instilling in us the holiness of commandments, by commanding us to recite Hallel.

Cantor: **Psalm 113** (ESV)
congregation speaks italics
Praise the LORD!
Praise, O servants of the LORD, praise the name of the LORD! Blessed be the name of the LORD from this time forth and forevermore!
From the rising of the sun to its setting, the name of the LORD is to be praised! The LORD is high above all nations, and his glory above the heavens!
Who is like the LORD our God, who is seated on high, who looks far down on the heavens and the earth?
He raises the poor from the dust and lifts the needy from the ash heap, to make them sit with princes, with the princes of his people.
He gives the barren woman a home, making her the joyous mother of children. Praise the LORD!

Cantor: **Psalm 114** (ESV)
congregation speaks italics
When Israel went out from Egypt, the house of Jacob from a people of strange language, Judah became his sanctuary, Israel his dominion.
The sea looked and fled; Jordan turned back. The mountains skipped like rams, the hills like lambs.
What ails you, O sea, that you flee? O Jordan, that you turn back? O mountains, that you skip like rams? O hills, like lambs?
Tremble, O earth, at the presence of the Lord, at the presence of the God of Jacob, who turns the rock into a pool of water, the flint into a spring of water.

Cantor: **Psalm 115:1-11** (ESV)
congregation speaks italics
Not to us, O LORD, not to us, but to your name give glory, for the sake of your steadfast love and your faithfulness!
Why should the nations say, "Where is their God?" Our God

Assorted Blessings for Chanukah

is in the heavens; he does all that he pleases.
Their idols are silver and gold, the work of human hands. They have mouths, but do not speak; eyes, but do not see.
They have ears, but do not hear; noses, but do not smell.
They have hands, but do not feel; feet, but do not walk;
and they do not make a sound in their throat. Those who make them become like them; so do all who trust in them.
O Israel, trust in the LORD! He is their help and their shield.
O house of Aaron, trust in the LORD! He is their help and their shield.
You who fear the LORD, trust in the LORD! He is their help and their shield.

Cantor:
congregation speaks italics

Psalm 115:12-18 (ESV)
The LORD has remembered us; he will bless us; he will bless the house of Israel;
he will bless the house of Aaron; he will bless those who fear the LORD, both the small and the great.
May the LORD give you increase, you and your children! May you be blessed by the LORD, who made heaven and earth!
The heavens are the LORD's heavens, but the earth he has given to the children of man.
The dead do not praise the LORD, nor do any who go down into silence.
But we will bless the LORD from this time forth and forevermore. Praise the LORD!

Cantor:
congregation speaks italics

Psalm 116:1-11 (ESV)
I love the LORD, because he has heard my voice and my pleas for mercy. Because he inclined his ear to me, therefore I will call on him as long as I live.
The snares of death encompassed me; the pangs of Sheol laid hold on me; I suffered distress and anguish.
Then I called on the name of the LORD: "O LORD, I pray, deliver my soul!"
Gracious is the LORD, and righteous; our God is merciful.
The LORD preserves the simple; when I was brought low, he saved me.
Return, O my soul, to your rest; for the LORD has dealt bountifully with you.
For you have delivered my soul from death, my eyes from tears, my feet from stumbling; I will walk before the LORD in the land of the living.
I believed, even when I spoke, "I am greatly afflicted"; I said in my alarm, "All mankind are liars."

Messianic Winter Holiday Helper

Cantor:　　　　**Psalm 116:12-19** (ESV)
congregation speaks italics

What shall I render to the LORD for all his benefits to me?
> *I will lift up the cup of salvation and call on the name of the LORD, I will pay my vows to the LORD in the presence of all his people.*

Precious in the sight of the LORD is the death of his saints.
> *O LORD, I am your servant; I am your servant, the son of your maidservant. You have loosed my bonds. I will offer to you the sacrifice of thanksgiving and call on the name of the LORD.*

I will pay my vows to the LORD in the presence of all his people,
> *in the courts of the house of the LORD, in your midst, O Jerusalem. Praise the LORD!*

Cantor:　　　　**Psalm 117** (ESV)

Praise the LORD, all nations! Extol him, all peoples! For great is his steadfast love toward us, and the faithfulness of the LORD endures forever. Praise the LORD!

Cantor:　　　　**Psalm 118:1-20** (ESV)
congregation speaks italics

The beginning of the Hodu is canted in Hebrew

Hodu l'ADONAI ki tov, ki l'olam chasdo.

Oh give thanks to the LORD, for he is good; for his steadfast love endures forever! Let Israel say, "His steadfast love endures forever." Let the house of Aaron say, "His steadfast love endures forever." Let those who fear the LORD say, "His steadfast love endures forever."

Out of my distress I called on the LORD; the LORD answered me and set me free. The LORD is on my side; I will not fear. What can man do to me?
> *The LORD is on my side as my helper; I shall look in triumph on those who hate me.*

It is better to take refuge in the LORD than to trust in man. It is better to take refuge in the LORD than to trust in princes.
> *All nations surrounded me; in the name of the LORD I cut them off!*

They surrounded me, surrounded me on every side; in the name of the LORD I cut them off!
> *They surrounded me like bees; they went out like a fire among thorns; in the name of the LORD I cut them off! I was pushed hard, so that I was falling, but the LORD helped me.*

The LORD is my strength and my song; he has become my salvation.
> *Glad songs of salvation are in the tents of the righteous: "The right hand of the LORD does valiantly, the right hand of*

Assorted Blessings for Chanukah

> the LORD exalts, the right hand of the LORD does valiantly!"

I shall not die, but I shall live, and recount the deeds of the LORD.

> The LORD has disciplined me severely, but he has not given me over to death.

Open to me the gates of righteousness, that I may enter through them and give thanks to the LORD.

> This is the gate of the LORD; the righteous shall enter through it.

Cantor: **Psalm 118:21-29 (ESV)**
congregation speaks italics

I thank you that you have answered me and have become my salvation.

> The stone that the builders rejected has become the cornerstone.

This is the LORD's doing; it is marvelous in our eyes.

cantor reads these lines first, then followed by the congregation
This is the day that the LORD has made; let us rejoice and be glad in it. Save us, we pray, O LORD! O LORD, we pray, give us success!

Ana ADONAI hoshi'ah na

Ana ADONAI hatzlichah na.

Blessed is he who comes in the name of the LORD! We bless you from the house of the LORD.

> The LORD is God, and he has made his light to shine upon us. Bind the festal sacrifice with cords, up to the horns of the altar!

You are my God, and I will give thanks to you; you are my God; I will extol you.

> Oh give thanks to the LORD, for he is good; for his steadfast love endures forever!

Cantor: May all Creation praise You, Lord our God. May the pious, the righteous who do Your will, and all Your people, the House of Israel, join in acclaiming You with joyous song. May they praise, revere, adore, extol, exalt and sanctify Your glory, our Sovereign. To You it is good to chant praise; to Your glory it is fitting to sing. You are God, from age to age, everlastingly. Praised are You Lord, Sovereign acclaimed with songs of praise.

The Dreidel Game

Each *dreidel* top has the four letters *nun, shin, hey,* and *gimel,* standing for *nes, gadol, hayah, sham*: "A great miracle happened there." Playing the game is very simple.

Robert Zunikoff / Unsplash

(1) Distribute an equal amount of candy or nuts to each player. (2) Each player puts a piece in the pot. (3) Each player spins the *dreidel* and does what the *dreidel* says (see below). (4) When a *gimel* is spun, a player puts a piece into the pot. (5) Everyone gets a turn, and when finished you can eat your candy or nuts.

Nun: take all
Shin: take half
Hey: add 1 to pot
Gimel: take nothing

About the Editor

Margaret McKee Huey is one of the founders of Outreach Israel Ministries (OIM) and serves on its Board as the Office Manager.

Margaret is a multi-talented woman who exemplifies what a Proverbs 31 woman should be. Besides handling the business responsibilities of OIM and editing assignments with our publications, she operates an internationally known needlework sampler design business that she founded in 1985. Yet, she still finds time to successfully invest in raising her three children.

In addition to her business acumen, Margaret is spiritually gifted as an evangelist. She was actively involved in evangelism through the *Walk to Emmaus, Chrysalis Program* and the *Lay Witness Mission* while in the United Methodist Church. When asked what Biblical character she most identifies with, she demurely responds, "why John the Baptist, of course." The passion of her heart is communicating the "Gospel According to the Torah." In an inspiring and convicting way, she not only helps you understand the sacrifice of Yeshua and your salvation, but also helps you understand the mercy of the Holy One as one follows His Torah.

Margaret comes from a long line of Methodist preachers and teachers. Although raised in a Christian home, she did not come to true saving faith until the age of 30. She was immediately drawn into an appreciation of Israel, the Jewish people, understanding that Yeshua was the Messiah of Israel and even celebrating the Seder Passover with her first husband, Kim McKee, at their Methodist church beginning in 1986.

Lamentably, in 1992 Margaret was widowed at the age of 39 with the responsibility for three young children. This unexpected tragedy did not detour her from her relationship with God, but instead prompted her into even greater dependency upon Him as her provider and comforter. As a result of her life experiences, she is gifted in grief counseling and deliverance issues.

Margaret is the editor for the upcoming Messianic cookbook, *Kosher Your Plate*, as well as editor for the *Messianic Helper Series*. Some of the titles for this series include: *Messianic Winter Holiday Helper, Messianic Spring Holiday Helper, Messianic Fall Holiday Helper*, and the *Messianic Sabbath Helper*.

Margaret is a graduate of Vanderbilt University with a Bachelor of Science degree in Geology. She is the wife of William Mark Huey and the mother of John McKee, Jane McKee, and Maggie Willetts, and now resides in Dallas, Texas.

Margaret can be reached at Outreach Israel Ministries.

Messianic Winter Holiday Helper

Contributors to this Volume

William Mark Huey became a Believer in the Messiah of Israel in 1978, but it was a Zola Levitt tour to Israel in 1994 with his wife Margaret, which sparked an ardent search for answers about the Hebraic and Jewish Roots of our faith, and the significance of the Torah, Biblical festivals, and the seventh-day Sabbath/*Shabbat*—among other things. By 1995, his family became members of a Messianic Jewish congregation in Dallas, Texas, and their pursuit for truth intensified. Within a year, Mark formed a conference-producing enterprise called "The Remnant Exchange," and began hosting prophecy conferences and seminars with increasing Messianic understanding and emphasis. Mark's business experience, owning a commercial real estate brokerage company, coupled with Margaret's ownership of a cross-stitch design company, led them to form a ministry consulting business which worked with a variety of Messianic ministries from 1997-2002. Mark and Margaret have dedicated their lives to serving the Lord in order to use their God-given gifts, talents, and abilities to advance His Kingdom until the Messiah returns.

By 2002, after years of exposure to tangible evidence that the prophesied "restoration of all things" (Acts 3:21) was becoming a reality, the impetus to focus energy and attention on Israel, the people, the Land, and Torah-centered Messianic teachings merged together. The outcome was the formation of **Outreach Israel Ministries**, of which Mark serves as Director, and Margaret as Business Manager. *From the beginning of Outreach Israel Ministries, the need to educate and to minister to the expanding number of Messianics has always been at the heart of the mission.* The merger with TNN Online in 2003 (now **Messianic Apologetics**) substantially enhanced the capabilities. Today, both Outreach Israel Ministries and Messianic Apologetics have a significant role to play in aiding the people of the broad Messianic movement, in the theological and spiritual issues that they face—as many Jewish people are coming to faith in Israel's Messiah, and many evangelical Christians embrace their faith heritage in Israel's Scriptures in tangibly new ways.

Mark is the author of a number of books which focus on encouraging others to embrace the Hebraic and Jewish roots of our faith. These include the commentaries, *TorahScope, Volumes I, II, & III, TorahScope Haftarah Exhortations, TorahScope Apostolic Scriptures Reflections,* and the devotionals, *Counting the Omer and Sayings of the Fathers: A Messianic Perspective on the Pirkei Avot.*

Mark is a graduate of Vanderbilt University with a B.A. in history, with graduate studies toward a master's degree in aviation management completed at Embry-Riddle Aeronautical University. Mark has served in leadership roles at Messianic congregations and fellowships. Mark serves as the Director of Partner Relations for the Joseph Project, a ministry of the Messianic Jewish Alliance of America (MJAA). Mark and Margaret Huey currently reside in Dallas, TX and have five grown children and two grandchildren.

John Kimball McKee is an integral part of Outreach Israel Ministries, and serves as the editor of Messianic Apologetics. He is a graduate of the University of Oklahoma (Class of 2003) with a B.A. in political science, and holds an M.A. in Biblical Studies from Asbury Theological Seminary (Class of 2009). He is a 2009 recipient of the Zondervan Biblical Languages Award for Greek. John has held memberships in the Evangelical Theological Society, the Evangelical Philosophical Society, and Christians for Biblical Equality, and is a longtime supporter of the perspectives and views of the Creationist ministry of Reasons to Believe. In 2019, John was licensed as a Messianic Teacher with the International Alliance of Messianic Congregations and Synagogues (IAMCS).

Since the 1990s, John's ministry has capitalized on the Internet's ability to reach people all over this planet. He has spoken with challenging and probing articles to a wide Messianic audience, and those evangelical Believers who are interested in Messianic things. Given his generational family background in evangelical ministry, as well as in academics and the military, John carries a strong burden to assist in the development and maturation of our emerging Messianic theology and spirituality. John has had the profound opportunity since 1997 to engage many in dialogue, so that they will consider the questions he postulates, as his only agenda is to be as Scripturally sound as possible. John believes in demonstrating a great deal of honor and respect to both his evangelical Protestant, Wesleyan and Reformed family background, as well as to the Jewish Synagogue, and together allowing the strengths and virtues of our Judeo-Protestant heritage to be employed for the Lord's plan for the Messianic movement in the long term future.

J.K. McKee is the son of the late K. Kimball McKee (1951-1992) and Margaret Jeffries McKee Huey (1953-), and stepson of William Mark Huey (1951-), who married his mother in 1994, and who is the executive director of Outreach Israel Ministries. Mark Huey is the Director of Partner Relations for the Joseph Project, a ministry of the Messianic Jewish Alliance of America (MJAA).

John has a very strong appreciation for those who have preceded him. His father, Kimball McKee, was a licensed lay minister in the Kentucky Conference of the United Methodist Church, and was a very strong evangelical Believer, most appreciable of the Jewish Roots of the faith.

Messianic Winter Holiday Helper

Among his many ministry pursuits, Kim brought the Passover *seder* to Christ United Methodist Church in Florence, KY, was a Sunday school teacher, and was extremely active in the Walk to Emmaus, leading the first men's walk in Madras, India in 1991. John is the grandson of the late Prof. William W. Jeffries (1914-1989; CDR USN WWII), who served as a professor at the United States Naval Academy in Annapolis, MD from 1942-1989, notably as the museum director and founder of what is now the William W. Jeffries Memorial Archives in the Nimitz Library. John is the great-grandson of Bishop Marvin A. Franklin (1894-1972), who served as a minister and bishop of the Methodist Church, throughout his ministry serving churches in Georgia, Florida, Alabama, and Mississippi. Bishop Franklin was President of the Council of Bishops from 1959-1960. John is also the first cousin twice removed of the late Charles L. Allen (1913-2005), formerly the senior pastor of Grace Methodist Church of Atlanta, GA and First Methodist Church of Houston, TX, and author of numerous books, notably including *God's Psychiatry*. John can also count among his ancestors, Lt. Colonel, By Brevet, Dr. James Cooper McKee (1830-1897), a Union veteran of the U.S. Civil War and significant contributor to the medical science of his generation.

J.K. McKee is a native of the Northern Kentucky/Greater Cincinnati, OH area. He has also lived in Dallas, TX, Norman, OK, Kissimmee-St. Cloud, FL, and Roatán, Honduras, Central America. He presently resides in McKinney, TX, just north of Dallas.

Bibliography

Articles
Einhorn, Yitzhak. "Hannukah Lamp," in *EJ*.
Grayson, A. Kirk. "Mesopotamia, History of (Babylonia): Religion," in *ABD*.
Herr, Moshe David. "Hanukkah," in *EJ*.
Huggins, Ronald V. "Christmas," in *EDB*.
Hyatt, J.P. "Circumcision," in *IDB*.
"John Hyrcanus," in *Dictionary of Judaism in the Biblical Period*.
Mueller, J. Theodore. "Christmas," in *Baker's Dictionary of Theology*.
Oppenheim, A.L. "Assyria and Babylonia: Religion," in *IDB*.
Porcella, Brewster. "Alexander the Great," in *NIDB*.
Provance, Brett Scott. *Pocket Dictionary of Liturgy & Worship*.
Rappaport, Uriel. "Mattathias," in *ABD*.
Smith, L. (2001). *The History of Christmas*. Christian Study Center. Retrieved 02 December, 2001 from <http://www.christianstudycenter.com>.
Stigers, Harold G. "*tz-d-q* (root)," in *TWOT*.
"Virgin Birth of Christ," in *Baker Encyclopedia of Christian Apologetics*.

Bible Versions and Study Bibles
American Standard Version (New York: Thomas Nelson & Sons, 1901).
Barker, Kenneth L., ed., et. al. *NIV Study Bible* (Grand Rapids: Zondervan, 2002).
Berlin, Adele, and Marc Zvi Brettler, eds. *The Jewish Study Bible*, NJPS (Oxford: Oxford University Press, 2004).
Esposito, Paul W. *The Apostles' Bible, An English Septuagint Version* (http://www.apostlesbible.com/).
God's Game Plan: The Athlete's Bible 2007, HCSB (Nashville: Serendipity House Publishers, 2007).
Green, Jay P., trans. *The Interlinear Bible*. (Lafayette, IN: Sovereign Grace Publishers, 1986).
Harrelson, Walter J., ed., et. al. *New Interpreter's Study Bible*, NRSV (Nashville: Abingdon, 2003).
Holman Christian Standard Bible (Nashville: Broadman & Holman, 2004).
Holy Bible, Contemporary English Version (New York: American Bible Society, 1995).
Holy Bible, King James Version (edited 1789).
Holy Bible, New International Version (Grand Rapids: Zondervan, 1978).
JPS Hebrew-English Tanakh (Philadelphia: Jewish Publication Society, 2000).
LaHaye, Tim, ed. *Tim LaHaye Prophecy Study Bible*, KJV (Chattanooga: AMG Publishers, 2000).
New American Standard Bible (La Habra, CA: Foundation Press Publications, 1971).
New American Standard, Updated Edition (Anaheim, CA: Foundation Publications, 1995).
New King James Version (Nashville: Thomas Nelson, 1982).
New Revised Standard Version (National Council of Churches of Christ, 1989).
Packer, J.I., ed. *The Holy Bible, English Standard Version* (Wheaton, IL: Crossway Bibles, 2001).
Ryrie, Charles C., ed. *The Ryrie Study Bible*, New American Standard (Chicago: Moody Press, 1978).
Scherman, Nosson, and Meir Zlotowitz, eds. *ArtScroll Tanach* (Brooklyn: Mesorah Publications, 1996).
Siewert, Frances E., ed. *The Amplified Bible* (Grand Rapids: Zondervan, 1965).

Stern, David H., trans. *Jewish New Testament* (Clarksville, MD: Jewish New Testament Publications, 1995).
_____, trans. *Complete Jewish Bible* (Clarksville, MD: Jewish New Testament Publications, 1998).
Suggs, M. Jack, Katharine Doob Sakenfeld, and James R. Mueller, eds. *The Oxford Study Bible*, REB (New York: Oxford University Press, 1992).
Tanakh: The Holy Scriptures (Philadelphia: Jewish Publication Society, 1999).
The Holy Bible, Revised Standard Version (Nashville: Cokesbury, 1952).
Young, Robert, trans. *Young's Literal Translation*.
Zodhiates, Spiros, ed. *Hebrew-Greek Key Study Bible*, NASB (Chattanooga: AMG Publishers, 1994).

Books

Bacchiocchi, Samuele. *From Sabbath to Sunday* (Rome: Pontifical Gregorian University Press, 1977).
Berkowitz, Ariel and D'vorah. *Torah Rediscovered* (Lakewood, CO: First Fruits of Zion, 1996).
_____. *Take Hold* (Littleton, CO: First Fruits of Zion, 1999).
Brown, Michael L. *Our Hands Are Stained With Blood* (Shippensburg, PA: Destiny Image, 1990).
Bruce, F.F. *New Testament History* (New York: Doubleday, 1969).
Carson, D.A., ed. *From Sabbath to Lord's Day* (Eugene, OR: Wipf and Stock, 1999).
_____, and Douglas J. Moo. *An Introduction to the New Testament*, second edition (Grand Rapids: Zondervan, 2005).
Dillard, Raymond B., and Tremper Longman III. *An Introduction to the Old Testament* (Grand Rapids: Zondervan, 1994).
Dunn, James D.G. *The New Perspective on Paul* (Grand Rapids: Eerdmans, 2005).
Egan, Hope. *Holy Cow! Does God Care About What We Eat?* (Littleton, CO: First Fruits of Zion, 2005).
Fee, Gordon D., and Douglas Stuart. *How to Read the Bible for All Its Worth* (Grand Rapids: Zondervan, 2003).
Friedman, David. *They Loved the Torah* (Baltimore: Lederer Books, 2001).
Guthrie, Donald. *New Testament Introduction* (Downers Grove, IL: InterVarsity, 1990).
Harrison, R.K. *Introduction to the Old Testament* (Grand Rapids: Eerdmans, 1969).
Hegg, Tim. *Introduction to Torah Living* (Tacoma, WA: TorahResource, 2002).
_____. *The Letter Writer: Paul's Background and Torah Perspective* (Littleton, CO: First Fruits of Zion, 2002).
_____. *It is Often Said: Comments and Comparisons of Traditional Christian Theology and Hebraic Thought*, 2 vols. (Littleton, CO: First Fruits of Zion, 2003).
_____. *Fellow Heirs: Jews & Gentiles Together in the Family of God* (Littleton, CO: First Fruits of Zion, 2003).
Huey, William Mark, and J.K. McKee. *Hebraic Roots: An Introductory Study* (Kissimmee, FL: TNN Press, 2003, 2009).
Juster, Daniel C. *Growing to Maturity* (Denver: The Union of Messianic Jewish Congregations Press, 1987).
_____. *Jewish Roots* (Shippensburg, PA: Destiny Image, 1995).
Kaiser, Walter C. *Toward Old Testament Ethics* (Grand Rapids: Zondervan, 1983).
_____. *The Old Testament Documents: Are They Reliable and Relevant?* (Downers Grove, IL: InterVarsity, 2001).
_____. *The Promise-Plan of God: A Biblical Theology of the Old and New Testaments* (Grand Rapids: Zondervan, 2008).
Kaiser, Walter C., and Moisés Silva. *An Introduction to Biblical Hermeneutics* (Grand Rapids: Zondervan, 1994).

Bibliography

Kitchen, K.A. *The Bible in Its World: The Bible & Archaeology Today* (Eugene, OR: Wipf & Stock, 1977).

Ladd, George Eldon. *The Blessed Hope* (Grand Rapids: Eerdmans, 1956).

Lancaster, D. Thomas. *The Mystery of the Gospel: Jew and Gentile in the Eternal Purpose of God* (Littleton, CO: First Fruits of Zion, 2003).

_____. *Restoration: Returning the Torah of God to the Disciples of Jesus* (Littleton, CO: First Fruits of Zion, 2005).

Levitt, Zola. *The Seven Feasts of Israel* (Dallas: Zola Levitt Ministries, 1979).

McKee, J.K. *The New Testament Validates Torah* (Kissimmee, FL: TNN Press, 2004, 2008).

_____. *James for the Practical Messianic* (Kissimmee, FL: TNN Press, 2005).

_____. *Hebrews for the Practical Messianic* (Kissimmee, FL: TNN Press, 2006).

_____. *A Survey of the Apostolic Scriptures for the Practical Messianic* (Kissimmee, FL: TNN Press, 2006).

_____. *Philippians for the Practical Messianic* (Kissimmee, FL: TNN Press, 2007).

_____. *When Will the Messiah Return?*, academic edition (Kissimmee, FL: TNN Press, 2007).

_____. *Galatians for the Practical Messianic*, second edition (Kissimmee, FL: TNN Press, 2007).

_____. *A Survey of the Tanach for the Practical Messianic* (Kissimmee, FL: TNN Press, 2008).

_____. *Ephesians for the Practical Messianic* (Kissimmee, FL: TNN Press, 2008).

_____. *Colossians and Philemon for the Practical Messianic* (Kissimmee, FL: TNN Press, 2010).

_____. *Acts 15 for the Practical Messianic* (Kissimmee, FL: TNN Press, 2010).

Oswalt, John N. *The Bible Among the Myths: Unique Revelation or Just Ancient Literature?* (Grand Rapids: Zondervan, 2009).

Provan, Iain, V. Philips Long, and Tremper Longman III. *A Biblical History of Israel* (Louisville, KY: Westminster John Knox, 2003).

Richardson, Susan E. *Holidays & Holy Days* (Ann Arbor, MI: Servant Publications, 2001).

Scarlata, Robin, and Linda Pierce. *A Family Guide to the Biblical Holidays with Activities for all Ages* (Madison, TN: Family Christian Press, 1997).

Stern, David H. *Restoring the Jewishness of the Gospel* (Clarksville, MD: Jewish New Testament Publications, 1990).

_____. *Messianic Jewish Manifesto* (Clarksville, MD: Jewish New Testament Publications, 1992).

Thompson, David L. *Bible Study That Works* (Nappanee, IN: Evangel Publishing House, 1994).

Walvoord, John F. *Every Prophecy of the Bible* (Colorado Springs: Chariot Victor Publishing, 1999).

White, Lew. *Fossilized Customs: The Pagan Sources of Popular Customs* (Louisville, KY: Strawberry Islands, 2001).

Wilson, Marvin R. *Our Father Abraham* (Grand Rapids: Eerdmans, 1989).

Wright, N.T. *What Saint Paul Really Said* (Grand Rapids: Eerdmans, 1997).

_____. *Paul in Fresh Perspective* (Minneapolis: Fortress Press, 2005).

Christian Reference Sources and Cited Commentaries

Alexander, T. Desmond, and David W. Baker, eds. *Dictionary of the Old Testament Pentateuch* (Downers Grove, IL: InterVarsity, 2003).

Arnold, Bill T., and H.G.M. Williamson, eds. *Dictionary of the Old Testament Historical Books* (Downers Grove, IL: InterVarsity, 2005).

Bercot, David W., ed. *A Dictionary of Early Christian Beliefs* (Peabody, MA: Hendrickson, 1998).

Bromiley, Geoffrey, ed. *International Standard Bible Encyclopedia*, 4 vols. (Grand Rapids: Eerdmans, 1988).

Bruce, F.F. *The Gospel of John* (Grand Rapids: Eerdmans, 1983).

_____. *New International Commentary on the New Testament: The Epistles to the Colossians, to Philemon, and to the Ephesians* (Grand Rapids: Eerdmans, 1984).
Buttrick, George, ed., et. al. *The Interpreter's Dictionary of the Bible*, 4 vols. (Nashville: Abingdon, 1962).
Cairns, Alan. *Dictionary of Theological Terms* (Greenville, SC: Ambassador Emerald International, 2002).
Crim, Keith, ed. *Interpreter's Dictionary of the Bible: Supplementary Volume* (Nashville: Abingdon, 1976).
deSilva, David A. *Perseverance in Gratitude: A Socio-Rhetorical Commentary on the Epistle "to the Hebrews"* (Grand Rapids, Eerdmans, 2000).
Dunn, James D.G. *Black's New Testament Commentary: The Epistle to the Galatians* (Peabody, MA: Hendrickson, 1993).
_____, and John W. Rogerson, eds. *Eerdmans Commentary on the Bible* (Grand Rapids: Eerdmans, 2003).
Evans, Craig A., and Stanley E. Porter, eds. *Dictionary of New Testament Background* (Downers Grove, IL: InterVarsity, 2000).
Freedman, David Noel, ed. *Anchor Bible Dictionary*, 6 vols. (New York: Doubleday, 1992).
_____, ed. *Eerdmans Dictionary of the Bible* (Grand Rapids: Eerdmans, 2000).
Geisler, Norman L., ed. *Baker Encyclopedia of Christian Apologetics* (Grand Rapids: Baker, 1999).
Green, Joel B., Scot McKnight, and I. Howard Marshall, eds. *Dictionary of Jesus and the Gospels* (Downers Grove, IL: InterVarsity, 1992).
Grenz, Stanley J., David Guretzki, and Cherith Fee Nordling. *Pocket Dictionary of Theological Terms* (Downers Grove, IL: InterVarsity, 1999).
Guthrie, D. and J.A. Motyer, eds. *The New Bible Commentary Revised* (Grand Rapids: Eerdmans, 1970).
Harrison, Everett F., ed. *Baker's Dictionary of Theology* (Grand Rapids: Baker Book House, 1960).
Hawthorne, Gerald F., Ralph P. Martin, and Daniel G. Reid, eds. *Dictionary of Paul and His Letters* (Downers Grove, IL: InterVarsity, 1993).
Keener, Craig S. *The IVP Bible Background Commentary: New Testament* (Downers Grove, IL: InterVarsity, 1993).
Keil, C., and F. Delitzsch, eds. *Commentary on the Old Testament*, 10 vols.
Laymon, Charles M., ed. *The Interpreter's One-Volume Commentary on the Bible* (Nashville: Abingdon, 1971).
Longman III, Tremper, and Peter Enns, eds. *Dictionary of the Old Testament Wisdom, Poetry & Writings* (Downers Grove, IL: InterVarsity, 2008).
Marshall, I. Howard. *Tyndale New Testament Commentaries: Acts* (Grand Rapids: Eerdmans, 1980).
Martin, Ralph P., and Peter H. Davids, eds. *Dictionary of the Later New Testament & Its Developments* (Downers Grove, IL: InterVarsity, 1997).
Roberts, Alexander, and James Donaldson, eds. *The Apostolic Fathers*, American Edition.
Schaff, Philip. *History of the Christian Church*, 8 vols. (Grand Rapids: Eerdmans, 1995).
Tenney, Merrill C., ed. *The New International Dictionary of the Bible* (Grand Rapids: Zondervan, 1987).
Unger, Merrill F. *Unger's Bible Handbook* (Chicago: Moody Press, 1967).
Walton, John H., and Victor H. Matthews and Mark W. Chavalas. *The IVP Bible Background Commentary: Old Testament* (Downers Grove, IL: InterVarsity, 2000).
Wesley, John. *Explanatory Notes Upon the New Testament*, reprint (Peterborough, UK: Epworth Press, 2000).

Greek Language Resources
Aland, Kurt, et. al. *The Greek New Testament, Fourth Revised Edition* (Stuttgart: Deutche Bibelgesellschaft/United Bible Societies, 1998).

Bibliography

Balme, Maurice, and Gilbert Lawall. *Athenaze: An Introduction to Ancient Greek*, Book I (New York and Oxford: Oxford University Press, 1990).

Black, David Allan. *Learn to Read New Testament Greek*, expanded edition (Nashville: Broadman & Holman, 1994).

Brenton, Sir Lancelot C. L., ed & trans. *The Septuagint With Apocrypha* (Peabody, MA: Hendrickson, 1999).

Bromiley, Geoffrey W., ed. *Theological Dictionary of the New Testament*, abridged (Grand Rapids: Eerdmans, 1985).

Brown, Robert K., and Philip W. Comfort, trans. *The New Greek-English Interlinear New Testament* (Carol Stream, IL: Tyndale House, 1990).

Danker, Frederick William, ed., et. al. *A Greek-English Lexicon of the New Testament and Other Early Christian Literature*, third edition (Chicago: University of Chicago Press, 2000).

Liddell, Henry George, and Robert Scott, eds. *Liddell and Scott's Greek-English Lexicon*, abridged (Oxford: Clarendon Press, 1953).

Metzger, Bruce M. *A Textual Commentary on the Greek New Testament* (London and New York: United Bible Societies, 1975).

Nestle, Erwin, and Kurt Aland, eds. *Novum Testamentum Graece, Nestle-Aland 27th Edition* (Stuttgart: Deutche Bibelgesellschaft, 1993).

Nestle-Aland Greek-English New Testament, NE27-RSV (Stuttgart: United Bible Societies/Deutche Bibelgesellschaft, 1981).

Newman, Jr., Barclay M. *A Concise Greek-English Dictionary of the New Testament* (Stuttgart: United Bible Societies/Deutche Bibelgesellschaft, 1971).

Rahlfs, Alfred, ed. *Septuaginta* (Stuttgart: Deutche Bibelgesellschaft, 1979).

Rogers, Cleon L., Jr., and Cleon L. Rogers III. *The New Linguistic and Exegetical Key to the Greek New Testament* (Grand Rapids: Zondervan, 1998).

Thayer, Joseph H. *Thayer's Greek-English Lexicon of the New Testament* (Peabody, MA: Hendrickson, 2003).

Vine, W.E. *Vine's Expository Dictionary of New Testament Words* (Nashville: Thomas Nelson, 1968).

Wallace, Daniel B. *Greek Grammar Beyond the Basics* (Grand Rapids: Zondervan, 1996).

Zodhiates, Spiros, ed. *Complete Word Study Dictionary: New Testament* (Chattanooga: AMG Publishers, 1993).

Hebrew Language Resources

Arnold, Bill T., and John H. Choi. *A Guide to Biblical Hebrew Syntax* (New York: Cambridge University Press, 2003).

Baker, Warren, and Eugene Carpenter, eds. *Complete Word Study Dictionary: Old Testament* (Chattanooga: AMG Publishers, 2003).

Brown, Francis, S.R. Driver, and Charles A. Briggs. *Hebrew and English Lexicon of the Old Testament* (Oxford: Clarendon Press, 1979).

Davidson, Benjamin. *The Analytical Hebrew and Chaldee Lexicon* (Grand Rapids: Zondervan, 1970).

Dotan, Aron, ed. *Biblia Hebraica Leningradensia* (Peabody, MA: Hendrickson, 2001).

Elliger, Karl, and Wilhelm Rudolph, et. al., eds. *Biblica Hebraica Stuttgartensia* (Stuttgart: Deutche Bibelgesellschaft, 1977).

Gabe, Eric S., ed. *New Testament in Hebrew and English* (Hitchin, UK: Society for Distributing the Hebrew Scriptures, 2000).

H.F.W. Gesenius: *Gesenius' Hebrew-Chaldee Lexicon to the Old Testament*, trans. Samuel Prideaux Tregelles (Grand Rapids: Baker, 1979).

Harris, R. Laird, Gleason L. Archer, Jr., and Bruce K. Waltke, eds. *Theological Wordbook of the Old Testament* (Chicago: Moody Press, 1980).

Holladay, William L., ed. *A Concise Hebrew and Aramaic Lexicon of the Old Testament* (Leiden, the Netherlands: E.J. Brill, 1988).
Jastrow, Marcus. *Dictionary of the Targumim, Talmud Bavli, Talmud Yerushalmi, and Midrashic Literature* (New York: Judaica Treasury, 2004).
Kelley, Page H., Daniel S. Mynatt, and Timothy G. Crawford, eds. *The Masorah of Biblia Hebraica Stuttgartensia* (Grand Rapids: Eerdmans, 1998).
Koehler, Ludwig, and Walter Baumgartner, eds. *The Hebrew & Aramaic Lexicon of the Old Testament*, 2 vols. (Leiden, the Netherlands: Brill, 2001).
Seow, C.L. *A Grammar for Biblical Hebrew*, revised edition (Nashville: Abingdon, 1995).
Tov, Emanuel. *Textual Criticism of the Hebrew Bible* (Minneapolis: Fortress Press, 1992).
Torah Nevi'im Ketuvim v'ha'B'rit ha'Chadashah (Jerusalem: Bible Society in Israel, 1991).
Unger, Merrill F., and William White. *Nelson's Expository Dictionary of the Old Testament* (Nashville: Thomas Nelson, 1980).

Historical Sources
Bettenson, Henry, and Chris Maunder, eds. *Documents of the Christian Church* (Oxford: Oxford University Press, 1999).
Eusebius: *Ecclesiastical History*, trans. C.F. Cruse (Peabody, MA: Hendrickson, 1998).
Herodotus: trans. Aubrey de Sélincourt, *The Histories* (London: Penguin Books, 1954).
Irvin, Dale T., and Scott W. Sunquist. *History of the World Christian Movement*, Vol. 1 (Maryknoll, NY: Orbis Books, 2001).
Josephus, Flavius: *The Works of Josephus: Complete and Unabridged*, trans. William Whiston (Peabody, MA: Hendrickson, 1987).
Judaeus, Philo: *The Works of Philo: Complete and Unabridged*, trans. C.D. Yonge (Peabody, MA: Hendrickson, 1993).
Kerr, Hugh T., ed. *Readings in Christian Thought* (Nashville: Abingdon, 1990).
Plato: *Gorgias*, trans., James H. Nichols, Jr. (Ithaca and London: Cornell University, 1998).
Shanks, Hershel, ed. *Ancient Israel: From Abraham to the Roman Destruction of the Temple* (Washington, D.C.: Biblical Archaeology Society, 1999).
Tacitus, Cornelius: *The Histories*, trans. Kenneth Wellesley (London: Penguin Books, 1992).

Jewish Reference Sources and Cited Commentaries
Cohen, A. *Soncino Chmash* (Brooklyn: Soncino Press, 1983).
Cohen, Abraham. *Everyman's Talmud: The Major Teachings of the Rabbinic Sages* (New York: Schoken, 1995).
Eisenberg, Ronald L. *The JPS Guide to Jewish Traditions* (Philadelphia: Jewish Publication Society, 2004).
Encyclopaedia Judaica. MS Windows 9x. Brooklyn: Judaica Multimedia (Israel) Ltd, 1997.
Harlow, Jules, ed. *Maḥzor for Rosh Hashanah and Yom Kippur* (New York: The Rabbinical Assembly, 1992).
_____, ed. *Siddur Sim Shalom for Shabbat and Festivals* (New York: Rabbinical Assembly, 2007).
Hertz, J.H., ed. *Pentateuch & Haftorahs* (London: Soncino, 1960).
_____. ed. *The Authorised Daily Prayer Book*, revised (New York: Bloch Publishing Company, 1960).
Kolatch, Alfred J. *The Jewish Book of Why* (Middle Village, NY: Jonathan David Publishers, 1981).
_____. *The Second Jewish Book of Why* (Middle Village, NY: Jonathan David Publishers, 1985).
Lieber, David L., ed. *Etz Hayim: Torah and Commentary* (New York: Rabbinical Assembly, 2001).
Neusner, Jacob, trans. *The Mishnah: A New Translation* (New Haven and London: Yale University Press, 1988).

Bibliography

_____, ed. *The Tosefta: Translated from the Hebrew With a New Introduction*, 2 vols. (Peabody, MA: Hendrickson, 2002).

_____, and William Scott Green, eds. *Dictionary of Judaism in the Biblical Period* (Peabody, MA: Hendrickson, 2002).

Robinson, George. *Essential Judaism: A Complete Guide to Beliefs, Customs, and Rituals* (New York: Pocket Books, 2000).

Scherman Nosson, and Meir Zlotowitz, eds. *The Complete ArtScroll Siddur: Nusach Ashkenaz* (Brooklyn: Mesorah Publications, 1984).

Scherman, Nosson, ed. et. al., *Seif Edition of the ArtScroll Transliterated Siddur: Sabbath and Festival* (Brooklyn: Mesorah Publications, 1998).

_____, ed. et. al. *The ArtScroll Chumash, Stone Edition*, 5th ed. (Brooklyn: Mesorah Publications, 2000).

The Babylonian Talmud: A Translation and Commentary. MS Windows XP. Peabody, MA: Hendrickson, 2005. CD-ROM.

Messianic Reference Sources

Stern, David H. *Jewish New Testament Commentary* (Clarksville, MD: Jewish New Testament Publications, 1995).

Miscellaneous Texts and Lexicons

Young, Robert. *Young's Analytical Concordance to the Bible* (Grand Rapids: Eerdmans, 1977).

Software Programs

BibleWorks 5.0. MS Windows 9x. Norfolk: BibleWorks, LLC, 2002. CD-ROM.

BibleWorks 7.0. MS Windows XP. Norfolk: BibleWorks, LLC, 2006. CD-ROM.

E-Sword 7.6.1. MS Windows 9x. Franklin, TN: Equipping Ministries Foundation, 2005.

E-Sword 8.0.8. MS Windows 9x. Franklin, TN: Equipping Ministries Foundation, 2008.

Judaic Classics Library II. MS Windows 3.1. Brooklyn: Institute for Computers in Jewish Life, 1996. CD-ROM.

Libronix Digital Library System 1.0d: Church History Collection. MS Windows XP. Garland, TX: Galaxie Software. 2002.

QuickVerse 6.0. MS Windows 95. Hiawatha, IA: Parsons Technology, 1999. CD-ROM.

The Essential Christian Library. MS-Windows 95. Coeur d'Alene, ID: Packard Technologies, 1998. CD-ROM.

World Book 2003. CD-ROM, Chicago: World Book, Inc., 2003.

Messianic Winter Holiday Helper